D1785457

Accession

Accession

THE MAKING OF A QUEEN

John Hartley

Quartet Books

First published by Quartet Books Limited 1992
A member of the Namara Group
27/29 Goodge Street, London W1P 1FD

Copyright © by John Hartley 1992

All rights reserved. No part of this book may be reproduced
in any form or by any means without the prior written
permission of the publisher.

British Library Cataloguing in Publication Data
Hartley, John, *1920–*
    Accession: the making of a Queen.
    I. Title
    941.085092

        ISBN 0 7043 7009 3

Typeset in 11/13 Baskerville by
Contour Typesetters, Southall, London
Printed and bound in Great Britain by
BPCC Hazell Books
Aylesbury, Bucks, England
Member of BPCC Ltd.

Contents

List of Illustrations

Preface and Acknowledgements

THE ACCESSION OF Her Majesty Queen Elizabeth II on 6 February 1952 was for her an occasion so extraordinary, so isolated and so private, that the events of the first twenty-four hours of her reign could only be recalled in detail later through the personal recollections of a handful of people who were very close to her. At the time I was fortunate to be close to those eyewitnesses – which put me, in effect, at one remove from the Queen. My special privilege subsequently was to be given approval to discuss freely and fully with members of the royal entourage their memories, and to record their comments on the Queen's reactions. I believe the result is to provide the only comprehensive account (outside the Royal Archives) of the Queen's participation in the unique historic occasion that was her Accession.

Although I did not have and did not seek access to documents in the Royal Archives, I should emphasize that this is not a hearsay account. Normally the members of the Royal Household and entourage are not permitted to disclose publicly (nor would they under any circumstances) their knowledge of or views on any events involving the Queen or the Duke of Edinburgh to which they have had privileged access.

The Accession was a special situation, however. It was a singular moment that cannot recur and will be of enduring interest historically. I am grateful therefore that I was formally enabled by Buckingham Palace to discuss with some of those involved their recollections on a personal basis.

For some forty-eight hours around the start of her reign the Queen was virtually cut off from the world. It was a two-way separation. She knew very little of what was happening in England; and until she arrived home on the next day, almost nothing was known in England of how she had reacted to the news of her father's death and of her own Accession. She had spent the night of her Accession up a tree in an African jungle, watching wild animals come to a waterhole. By the time the news of the King's death reached Kenya, she was secluded in a forest lodge on the lower slopes of Mount Kenya. After a night with very little sleep and a day of great strain packing up and leaving Kenya, she then spent a second disturbed night in a long and tedious flight back to England, alighting the following afternoon to her public reception at London Airport and a drive to Clarence House. Moreover, during all these tiring hours the Queen had to come to terms with her own private emotions over the death of her father. Her intimate companions throughout this time had been the only close observers of her demeanour and response.

For their co-operation and assistance, I am most grateful to:

Lord Charteris of Amisfield, formerly Private Secretary to HRH Princess Elizabeth and then to HM the Queen. He gave me substantial assistance and a great deal of wise advice.

Commander Michael Parker (RN Rtd), an Australian, formerly Equerry to Princess Elizabeth and then the Queen, and Private Secretary to Prince Philip. His practical common sense helped me to keep everything in perspective. His vivid recall and his graphic description of the first dawn in the Queen's reign was tinged with a numinous awe which was in itself memorable.

Lady Pamela Hicks (née Mountbatten), a cousin of the Queen and Princess Elizabeth's Lady-in-Waiting in Kenya. She noticed perceptively and sympathetically the more subtle signs of emotional response.

Also present with the royal party in Kenya for part of the time was the late Edward Windley, then Provincial Commissioner for the Nyeri area, who was later killed tragically in a light-plane crash in Australia. He helped the royal party pack up at very short notice and leave the Sagana Lodge. He was still in a dazed condition on the following day in the lodge when we discussed the experience.

They were all with the Queen in Kenya. Lieutenant-Colonel Martin Charteris (as he then was) and Lieutenant-Commander Michael Parker had also accompanied the then Princess Elizabeth and the Duke of Edinburgh on their tour of Canada in 1951 (which I also covered on behalf of *The Times*).

I must record my gratitude to the late Sir John Colville, formerly Private Secretary to Sir Winston Churchill. He had also been Princess Elizabeth's first Private Secretary. From his diary notes and his recollections, he told me of Winston Churchill's reactions and thoughts at the time of the King's death and his feelings towards the new Queen. Sir John gave me valuable comments on an early draft of this book which he read.

During more recent stages of the writing I have been especially indebted to the Governor-General of Australia, Mr Bill Hayden, and to Sir David Smith (now retired), formerly Official Secretary to five successive Governors-General of Australia. Their comments on an embryo republican movement that came to the fore in Australia during 1991 were directly relevant as an illustration of what I had already drafted in my closing chapter.

In dealing with the royal tours in Canada and Kenya, I have drawn extensively on the contemporary accounts in *The Times*, most of which I wrote myself. I must also thank Reuters Ltd and particularly the late Ranald Maclurkin, who was Editor of Reuters in the 1970s when I met him. He had been Chief Reporter on desk duty twenty years earlier, when he put out the Reuters 'news-flash' that announced to the world, and to the royal party in Kenya, the death of King George VI. He then went to Sandringham to report on events there.

In Kenya I received considerable assistance from Mervyn Cowie, the first Director of the country's National Parks. I am most appreciative that he has permitted me to quote at length from his book *Fly, Vulture*. He recounted to me more than once his version of the trouble with the elephants as the royal party walked up the jungle path to Treetops, but his written account could hardly be bettered and I am grateful for his permission to use it.

I am indebted also to Colonel Jim Corbett, the legendary hunter of man-eating tigers and leopards in India (where a national park is now named after him). His books became famous and have provided me with some background to the man himself. He was one of the small party that spent the night at Treetops during which Princess Elizabeth became Queen. I am equally indebted to Eric Sherbrooke Walker, the then owner of the hotel. Both men gave me especial help on the next morning in the belief that this would provide additional material for the official book of the Australasian royal tour of 1952, which I had been commissioned to write but that was destined never to be written. Jim Corbett and Sherbrooke Walker both subsequently wrote books themselves (see Bibliography), which have been widely read and quoted and that in turn provided me with important source material. I have also drawn on Elspeth Huxley's *Out in the Midday Sun: My Kenya* for some background on Kenya and several personalities of that time and place.

On a return visit to Kenya in 1973 I was given further assistance by Mr Tubby Block and the late Mr Jack Block, then respectively Chairman and Managing Director of Block Hotels Ltd, the owners by that stage of Treetops and the Outspan Hotel. I am grateful to the present proprietors of Treetops for permission to use material from the Block Hotel archives and especially to reproduce from the visitors' book at Treetops the page on which Princess Elizabeth signed her name as Princess for the last time.

Collecting pictures after a lapse of many years and obtaining clearances for their use can have its difficulties. Some of the commercial picture agencies have changed hands or gone out of business. I have made every effort to obtain approvals, where needed. There are in fact very few pictures available. The professional photographing of royalty was not then the frenetic business it has since become. When the Queen left the jungle after her night at Treetops, only a handful of correspondents were there to see it. When she left Kenya, later in the day, it was requested that no pictures be taken, and this was respected. I have, however, received very substantial co-operation and assistance from Michael Roffey and David Clarke of the Picture Library of Times Newspapers, and I am grateful to Times Newspapers Limited for the supply of, and permission to reproduce, so many of their pictures. I am also grateful to my Australian friends: Aub McCarthy, former picture editor of *The Australian*, for his early help and advice with the pictures; and Ken Phillips for his initial help with the maps.

There were, of course, no press or official pictures taken of the Queen while she was at Treetops. The very rare pictures in this book of the Queen at Treetops have come from a private source. Copyright is reserved and they are reproduced by gracious permission of Her Majesty the Queen. I am grateful to the Queen's Private Secretary and Deputy Private Secretary and to Miss Frances Dimond, Curator of the Royal Photograph Collection, Queen's Archive at Windsor Castle, for their co-operation. I am honoured and grateful to have been allowed to use these pictures from the Queen's Photographic Collection.

Other privately owned pictures used here include a number that I myself took at Treetops and in the Aberdare forest on that morning of 6 February 1952 (although I am no photographer), about an hour after the Queen had left Treetops; and at the Sagana Lodge the following morning. The rooms there had been tidied, but the flowers and everything else were then still just as they had been on the previous afternoon.

In the past, the former BOAC (British Overseas Airways Corporation) gave me much help with details of the aircrews flying the royal party to Kenya, and especially on their return journey. I was also given a summary of the log of the Argonaut *Atlanta*, the plane that so fortuitously was available at Mombasa and was diverted at very short notice to fly the Queen back to England.

I have also received valuable advice and assistance from the Canadian and Kenya High Commissions in Canberra as well as much incidental help from many friends and colleagues. To all of them I am grateful.

Thanks are inadequate for the invaluable encouragement, support and help I have received over the years from my wife Pamela.

The final links in the chain towards publication have been my literary agent in London, Anne Dewe of Andrew Mann Ltd; the publisher of Quartet Books, Mr Naim Attallah; Peter Ford, whose practical advice and editing have been influential on the text in its final form; Anna-Thérèse Lowe, who has skilfully overseen the stages of the book's progress on a tight schedule; and Mark Stevens, who was responsible for the design and artwork. To them, and to all the other members of the staff of Quartet Books who have helped it on its way, I express my thanks.

Finally, in rounding off this Preface, I must add a word about history. This was a historic event, part of a whole cycle of Accessions, all different, going back over more than a thousand years. This story of the present Queen's Accession related here has been prepared from accounts provided out of respect and regard for the main personality involved.

When it comes to it, it is *people*, especially the leaders of nations, whether by inheritance, achievement or both, who create and change the course of history by the strengths and weaknesses of their characters and personalities. If we are to recognize and acknowledge the debt we owe to good leaders – and I hope this book does that for one good leader in particular – it is essential to have some understanding of their personalities and sources of inspiration.

Bundanoon   J.H.
New South Wales
Australia   *September 1991*

Foreword

THE PASSING OF TIME has made it possible forty years on to review in perspective the Queen's reactions to the dramatic events that occurred in Kenya in February 1952, and to recognize the significance of them for the years that were to follow.

I had been accredited to the royal party as Special Correspondent for *The Times*, covering the proposed tour of Australasia by Princess Elizabeth and the Duke of Edinburgh. I had also been commissioned by the King George's Jubilee Trust (with the King's approval) to write the official book of the tour.

On the first morning of the Queen's reign, we stood, a small group of newspaper correspondents (it was still the pre-television era – which in itself indicates the length of time that has passed), on the corner of an unmade dirt road and a stony grass track that led towards the dark line of the Aberdare forest. We were waiting for Princess Elizabeth and the Duke of Edinburgh to leave Treetops, the hut in the jungle where they had spent the night, and we would then go up to it.

An African bus had been stopped to allow the royal car right of passage along the narrow dusty road ahead, but the royal party was well behind schedule and the Africans had got out of the bus. They sat or stood passively by the roadside. We kicked stones and chatted. We all just waited.

Eventually a large, black, shining limousine came bumping along the track, incongruously out of place against the jungle background. Members of the press were not accustomed to wave at royalty. Indeed, by custom and training, they strove in those days to remain for the most part inconspicuous spectators. But here we were, dressed very casually and nothing if not conspicuous. The Princess was perfectly aware of who we were and why we were there. As the car slowly drew level and virtually paused to turn on to the road from the track, we waved somewhat awkwardly and self-consciously. In return we received a dazzling, happy smile. The Princess seemed to seek us out individually, each for a personal wave. It was all most relaxed and informal – and very unusual and unexpected.

It is interesting and appropriate now to look back on those critical days for Princess Elizabeth, when the facets and strengths of character that were to be the foundation of her very successful reign were to become immediately apparent from her unguarded reactions during that emotionally traumatic period. In a somewhat different context, C.E. Montague, the great dramatic critic of the old *Manchester Guardian* under C.P. Scott's editorship, wrote that it is interesting to see the first draft of a masterpiece before the magic has been put into it. It is the 'magic' in a personality that makes a subsequent career interesting.

A few months earlier, in the autumn of 1951, I had covered the highly successful tour of Canada by the Princess and the Duke. That earlier tour had been a fortuitous and testing induction for Princess Elizabeth into acting in a major role on her own. She had previously been in the shadow of the King and Queen on big State occasions. The visit to Canada, however, was only the second royal tour of a Dominion in twelve years. The previous tour had been the King and Queen's visit to South Africa in 1947, the one before that their visit to Canada in 1939.

Princess Elizabeth had always been a very private person. The family had referred to her among themselves as 'the cat that walks alone'. The King once commented in sympathy for his daughter, before her marriage, 'There she goes, Elizabeth, poor lonely girl, she will be lonely all her life.' He made this comment in 1947 to Mr P.B. Fletcher, a Minister of the Southern Rhodesian Government, as they stood by the grave of Cecil Rhodes. Mr Fletcher asked the King if he should go and accompany the Princess. The King replied, 'Yes, I would like that.' Princess Elizabeth did not turn as Mr Fletcher approached, but said, 'Mr Fletcher, what a wonderful shrine you have here.' He asked how she knew it was he who approached and she replied, 'I saw you with the King, and I knew he would send you down to me.' This self-isolating tendency was to change with her marriage, but she still preserved considerable personal reserve.

The Canadian tour was to change even this, and it was fascinating to watch as her qualities of inner self were gradually drawn to the surface. The tour had been intended to have a 'simple itinerary', but so insistent were the Canadians all over that vast country to see and greet the Princess that it eventually became the most strenuous royal tour ever carried out, before or since. The significance of this for the Princess was that it provided her with a 'shock' experience that was to prove invaluable a few months later when she became Queen. When the Canadian tour ended in November 1951, the Canadians claimed they were sending back 'a new Princess'.

The King and Queen had originally been due to carry out the Australasian tour in the following year, but, with the King's general state of health causing continuing anxiety, the responsibility was taken over by Princess Elizabeth and the Duke of Edinburgh. After only a few weeks' respite between tours, they therefore set out once more in January 1952. The King was to have travelled mostly by sea and train, but the Princess and the Duke had shown in Canada that they could stand up to the rigours of a more concentrated itinerary with the use of aircraft. A number of additions were made to the schedule, among them the inclusion of a visit to Kenya at the beginning of the tour.

The Princess had just concluded her programme in Kenya and was preparing to move on to Ceylon when the news reached her that the King had died. She was isolated in a forest lodge on the lower slopes of Mount Kenya, having spent the previous night up a giant fig tree in the jungle, watching animals at a waterhole. All communications with Kenya – by telephone, cable and air travel – were extremely poor at the time. Princess Elizabeth must have been one of the last persons awake in the British Commonwealth to learn she was Queen.

Because she was inaccessible, and because of the great popularity of the King whose sudden death came as an immense shock to the nation, the whole focus of attention at the time was fixed on London. In Kenya, however, desperate efforts were being made to find a way to fly the Queen home. Very little was said or written at the time of what was being done there, and very little in particular was known of the Queen's reactions, feelings and behaviour. I had been fortunate in being fairly close to the Princess on her visits to Canada and Washington, and also in Kenya. The changes and developments in her personality had been absorbing to observe.

The fortieth anniversary of the Queen's Accession seems an appropriate moment to recall the start of a reign which, far from being complete, nevertheless has run its major course. It has been a reign that has seen momentous changes in the world. It started with the last days of the crumbling British Empire, which was reformed into the British Common-wealth, and has seen the decline and break-up of the monolithic Soviet Empire, including the whole of Eastern Europe, which was still in the iron grip of Stalin himself when she came to the Throne.

I am not a historian, but am very much aware (after having subsequently spent more than thirty years in the news and television industry) that the Queen has, in a subtle and distinguished way, been enormously influential on the affairs of the British Commonwealth during a critical period of change. It is illuminating to look back and see why.

It was by chance that I became involved with the royal tours. *The Times* did not have a 'Royal Correspondent', and this was in fact before the days of the frenzied pursuit of the royal family by photographers, reporters, gossip columnists and others. The then two domestic news agencies each had a regular Court Correspondent who passed on all routine announcements and information. These two reporters were often dressed in black coats and striped trousers and wore bowler hats or black homburgs. They moved about together and were known in Fleet Street as 'The Penguins'.

In the summer of 1951, I had been on the staff of *The Times* for about five years. The growth of television had not yet eroded the power and influence of newspapers generally, to the extent it did later. We believed sincerely (with many others around the globe) that *The Times* was not only the best newspaper in the world, but also the most influential of all the news media. It was regarded as an honour to work on *The Times*. A high standard of writing was expected, but a fair degree of latitude was permitted to become involved in areas of one's own personal interests provided these were appropriate. I had been concerned with social welfare and had been specializing in the development of New Towns in post-war Britain; I had also recently been preparing two major series of leader-page articles: one on prison reform, the other on reforms in the treatment of young offenders.

This latter sprang from an interest I had taken for several years as a voluntary helper in a very large boys' club in Hertfordshire. It began with my coaching in athletics and cricket, but had been extended by the then Warden of the club, Colonel Ronald Menday, a former Commando officer with a distinguished war record. (He had taken over command of the D-Day Commandos on the first day when his colonel was wounded on the beaches, and had then led the Commandos for another two months, during which time he earned the Military Cross and Croix de Guerre (*avec Palme*), before being blown up and wounded himself.) He was an inspiring leader of men and of boys. After the war he was offered several highly-paid jobs, but chose the one with the least money but which for him offered the most satisfying opportunities.

We discovered that we shared the same belief that everyone has some creative 'gift', and that if this aptitude remains undiscovered and unused it can lead to frustration and problems. On the other hand, the discovery and development of any creative aptitude can open up new worlds of satisfaction and achievement. Ron Menday therefore introduced a wide range of cultural activities into a club that was noted in the county for its football and boxing teams, and very soon it had one of the largest and best youth drama groups in the country. He inveigled me into the drama activity, and when he was asked to go to Germany to take charge of the resettlement of several hundred thousand displaced persons in various countries around the world, he left me with all the drama problems (for which I had discovered to my surprise that I had a concealed aptitude).

In that summer of 1951 we had been taking part in various one-act-play festivals and competitions. As it was Festival of Britain Year, we invited the local girls' club to join with us in something more ambitious. The boys converted a dell in a local pine wood into an open-air theatre with terraced seating, apron stage, grassy banks, brushwood screens, and several hundred metres of power lines laid for lighting. For a whole week we put on evening performances of a full production of *A Midsummer Night's Dream*, produced by a local thespian who hadn't realized what he was letting himself in for, but who rose to the occasion magnificently.

We were fortunate to have beautiful summer nights, and the air was heavy with the biting scent of pine (and mosquitoes!) The long path through the woods to the dell was strewn with pine needles and the trees were mysteriously lit. The whole setting for the *Dream* was magical and the performance was extraordinarily successful.

While this was going on, I was struggling with a production of Benjamin Britten's *Let's Make an Opera* with a group of junior boys and girls; I was also trying to start writing the script for the annual Christmas pantomime that the boys' club put on to packed houses every year and which financed our drama activities for the rest of the season. My co-writer and co-producer (and also Ron Menday's successor as Widow Twankey) was a man called George Faldo. George was particularly taken at that time with comedian Sid Field's golfing sketch – a classic of its kind. He and his wife subsequently had a son called Nick who was not as funny as Sid Field, but is a much better golfer!

I was also playing duplicate contract bridge for Hertfordshire, but had had to give up my own athletic interests. I did not have time for everything, though somehow I had recently managed to become engaged to be married. In between all these activities I was working full-time for *The Times*. Into this carefully dovetailed personal schedule came the bombshell that the Editor had approved my covering the hastily arranged five-week tour of Canada and the United States for the Princess Elizabeth and the Duke of Edinburgh, due to begin in September.

I had not expected to be chosen. The royal tour of South Africa by the King and Queen in 1947 had been covered by Dermot Morrah, a Fellow of All Souls College, Oxford, a distinguished leader-writer for *The Times* and also a fine descriptive writer. Later, as Arundel Herald Extraordinary, he carried a 'wand' in the royal procession at the Queen's Coronation. He came straight back to the office from Westminster Abbey after the ceremony, still attired in his scarlet knee-breeches and looking like a playing card, to dictate his description of a scene he had observed at very close quarters.

It was known that he was not available for Canada. It had been expected during the early days of planning the tour, when a 'simple itinerary' was contemplated, that Alan Pitt Robbins, the Home News Editor, who was about to retire, would go as it would help him renew on behalf of *The Times* his many contacts with Canadian newspapermen who were members of the Commonwealth Press Union, of which *The Times* was a leading supporter. But it was not to be that sort of a tour and fortunately for him a General Election in Britain was announced as being about to take place so he had to withdraw. I say 'fortunately', because Alan Robbins was a big man weighing nearly twenty stone and the Canadian tour as it eventuated would surely have taken years off his life.

I had to make all my own arrangements. *The Times* was not a wealthy newspaper and was perforce parsimonious with expenses. I did not have a portable typewriter, neither were *The Times* or the management prepared to pay for one. When would it be used again? And by whom? In the end I bought a second-hand, pre-war, reconditioned typewriter for £10 from one of the office messengers. Armed with this, and with careful instructions on the cheapest way to send dispatches from Canada to London, I set off to represent the world's greatest newspaper in the senior Dominion of the British Commonwealth.

The experience was a revelation and I tried in my dispatches to convey something of the excitement of the people of Canada, the atmosphere of that great country, and also the gradual changes taking place in the personality of Princess Elizabeth. I received very little 'feed-back' reaction from London, except for a message sent early on (at the specially reduced press cable rate of a penny a word) to remind me to mention the weather.

Someone must have been pleased, however, for I was later told that I would be going on the Australasian tour starting in January. Thanks to my fiancée's acumen, I just had time to get married and have a fortnight's honeymoon before I was back at the airport bidding fond farewells and expecting to be away for four months.

I had had lunch in the meantime with the Director of the King George's Jubilee Trust, who had asked me if I would accept the commission to write the official book of the tour, which, it was hoped, would be published shortly after the tour ended. To achieve this deadline was going to mean sending a chapter at a time at the end of each stage of the tour. Having returned exhausted from Canada, I was none too happy with the arrangement, but I nevertheless accepted. I was particularly apprehensive when told that the first uncorrected proofs would have to be sent progressively to the King for approval.

That particular book, of course, was destined never to be written. On the last day of the Kenyan part of the tour, while Princess Elizabeth was sitting at the desk in the Sagana Lodge in the jungle writing home to her mother and father describing her exciting news of the night before, I was sitting not many miles away at a desk at the Outspan Hotel at Nyeri, looking at a stunning view of Mount Kenya and trying to do the same thing – but feeling somewhat hungry as I had gone without lunch in order to complete the Kenya chapter of the book I was typing on my very staunch antique typewriter. It was then that I heard the news that the King had died. The Queen heard some time later still.

After my return to England, I was having a quiet private moan to the Editor of *The Times Weekly Edition* about how little interest the London office seemed to have taken in events in Kenya, when he gave me some elder-statesman advice. He said, 'Sit down and write up all your notes while they are still fresh in your mind – and keep hold of them. Whatever else happens, they are part of British history, and you have a better record of that than anyone else.' He added: 'The Accession of a Monarch is always an important and historic event, and goodness alone knows when we will get another one.' Forty years on this remains, thankfully, a very open question.

I took his advice and have since then been able to add to those original notes. They record in detail an important moment of British history. I have always thought, however, that history – as I learned it at school – was a dull subject, and when I started writing this book I felt that while I knew the facts were of very great interest, I might have to try to make the recounting of them 'readable'. As I progressed I realized what an inadequate idea that had been.

The subject developed not just as a record of dates and happenings, but as an intensely human story. Between the summer of 1951 and the mid-winter of 1952, Princess Elizabeth changed and matured so that at the moment when she acceded to the Throne her personality was ready to take on another dimension and she immediately attained the full stature of a Queen; and as the subsequent years have shown, of a great Queen.

Part One

One

Succession

W HEN QUEEN ELIZABETH II ascended to the Throne in 1952, it was the start of an era that was to see some remarkable women rising to leadership and prominence in various countries of the world.

The post-war years provided opportunities for women leaders to emerge and reach positions of great political power, both nationally and internationally. Those women had the courage, strength of character and personality, and the necessary determination to succeed – and they took their opportunities: Golda Meir of Israel in a new state surrounded by hostile neighbours; Indira Gandhi in India and Benazir Bhutto in Pakistan; Cory Aquino with a courageous and peaceful *coup* in the Philippines; and Margaret Thatcher, the first woman Prime Minister in Britain, serving a record three terms and giving her name to a new and tough form of government.

Unlike these women politicians, the Queen did not have to battle her way to the top. On the contrary, as the mother of two small children, a young and rather inexperienced public figure, she was thrust forward somewhat reluctantly in 1952 into a position of great authority and influence. Throughout the decades of immense change that have followed, she has nevertheless become the most influential non-political woman leader in the world.

Without exception, the women Prime Ministers in the different countries of the world have all had in their respective ways a tigerish fighting quality that has enabled them to take on and succeed against all comers in their own political arenas. The Queen has this fighting quality also, but with her it has been more subtly deployed and is rarely, if ever, seen in public. She does not need to have the killer instinct so necessary in politics, nor does she have to be competitive. This enables her to temper the pragmatic approaches of others with a greater understanding of both sides. It also enables her to exercise a very real sense of compassion. She is, however, no soft touch. In fact she is formidably resolute. It is said she can freeze the strongest male with a single glance at twenty paces if ever the occasion arises. She has to lead and suggest and use her power more by example and influence. The strength of the power she holds lies in its presence rather than its use, while subtle persuasion is a woman's natural weapon.

The role of Monarchy has changed greatly during the Queen's reign. She has less direct power than her monarchical predecessors, but her influence is enormous and her responsibilities are more complex and require greater sophistication in their handling. The dignity of the position she holds, and the constitutional authority she represents, have to be maintained and respected at all times. Whether in public or in private she is always the Queen – because it is her duty to be so.

Selection of the next King or Queen is never by popular vote or government appointment. It is determined by primogeniture succession: the principle of hereditary succession introduced after the Norman Conquest over nine hundred years ago. Since then five royal dynasties have sat on the Throne of England, all with related links, however tenuous. Over the centuries the powers of Parliament and the Church have increased, and the direct power to rule of the Monarch has decreased. Instead, the responsibilities of Monarchy have widened to provide a unique structure with safeguards for both the Monarchy and the people.

By happy chance, when the present Queen came to the Throne on 6 February 1952, she was the right person to succeed, and it came at the right moment in her life. Furthermore, she had also just had the right kind of experience to prepare her for her new role – an advantage which seems to have been shared by very few of her predecessors. Nor was the national excitement that greeted her Accession a transient emotion destined to turn to disappointment. On the contrary, the outcome was more successful than all the hopeful anticipations could have dreamed, though it has been quite different from anything that was expected. The result was a reign notable for the quality of the work the Queen has carried out as well as for being the busiest and most prominent in terms of public involvement in the history of the Crown.

The principle of hereditary succession, with precedence being given to the male line in order of age and seniority, would seem to provide a fairly clear procedure for succession. It is, however, somewhat arbitrary when it comes to assessing suitability or worth. Moreover, with so much power, status, privilege and possessions as well as responsibilities residing with the Monarch, there have inevitably been a great many attempts to manipulate the system.

The critical points in any reign lie at the beginning and the end. These have in history been accompanied by battles, murder, executions, persecutions, usurping of the Throne, imprisonments, scandal, and a great deal of intrigue, as well as popular rejoicings and celebrations. Any review of the various Accessions to a Throne that has endured for over a thousand years must also become a study of personalities. And because these changes involve deaths as well as the opening up of new horizons, the times are sad as well as happy, and on occasions tragic as well as inspiring and heroic.

One particular factor that has caused an immense amount of strife and been divisive and decisive in determining the rights of Accession from the time of Henry VIII onwards has been religion. Ever since Henry VIII split with the Pope and the Roman Catholic Church over the matter of his divorce from Catherine of Aragon, Catholics and Protestants have been divided. For a century and a half after Henry VIII's death, bitter religious conflict developed at times into murderous persecution. In the end, Parliament stepped in and called a halt to the feuding by passing the Act of Settlement of 1701. This specified that in future all British Monarchs must be members of the Church of England. It also laid down a Protestant hereditary line of succession that by-passed the deposed Catholic convert James II and his heirs and introduced a somewhat removed, but Protestant, line of succession. This dated from James I's daughter Elizabeth, who had married the Elector of Hanover.

In due course after the death of Queen Anne – who left no heirs despite having had seventeen children – the then Elector of Hanover succeeded to the Throne of England as George I – a King who had never been to England, who spoke little English and never bothered to learn much of the language. He was nevertheless the first Monarch in the long Hanoverian dynasty, which changed its family name to Windsor during the First World War.

In 1910, when George V ascended to the Throne some two hundred years after the passing of the Act of Settlement debarring Catholics from succeeding, it was estimated that in the region of a thousand descendants of Charles I (father of James II and brother of Elizabeth) would have had superior claims to succeed.

The manner of Accession of each new Monarch has special historical significance and has often been accompanied by moments of enthralling high drama.

The first King of England is generally accepted as having been Egbert, who reigned from AD 802–39. Egbert was King of Wessex, which was the only kingdom in England to hold out successfully against the Danish invaders. He alone, therefore, was able to represent England. His grandson Alfred the Great later defeated the Danes and not only confirmed the title but established himself as one of the best known of all English kings.

Before the Norman Conquest in 1066, the law of primogeniture succession did not apply to the Saxon kings. The Witan, or Council, elected the most suitable successor, though he had to be of royal blood. Fewer than half the Saxon kings of England had succeeded their fathers. William the Conqueror introduced not only some strange bedfellows but also new blood into the

Monarchy. His innovations opened the door as well to a great deal of female intrigue and in-fighting.

Royal offspring in the Middle Ages (and even later) must have reconciled themselves to the thought that their future marriages would almost certainly be arranged for political, diplomatic, financial and property or title reasons. Inter-marriage within the noble houses not only of England but of the whole of Europe was common then, and continued up to the present century. Queen Victoria was survived by six children, forty grandchildren and thirty-seven great-grandchildren. Descendants of hers included the Empress of Germany (and mother of Kaiser Wilhelm II), the Tsarina of Russia (assassinated in 1918), and the Queens of Norway, Sweden, Greece, Romania, Yugoslavia and Spain.

Marriages frequently took place at a very young age. Edward III was only sixteen and his bride fourteen when they married in the year after his Accession in 1327. Henry Bolinbroke (who deposed Richard II in 1399 and became Henry IV) was only fourteen when he married Mary de Bohun. Their first son was to become the famous Henry V, and they had three more sons and two daughters before Mary was to die in childbirth, still in her early twenties.

The remarkable Lady Margaret Beaufort, granddaughter of John of Gaunt (fourth son of Edward III), was only thirteen when she became a widow and already pregnant. The son born to her in 1457 when she was just fourteen was Henry Tudor. He became Henry VII, victor over the infamous Richard III, founder of the great Tudor dynasty and father of Henry VIII.

Henry VII's own marriage was set up by the scheming and revengeful Queen who was widow of Edward IV. She was mother of the two Princes in the Tower (one was the twelve-year-old Edward V), who had been seized and thrown in the Tower by Richard III, and there murdered. She plotted, not unnaturally, to bring about the downfall of Richard III. Upon the disappearance and death of her two sons, her eldest daughter Elizabeth became heiress to the House of York, which had been locked for decades in the bloody Wars of the Roses with the House of Lancaster. The widowed Queen fled to France with her remaining children, where Henry Tudor, head of the House of Lancaster, was already in exile. The Queen then cleverly 'arranged' the betrothal of her daughter Elizabeth to Henry and he swore solemnly at a ceremony in Rennes Cathedral to marry Elizabeth after he became King of England.

This final unification of the Houses of York and Lancaster after years of civil strife was to bring to an end the Wars of the Roses. It was an appealing prospect in England, and for Richard III it spelled the doom that came to him at Bosworth Field, where his naked body was carried ignominiously from the battlefield slung across the back of a pack-horse. The Crown of England, recovered from underneath a gorse bush, was immediately placed upon

Henry's head. Parliament subsequently ratified this act and the Pope threatened to excommunicate anyone who challenged the claim.

Henry duly married Elizabeth. What had started as a skilfully arranged marriage finished up as a tender loving married life and epitomized the First Rule of Courtly Love as adumbrated by Andreas Capellanus in the twelfth century: 'Marriage is no real excuse for not loving.' Such arrangements did not always work out so happily, however. For romantically minded young girls there were frequently tears. Mary, the attractive eldest daughter of James II, for instance, cried for two days when told at the age of fifteen that she had to marry her cousin, the slightly hunchbacked and asthmatic Dutch Prince William of Orange. William became the Protestant champion in Europe. Because Mary had been brought up a Protestant, she became Queen Mary II when William of Orange was invited to England to depose her father, who was a Catholic.

Some little girls were too young to understand. Henry VIII arranged the betrothal of his daughter Mary by his first wife, Catherine of Aragon (Mary was later to become Mary I and known as 'Bloody Mary'), in a series of abortive proxy marriages. Mary was not three years old when she was betrothed to the Dauphin, heir to the Throne of France. As Cardinal Wolsey lifted her up so that a tiny ring could be slipped on to her finger, she asked the French Admiral Bonnivet, who was holding the ring, 'Are you the Dauphin? If you are, I want to kiss you.'

As a mature woman, Mary became desperately anxious to marry, but was not able to do so until after she became Queen. In her late thirties she married her cousin Prince Philip (later Philip II) of Spain, who left her after fourteen months when Parliament refused to allow him to be crowned. Years later he tried to take by force what he had failed to obtain by marriage, but his mighty Armada was defeated by Mary's half-sister Queen Elizabeth I.

Elizabeth I shares with Queen Victoria and the present Queen the distinction of being among the three female monarchs who have reigned for more than forty years. A reign of forty years is a long time, and Queen Elizabeth II, perhaps more than any of her predecessors, has been confronted with enormous changes during her life on the Throne.

Elizabeth I was aptly nicknamed 'Gloriana' and reigned for forty-four years from 1558 to 1603. She came to the Throne at the age of twenty-five – the same age as her namesake Elizabeth II – and died aged seventy. She had inherited a Throne which her father Henry VIII had imbued with almost absolute powers. Her ships roamed the seas and circumnavigated the globe, bringing much wealth, power and prestige to England. It was the great literary era of Shakespeare, Marlowe and Spencer.

Queen Victoria ascended the Throne in 1837 and died in 1901 aged eighty-one after a reign of sixty-three years – the longest in British history. In contrast to Elizabeth I, Queen Victoria inherited a Throne that had been brought into disrepute by a series of kings who were happy to lead society, the aristocracy and the Established Church, but who failed to be popular or true leaders of the nation. The Throne was almost at its lowest ebb.

Queen Victoria's reign was to see the extraordinary developments in wealth through the Industrial Revolution when – mainly from the efforts of the Dissenters, or the trading classes – England was leading the world in new inventions and manufacturing processes. The British Empire doubled in size and Queen Victoria became Empress of India. The jingoism of Empire was to sweep the country towards the end of her reign and into the succeeding Edwardian era with 'Land of Hope and Glory', 'Rule Britannia' and Rudyard Kipling's patriotic poetry.

The reigns of both these Queens were to contribute greatly to the cultural heritage of the country, but England's greatest gift to the world from all periods of history started earlier than either of them: with the growth of parliamentary government and the principle of free speech.

The first 'Model Parliament' was convened in 1295 by an English Monarch – Edward I – in the Middle Ages. It was a creation that was in due course to usurp many of the powers and functions of the Monarchy itself. Edward I reigned for thirty-five years from 1272 to 1307 and became known as the father of the 'Mother of all Parliaments'. He was a splendid figure of a man, standing head and shoulders above his contemporaries. He loved the martial arts and tournaments and was a great soldier, statesman and lawyer. It was he who made his eldest son the first Prince of Wales in 1301, a title since held by all Heirs to the Throne.

Edward I's father, Henry III, reigned for fifty-six years and was much more interested in building castles and cathedrals than in some of the more militant and administrative sides of kingship. He was the greatest patron of Gothic architecture in the Middle Ages. Under his watchful eye, the flying buttresses, pointed arches and vaulted roofs that remain the glories of cathedral architecture began to appear all over England. Nevertheless he did not meet the current mood for a King who would go out and conquer. His son Edward did. When the King and Prince Edward were captured by a force led by Simon de Montfort, the King was summoned to appear before a 'parlement' – or 'speaking' – comprised of two knights from each shire, and two burgesses from each of certain towns, to try to persuade him to act with a Council of Nobles. Edward escaped, killed de Montfort, and rescued his father.

When he became King, Edward revived the 'parlement' idea and in 1295 summoned representatives from the nobility, the clergy, knights of the shires and burgesses of the cities, to the 'Model Parliament' in Westminster which brought the Lords and Commons together for the first time. Edward I was perhaps the most appropriate man to inspire such a gathering for he subsequently acquired a reputation for deviousness that placed him several centuries ahead of his time.

The creation of the parliamentary institution was to be as fundamental in importance to the future of the Monarchy in the distribution and use of power as Henry VIII's split with the Roman Catholic Church and the Pope some two and a half centuries later, the latter in due course leading to the barring of Catholics from succeeding to the Throne. The gradual transfer of power from the Monarchy to Parliament (with some involvement of religious dispute) reached a climax during the reign of Charles I, who was seized by Oliver Cromwell at the head of a faction of Parliamentarians and a strong force of Roundhead soldiers, and publicly beheaded in 1649. After Cromwell's death, the Monarchy returned with Charles II, but the progressive erosion of direct political power from the Monarch continued up to the twentieth century. This, of course, affected the status of the Crown and progressively changed the public perception of, and attitude towards, the Monarchy.

The 'image' of Monarchy, and indeed of any leadership, relies to some extent on a mystique based on confidence. This is derived extensively from what is seen or heard, but also partially from a concealment which leaves much to be imagined or supposed. In the early days of the Monarchy, the panoply and ceremony were developed to heighten the sense of position and importance and power of the Monarch. The medieval kings were gorgeously visible, but at the same time they were 'concealed' by the surroundings of finery and power that made them awesome (and sometimes fearsome).

When Richard II ascended to the Throne in 1377 at the age of ten, he very soon learned to strengthen his position by preaching the doctrine of the Divine Right of Kings to Rule – which he seems to have believed. He developed the sense of pageantry to bolster his own self-glory and even had a huge throne built on a raised platform so that on feast days all who approached him might kneel at his feet. When he tried to usurp the rights of Parliament and make his own laws, he was deposed. Adam of Usk related how he was carried away on the Thames, 'in the silence of dark midnight, weeping and loudly lamenting that he had ever been born'. Later, Adam said, 'He grieved more sorely even to death, which came to him most miserably on the last day of February [AD 1400] as he lay in chains in the castle of Pontefract, tortured by Sir N. Swinford with scant fare.'

While the traditions and ceremonials of Monarchy have changed over the centuries, the public has rarely been deceived by outward show, or not for long. Kings from George I to George IV, though they were leaders of society, were never popular leaders of the nation. They were a source of constant gossip and ridicule in London's coffee houses, and the subject of lampoons right from the start. When George I arrived in England from Hanover in 1714, he brought no Queen with him. He had divorced his wife, whose lover had disappeared and was believed to have been hacked to pieces and buried under the floor-boards. She herself was locked away in a moated castle for the remainder of her life. Instead, George I brought along two German mistresses. One was very thin and was promptly nicknamed 'The Maypole'. The other was very stout and became known as 'The Elephant and Castle' after the well-known public house.

George IV's Coronation may have been one of the most magnificent ever attempted, but it was a flawed performance. As Prince Regent, George, a man of style and taste, had been, along with Beau Brummell, a leader of fashion and an extrovert greatly given to display. The Prince became, however, a gross man, a heavy drinker, a gargantuan eater and wildly extravagant. He agreed to marry Caroline of Brunswick in order to placate Parliament over his debts, but when he met her he was appalled. She was fat and unwashed, and he became drunk at his own wedding. After the birth of their daughter Charlotte they ceased to live together. When he became King, George IV tried unsuccessfully to get a Bill through Parliament saying Caroline should not be Queen.

The splendour of his Coronation in 1821 was marred by the unseemly spectacle of the uninvited Queen trying to force her way into Westminster Abbey and being turned away at the doors. The reception at Westminster Hall was notable for the presence of prize-fighters engaged to keep the peace between the noble guests.

Other royal rituals of that time also failed to be particularly edifying. David Cannadine relates in an essay (see Bibliography) how the undertakers were drunk at the funeral of Princess Charlotte in 1817. When the Duke of York died some years later, the chapel at Windsor was so damp that most of the mourners caught cold. Canning developed rheumatic fever and the Bishop of London died. At George IV's funeral his brother, the new King, William IV, talked all the way through the service and left early. *The Times* newspaper said of the mourners, 'We never saw so motley, so rude, so ill-mannered, a body of persons.' The funerals of the popular heroes Nelson and Wellington were, by contrast, far more splendid and dignified affairs.

When William IV, uncle to the future Queen Victoria, succeeded to the Throne in 1830 at the age of sixty-four, he could hardly believe his luck. He drove up and down the streets of London in an open carriage with a broad smile on his face, kissing the passers-by. He became known as 'Silly Billy'. Unlike George IV, he did not like ceremonials and did not want a Coronation at all, much to the dismay of the nobility who had so much enjoyed the previous one. Finally he agreed to one, provided it cost no more than one tenth of that of his brother. It was so parsimonious that it became known as the 'Half-Crownation'.

Queen Victoria's Accession to the Throne was itself marked by complaints about further cost to the public purse from yet another Coronation. The 1838 ceremony was unrehearsed and incompetently conducted. The clergy lost their places, the ring turned out to be too small for the finger when the Archbishop of Canterbury tried to put it on, and the trainbearers talked throughout. The inept performance of the ceremonials reflected the low regard in public esteem into which the Monarchy had fallen.

It was only after Queen Victoria married Prince Albert of Saxe-Coburg-Gotha two years later that matters began to improve. He was an efficient Prince Consort with imagination and constructive ideas. He set about bringing order to the proceedings and achieved a new respect for the Monarchy as well as for the Monarch. Although Queen Victoria became almost a recluse after the death of Prince Albert, and opened Parliament only six times in twenty-five years, her Silver and Diamond Jubilees were marked by splendid celebrations and enthusiastic scenes of public esteem and loyalty; her death in 1901 was an occasion of profound national mourning.

Prince Albert not only restored the image of Monarchy to the status of national representation it had enjoyed in the great days of the Tudors (though without the absolute power of those times), he also directed the Monarchy along a new course which has been followed up to the present day. It has been noted by historians that, as the political powers of the Monarchy declined or were passed over to Parliament, so has the constitutional position of the Monarch developed, with an appropriate and improved ceremony to match. With the disappearance of the other major Monarchies of Europe, from Germany, Russia, Greece and France, for instance, the English Monarchy has been left as the only major 'traditional' royal ceremonial of ancient and genuine splendour. The honing and refining of these procedures has given the English Monarchy a somewhat exclusive presence in the world.

The role of the present Queen is far from being that of a ceremonial leader. She still has considerable constitutional powers and responsibilities, but by and large the strength of this power lies in its not having to be actively exercised. It needs to be exerted subtly by influence rather than by direct action.

In recent times, the Monarchy has suffered when politicians have persuaded the Queen to use her influence or powers directly on behalf of some political motive. Whatever the rights or wrongs of the dispute in 1975 between the Australian Prime Minister, Mr Gough Whitlam, and the then leader of the Opposition, Mr Malcolm Fraser, the removal of the Prime Minister of Australia from office by the Governor-General, Sir John Kerr, using his constitutional powers as the Queen's representative, certainly put a strain on the Australian understanding of the role of Monarchy, though the Queen's personal popularity remained undiminished.

The Queen was unwisely persuaded in 1978 to invite the Romanian President Nicolae Ceaușescu on a State visit. The Government's purpose was to persuade him to clinch a large order for aircraft that was then being negotiated. Romania was following a political line independent of Moscow and was in some favour in the West. The time that Ceaușescu spent at

Buckingham Palace as the guest of the Queen, with his entourage of secret police and (final insult) a food taster to ensure he was not being poisoned, were later said to have been regarded by the Queen as among the three worst days of her life.

Using the Queen's position at short notice to put out local bush fires or opportunistically to gain short-term trade advantages – whatever pragmatic arguments may be advanced about 'national interest' – has in practice set dangerous precedents. The watershed for such days has passed, and far more benefit has been and is being derived from developing her role as a constitutional Monarch. The Queen has had an enormous influence in public and behind the scenes in helping the crumbling British Empire to be reshaped as the British Commonwealth; and further, to be held together despite occasional or recurrent tensions. All of this has been achieved amid an unprecedented blaze of publicity, analysis, criticism and public interest. Indeed, the skilful use of the new communications facilities has often brought positive benefit.

One of the earliest innovations of the present Queen's reign occurred immediately after her Accession when the principle of the indivisibility of the Crown was abandoned and she was proclaimed separately in each country of the former British Empire as Queen of that country. She was confirmed as Head of the British Commonwealth by Statute in 1953, which enabled such independent republics as India and Pakistan to be members of the British Commonwealth, and permitted the admission also of those other countries that became independent subsequently. The modified role of Monarchy then fitted comfortably into the new concept of the British Commonwealth as it was reshaped under the existing leadership.

President Jomo Kenyatta, the first President of the newly independent Republic of Kenya, was known to have a special personal regard for the Queen. He had been the leader of the bloody uprising and battle for independence in Kenya in which the Mau Mau had taken part with so much bitterness. After the struggle was over, the Duke of Edinburgh was invited to participate in the Independence celebrations and ceremony for raising the new flag. The Queen and other members of the royal family were later welcomed back as visitors, for it had been in Kenya that she first heard she was Queen, coincidentally with the start of the Mau Mau uprising.

It has been instructive in modern times to compare the more recent development of other 'Empires' and power blocs. Some groups of countries, as in Western Europe, which have in the past been quite separate and independent, and even antagonistic towards each other, have already established close economic ties and are exploring and moving towards closer political union. Others, as in Eastern Europe and the Soviet Union, shackled together under a centralized control for so long, are moving inexorably towards greater individual independence. In Germany, the move towards reunification started with the breaking down of the Berlin Wall.

While the British Commonwealth no longer retains the international power it once held, it continues to have important responsibilities and influence in helping, especially, a large number of developing countries. The Queen's well-known concern and sincere sense of responsibility in this regard have been strong unifying forces, for she is held in high personal esteem throughout the Commonwealth. One of the factors which has been of particular unifying assistance has been the extent to which the Queen and the Duke of Edinburgh, separately or together, have travelled extensively around the world visiting the Commonwealth countries.

Two modern developments in the past forty years have enabled the Queen to travel more, and become increasingly visible and to meet and be seen by greater numbers of people than any of her predecessors: the use of giant jet airliners, which are fast and do not overtire the traveller; and the extraordinary growth of television combined with the use of satellites to bring the intimacy of immediate visual contact to events anywhere in the world. The world's newspapers and magazines have also developed investigative reporting and writing to a pitch where few personal secrets remain for anyone in whom they take an interest, except those which are protected by the law of libel – and sometimes not even then. The remarkable fact is that although the Queen is constantly seen on television all over the world, and is mentioned almost daily in the newspapers, she has still managed to preserve a great deal of her personal privacy. The effect of this has been to elevate her in public respect.

There seem to be two reasons for how this has come about. The first is the assiduous care and attention that the Duke of Edinburgh takes to ensure there is no intrusion on the Queen's privacy by anyone or anything. In modern parlance, he has been her 'Minder'. Although she is physically as 'visible' as anyone in the world, we are still conscious of seeing only the tip of the iceberg of her personality.

To achieve this, the Duke has engaged in a long-running love-hate relationship with the media. Having been a naval officer who saw action during the Second World War, he has shown that he is every bit as capable of fighting battles of the air waves as he is those of the sea. He understands the media intimately, and much of the credit for the present 'image' of the Monarchy must go to the Duke for his vigilant watch-dog management of the Queen's public appearances. What Prince Albert did for the image of Monarchy during the reign of Queen Victoria, the Duke of Edinburgh is doing for the present Queen in an age of bewildering scientific change.

It is not just a matter of negative protection. Television provides opportunities to present the Queen and members of the royal family to audiences that would never otherwise be able to see or hear them. The Queen gives her annual Christmas Message on television; there have been carefully produced, if sometimes rather contrived films of the private life of the royal family; and the Queen and the Duke have appeared in television documentaries, speaking about anything from art treasures to horses.

But the television appearances which, above all, attract world audiences numbering hundreds of millions are the great formal ceremonials. The first indicator of this was the unexpected popularity of the Queen's Coronation on early black-and-white television. It was televised at the Queen's wish, despite some advice to the contrary. The lesson was quickly learned. Gone now are the bungling efforts of the early days. Everything is planned and rehearsed down to the last detail and then timed with stop-watches. In 1969, when Prince Charles was inducted by the Queen as Prince of Wales in the spectacular setting of the centuries-old castle at Caernarvon, every single camera position and routine was carefully worked out in advance. Even the canopy over Prince Charles's head was made of transparent plastic for the benefit of the cameras.

When Prince Charles married Lady Diana Spencer at St Paul's Cathedral in 1981 at the 'Wedding of the Century', there were twenty-two television cameras in the cathedral and fifty countries around the world received the television transmissions. It was estimated that the total audience was in the order of 1,000 million.

After the wedding ceremony, huge crowds waited outside Buckingham Palace to see the royal couple on the balcony. Under the eyes of long-focus lenses of yet more television cameras, and encouraged by the crowd, Prince Charles kissed his bride – the first Prince ever to do so in public. The crowd cheered, and the world watched and loved it.

In an era when television and radio reporters climb over each other and everyone else to interview anyone in whom they are interested, it says much for the media and their respect for the personality of the Queen that the protocol request not to approach the Queen has been scrupulously observed. Only once has the Queen been confronted directly by a television reporter while the cameras were on her. This happened in Canada in 1987 when she was attending a Commonwealth Conference. She was walking down a corridor towards the conference room where the big item for discussion was going to be the recent *coup* in Fiji. As she came close to the camera, a British television reporter (out of vision) turned a hand microphone tentatively in her direction and asked politely but clearly the one question that was in everybody's mind: 'What is going to happen?'

Though taken by surprise, the Queen did not show it. She passed the moment off brilliantly. Slowing her step only slightly, she half-turned as she walked, smiled sweetly and said teasingly, as though talking to an inquisitive grandchild, 'We'll just have to wait and see, won't we?' From a television point of view, it was a stunning and unexpected moment of viewing, made memorable by the Queen's superb confidence and remarkable composure.

She was almost playing with the reporter and seemed quite at ease. It is not, however, a type of incident that is likely to be repeated very often, if at all.

The confidence displayed by the Queen comes of hard-won experience, and was in marked contrast to her feelings when she first went to Canada in 1951 a few months before her Accession. Then she was nervous and inexperienced and, like everyone else, taken totally by surprise by the overwhelming public reception and media coverage she received. It was a visit that proved to be critical for her future. The Queen learned a crucial lesson and acquired invaluable experience that was to serve her all her life.

The second, perhaps more important reason for the continuing popularity of the Queen, has been her own modest and quite objective respect for the Crown as an Office of State rather than for herself. She has always given the impression publicly that she is the representative of the Crown of State and that respect must first be paid to the Crown – by herself as well as by others. Her dedicated sense of duty is obsessive. The greatest offence to her would be through transgressing her standards of duty, or loyalty, or sense of responsibility. The dignity of the position she holds, and the constitutional authority she represents, have to be maintained, upheld and respected at all times.

Paradoxically, the Queen's most valuable and effective assets are factors that are intangible and cannot be seen, but can nevertheless be clearly sensed and felt. And appreciated! Her sense of duty and her self-discipline are the 'concealed' elements that create the mystique of her public personality.

When Elizabeth I addressed Parliament for the last time before her death in what has been described as her 'Golden Speech', she said that while being Queen was a glorious thing, it was the people's love and loyalty that mattered. 'There will never Queen sit in my seat with more zeal to my country,' she said, 'and though you have had, and may have, many Princes more mighty and wise sitting in this State, yet you never had, or shall have, any that will be more careful and loving.' It is a claim that explains why she was loved so greatly. But it is one that may now, close to four hundred years later, be challenged – by her namesake.

At the time the present Queen celebrated her twenty-first birthday in 1947, she was, as Princess Elizabeth, in South Africa, accompanying the King and Queen on a tour of that country. She marked the occasion by making her famous speech of Dedication to serve the people of the Commonwealth and Empire all her life. It was broadcast on the 'wireless' and heard all over the world. The Princess recalled that this traditional affirmation, with the motto 'I Serve', had been taken for centuries by all Heirs to the Throne when they came to manhood. She said, however, that she was by the invention of modern science able to do what none of her ancestors could have done: to make her Knightly Dedication with the whole Empire listening.

This sense of dedication to the Commonwealth was a virtue that appealed to Winston Churchill. He came to admire the Queen greatly after her

Accession, but he did not know her very well before then. Even so he managed to place his finger perceptively upon her future in a speech he made at Guildhall in 1951 when Princess Elizabeth and the Duke of Edinburgh were officially welcomed home from their triumphant tour of Canada, a tour which had been arranged at short notice during what would turn out to be the final months of the King's life.

This, Princess Elizabeth's first major tour on her own, had been a huge success, and Mr Churchill had recently been returned to power at a General Election and was once more Prime Minister. The Princess and the Duke drove in State and, despite light rain, in an open carriage with an escort of the Household Cavalry, through the streets of London to Guildhall. There was great public excitement, and also much personal interest, for the Canadians had been claiming exultantly, 'We are sending you home a new Princess!'

Speaking at the luncheon, in a voice full of emotion, Winston Churchill said, 'None has surpassed in brilliance and living force the mission you and your husband have discharged.' He continued grandiloquently, but nevertheless in strangely prophetic terms: 'The whole nation is grateful to you for what you have done for us, and to Providence for having endowed you with the gifts and personality which are not only precious to the British Commonwealth and Empire and its islands at home, but will play their part in assuring and mellowing the forward march of society all over the world.'

Mr Churchill had an acute sense of occasion. He also had a great feeling for history. But he did not know then how close was the time when his astute and perceptive comments would be shown to be most apt. The Princess's 'gifts and personality' were about to make their impact upon history and the many different forms of society all over the world to which Churchill had referred.

Part Two

Two

An Uncertain Summer

AFTER THE LONG GLOOM of the Second World War and the immediate post-war years, the exhilarating summer of 1951 was a strawberries-and-cream season at last. With blazing sunshine blessing the Henley Regatta, Test Match cricket and the Wimbledon tennis championships alike, it seemed too good to be true. Not everyone believed it. The Tennis Correspondent of *The Times* commented that, when the umpire at Wimbledon could walk on to the Centre Court on the sunniest day of the year carrying an umbrella, 'One feels that almost anything may happen!' As indeed it did. It was that sort of rain-and-shine, on-off summer.

Mrs Louise Brough, the Women's Singles champion at Wimbledon for the previous three years, was knocked out in the semi-finals. A little-known American, R. Savitt, making his first appearances on the Centre Court, won the Men's Singles title. Sugar Ray Robinson, to this day rated as possibly the greatest boxer of all time pound-for-pound (whatever that may mean), surprisingly lost his Middleweight Champion of the World boxing title in London to an under-dog Englishman, Randolph Turpin. Another Englishman, Max Faulkner, won the British Open golf title. At the Oval cricket ground, the veteran Len Hutton scored his hundredth century in first-class cricket with a magnificent cover-drive for four on the same ground on which he had made a Test Match record-breaking 364 runs against Australia in 1938. There was a record entry for the National Rose Show in London and at the National Sweet-Pea Society Show it was noted that the sweet-pea blooms were bigger than ever, with twelve stems to a vase now looking as good as fifteen stems had looked before the war.

The Korean War was ending and Dr Mosaddeq and Iranian oil appeared to be equally remote concerns. It was the busiest and brightest summer in Britain since before the war. It seemed like a return to yesteryear. Almost. While the resilience and buoyancy of former good times, for so long only a distant memory, had at last returned, there was still a degree of food rationing and the bookshop staff of 84 Charing Cross Road were writing grateful letters to Helen Hanff in New York to thank her for her Easter food parcels of tins of ham and tongue and packets of dried egg. Licences were still needed to build even the smallest house and, despite protests, inflation had forced the minimum bus fares on London Transport up to tuppence.

But the Festival of Britain, launched by the King on the steps of St Paul's Cathedral in May, had put the country into party mood, with open-air street parties, fireworks, and mock ducking-stool re-enactments along with dancing on the village greens. It was not the return to an old era, however – it was more to be the Indian summer of that era, and the transition stage into a whole new way of life.

Nevertheless, Ascot race course had been remodelled at great expense (after the issue of the appropriate licences). New stands had been built and the whole painted, for the first time since before the war, with pristine white picked out in gold ready not only for the Sport of Kings, but for that great event of the fashion and racing 'season', the opening of Royal Ascot. But when the royal carriage, drawn by four horses, drove down the centre of the course, the Queen was alone, without the King. During the whole of that exciting summer from the end of May onwards, a vaguely troubling shadow was to hang across the nation, caused by the King's persistent indisposition.

The King's health had been a matter for some concern ever since the end of 1948, when a disorder of his arteries was diagnosed and he was forced to cancel all engagements and to rest for several months. He had treatment which improved his condition, but was left reduced in strength. An important tour by the King and Queen to Australia and New Zealand planned for 1949 was postponed indefinitely, but was later reconsidered and arranged for 1952. On 29 May 1951, the King had contracted influenza after attending a service of the Order of the Bath at Westminster Abbey. No bulletins were issued at first, but a planned tour to Northern Ireland at the beginning of June was modified, the visit being carried out alone by the Queen accompanied by Princess Margaret.

A week after the first attack, a medical bulletin issued on 2 June said the King had a small catarrhal inflammation of the lung, 'but the constitutional disturbance is slight'. On 4 June it was stated that, on the advice of his doctors, the King had decided to cancel all engagements for at least four weeks. A bulletin by the doctors on 6 June said the King's condition continued to be satisfactory.

On 13 June, however, the doctors issued a further bulletin which contained the first hints of a deeper concern. They stated that the King continued to make progress and the inflammation in his lung had subsided, but then added the cautious comment that, in view of the attacks of catarrhal infection His Majesty had suffered during the present year, they were advising that a prolonged convalescence was essential.

Despite efforts to allay general anxiety, alarm bells were starting to ring in the public's mind. The King was greatly loved and it was recalled how, in 1948, he had been the first to insist that there should be no fuss about his condition during his previous illness, which began with his suffering from cramp in the feet. The specialists then called in had taken a serious view, for it was found he had Buerger's disease, a disorder of the arteries. But Princess Elizabeth was at that time expecting the birth of her first child very shortly, an event awaited with eagerness and excitement. The King would not allow anything to be said about his own health until after the birth of the child.

Prince Charles was born on 14 November. Even then the King insisted on waiting a further week until the general celebration and rejoicing was over before, on the 23rd, he allowed an announcement to be made about his health. It at once caused great public concern, stating, as it did, that not only would the King have to cancel all engagements for several months, but there was also danger of gangrene in the King's right leg involving the possibility of amputation.

The King was forced to rest and seemed to be progressing until the doctors announced in the following March of 1949 that, though the flow of blood had been restored to the left leg, the main artery in the right leg was still obstructed. With a view to improving the flow of blood to the right foot, the King was advised to have a lumbar sympathectomy performed on his right side. He agreed, and thereafter his health improved, though he was never really to be strong again. Nevertheless the Australian tour was reconsidered and arranged for early 1952, and in the meantime a visit to Northern Ireland was planned for 1951.

In the light of all that had gone before, it was not therefore surprising that, when the doctors advised prolonged convalescence after the King's attack of influenza in 1951, there should be doubts in the public mind about the seriousness of his condition. *The Times* felt impelled to carry a main leading article, stating categorically that there was no connection between the condition of the King's lungs and the flow of blood to his feet. Incongruous as this may seem, it was a reflection of the concern being felt and the need for reassurance. The public was familiar with influenza, but it did not know much about Buerger's disease. It was also aware of the King's modest insistence that no fuss should be made. So what was wrong? They could only wait and hope that, as before, he would recover in due course.

The effect of the King's illness was to throw a heavier burden of responsibility on to the other members of the royal family as they continued to undertake the King's various public engagements on his behalf. The Queen carried out the official visit to Northern Ireland and shortly afterwards received the elderly King Haakon of Norway – then nearly eighty – on an official visit in June. The Queen sat by King Haakon's side at the State

Banquet at Buckingham Palace in June while Princess Elizabeth read her father's speech.

The most dramatic moment of the summer, however, came on the next day, 8 June, when Princess Elizabeth represented the King at the Trooping the Colour ceremony on Horse Guards Parade. The Princess's appearance was a sensation. Mounted side-saddle on a chestnut police horse named Winston, she wore a scarlet tunic crossed with the blue ribbon of the Garter, a dark-blue skirt, and a black tricorne hat with a tall white plume fixed to a grenade emblem on the left side – a copy of a hat worn by a Colonel of Grenadiers in 1745. It was the first time she wore this uniform, which was specially designed for her for the occasion, and which never ceased afterwards to attract all eyes when she again wore it at future parades.

Even without her striking appearance, the presence of a woman mounted on horseback as the central figure of this traditional and very male military occasion was unique. Throughout an hour of highly precise ceremonial, she showed complete poise and composure. At another Trooping the Colour parade some years later, when a young man in the crowd fired several blank cartridge shots at her from a pistol at close range, she again showed perfect self-control. She said later of this occasion that the most disconcerting thing had been 'the sound of the cavalry' as the mounted Guard of Honour spurred up alongside her to act as a shield in her defence.

For Princess Elizabeth, the summer of 1951 was to foreshadow major changes in her life. She had been living quietly at home, in Clarence House in London, as Princess Elizabeth, Duchess of Edinburgh. She was the mother of two small children – Prince Charles was two years old and Princess Anne still a baby. The Duke of Edinburgh was serving with the Mediterranean Fleet in command of the frigate HMS *Magpie*. It had already been announced that he would return to London in August to be with Princess Elizabeth until after the King and Queen returned in mid-1952 from their deferred Australasian tour.

Princess Elizabeth had celebrated her twenty-fifth birthday the previous April during a two-week private holiday in Rome where she and the Duke were guests of the British Ambassador. Now, however, she was being drawn into greater prominence by undertaking more public duties on behalf of the King in addition to those already arranged for her.

One of the busiest days of the summer for the royal family was also to bring a major surprise announcement. On 4 July, American Independence Day, the Queen, accompanied by Princess Elizabeth and Princess Margaret, attended a commemoration service at St Paul's Cathedral where General Eisenhower, in military uniform, presented the cathedral with an illuminated Roll of Honour bound in leather containing the names of 28,000 US servicemen and women who had lost their lives during the war in operations from the United Kingdom. At the same service, the Archbishop of

Canterbury dedicated a silver cross and silver candelabra that were the King's gift to Washington Cathedral to commemorate the hospitality shown in the war by Washington Cathedral to British servicemen and women in the United States.

Later in the same day, the Queen visited the Tate Gallery; Queen Mary visited exhibitions of Chelsea china, and of the royal cabinet makers of France; the Duke and Duchess of Gloucester and the Princess Royal attended the opening of the Royal Agricultural Society Show at Cambridge; Prince Michael of Kent celebrated his ninth birthday; and, in the evening, Princess Elizabeth was present at a ball at the Royal Military College, Sandhurst.

During the evening of that hectic day, the joint announcement was made – routinely from Clarence House, but personally by the Prime Minister of Canada, Mr St Laurent, in Ottawa – that Princess Elizabeth and the Duke of Edinburgh were to visit Canada in the autumn. The news was received in Canada with the utmost delight.

Royal tours overseas were a rare event at that time. The King and Queen had had their very successful visit to Canada and the United States in 1939, when neither of the Princesses accompanied them. The only visit to a Dominion since then had been to South Africa in 1947 when the King and Queen were accompanied by both Princess Elizabeth and Princess Margaret. It was while on that tour that Princes Elizabeth had celebrated her twenty-first birthday with her famous broadcast of Dedication: 'I declare before you all that my whole life, whether it be long or short, shall be devoted to your service and the service of our great Imperial family to which we all belong.'

The King and Queen's proposed then deferred visit to Australia and New Zealand by sea was still in preparation. The itinerary had been issued on 19 June, less than a week after the doctors recommended a prolonged convalescence, and the prospect of its being carried out as planned was beginning to seem increasingly unlikely. The Canadians were therefore all the more pleased to be having a visit from Princess Elizabeth and the Duke of Edinburgh. No itinerary had yet been worked out, but the efforts to honour the royal request that the tour should be kept 'as simple as possible' soon came under immense pressure from the enthusiastic clamour by Canadians from all parts of the country to receive a visit from the Princess and the Duke.

It was not practicable to meet all the requests, and the Princess and the Duke were themselves disappointed that they were not going to be able to visit the Yukon and the far north in the time available. Nevertheless the itinerary, when it was finally completed, allowed for fifty-four towns to be visited in thirty-five days, with many thousands of miles being covered by air, royal train, sea and car in the second largest country in the world, spanning nearly 3,000 miles. Even in the planning stage, without the final realization, it was clearly seen to be a most strenuous undertaking. Moreover, it was announced early in August that Princess Elizabeth had accepted an invitation from

President Truman to make a two-day visit to Washington, to be fitted in towards the end of the Canadian tour.

At the beginning of August, the King and Queen went on holiday to Balmoral, where, on 21 August, Princess Margaret celebrated her twenty-first birthday. The King had not expected to return to London until 10 October, but even the beautiful clear air of Scotland could not cure his chest and on 1 September he was visited at Balmoral by a radiologist and a chest specialist. A week later the King travelled to London by royal train for further examination, but flew back to Balmoral the same day. A few days later he returned to London for further treatment.

The Queen followed him on 11 September – the day on which an ominous bulletin signed by nine doctors stated that a series of examinations had been carried out on the King, including radiology and bronchoscopy, which showed that structural changes had occurred in one of the King's lungs. The Queen was accompanied by Princess Elizabeth and the Duke of Edinburgh, who had been due to return to London on that day in any case to prepare for departure by sea for Canada on Tuesday, 25 September.

Ten days later, on Friday, 21 September, a very short medical bulletin signed by seven doctors conveyed the alarming news that the condition of the King's lung gave cause for concern. 'In view of the structural changes referred to in the last bulletin,' it said, 'we have advised His Majesty to undergo an operation in the near future. This advice the King has accepted.'

A simultaneous announcement from Buckingham Palace referred to the two royal tours then in preparation. It said that a final decision on the possibility of the King undertaking his projected tour of Australia and New Zealand in 1952 would be announced within a week or two. It added the reassuring statement that the projected tour of Canada by Princess Elizabeth and the Duke of Edinburgh would still be carried out in full, but instead of leaving by sea on the following Tuesday, they hoped to fly on a later day so as to arrive at Quebec in time to begin the tour on 2 October.

Canadian reaction was generous. Mr St Laurent stated that the Canadian people were relieved and pleased that the King's health was considered not so serious as to cause the tour's abandonment. They all hoped the treatment would bring about such beneficial results that Princess Elizabeth would not have occasion to feel undue concern about the King's health during her stay in their country.

On the afternoon of Saturday, 22 September, Queen Mary and Princess Elizabeth went to Buckingham Palace to visit the King, and Princess Margaret flew down from Balmoral to be with him in the evening. Only Prince Charles and Princess Anne remained at Balmoral. During the evening Princess Elizabeth and the Duke of Edinburgh attended the film entitled appropriately *The Lady with a Lamp*, starring Anna Neagle as Florence

Nightingale. To one inquirer expressing sympathy, the Princess replied, 'Yes. This is a worrying time.'

The operation on the King was carried out on the following morning, Sunday, 23 September, at about 10 a.m. while prayers for the King's recovery were being offered in churches of all denominations throughout the country, and during the day throughout the world. It was performed in a room in the north wing of Buckingham Palace which had been specially prepared as an operating theatre. The Queen, accompanied by Princess Elizabeth, the Duke of Edinburgh and Princess Margaret, had attended early-morning service in the chapel of Lambeth Palace, the London home of the Archbishop of Canterbury, who conducted the service. The Queen was the first person to hear from the doctors how the King had withstood the operation. Then other members of the royal family were told, and the Prime Minister, Mr Attlee, was informed.

The doctors' bulletin was posted on the gates of Buckingham Palace at about 4.30 p.m., where it was read by several hundred people waiting patiently outside the railings despite a cool breeze. It stated briefly that an operation for 'lung resection' had been carried out, and that while anxiety must remain for some days, 'His Majesty's post-operative condition is satisfactory.' What was not said, but was kept a very closely guarded secret, was that the doctors had found cancer in the lung they removed. The Queen and Princess Elizabeth were told the grave news, but the King himself was not informed.

During the next few days, moderately reassuring bulletins were issued about the King's progress and Mr St Laurent and Mr Attlee were in telephone discussions about the King's health and its possible consequences for the royal tour of Canada. In an effort to ease any anxiety in the King's mind about the Australasian tour, the Australian Prime Minister, Mr Menzies, wrote to him on 21 September, referring to a letter which he and and the Prime Minister of New Zealand had sent jointly to him in June, saying that if the King's health precluded him from making the tour of Australasia early in 1952, both countries would welcome the tour being carried out by Princess Elizabeth and the Duke of Edinburgh. He now reaffirmed that welcome.

On Wednesday, 26 September, a cautionary statement was issued from Buckingham Palace saying it should be remembered that, while the King's gradual progress towards recovery had been uninterrupted, and although no complications had arisen so far, 'there will inevitably be a period of some anxiety for the next week or ten days'. Shortly afterwards on the same day it was announced from Clarence House that Princess Elizabeth and the Duke of Edinburgh had accepted a suggestion, made to them by the Prime Minister of Canada, to postpone the start of the Canadian tour by one or two weeks. It was added that they both hoped very much that arrangements could still be made for a visit to Washington.

The Canadian reaction remained one of understanding. No one wanted to see the tour cancelled, though there were advocates for postponement until the following spring when the weather would be better and more reliable. If the tour was carried out as planned, but set back by two weeks, it would extend it beyond the Canadian 'Fall' and bring it into the approaching cold weather of early winter. On the other hand, postponement of the Canadian tour until the spring of 1952 would create a clash of dates with the proposed tour to Australasia by the King and Queen.

The attitude in Canada was mainly one of personal sympathy for the King and the Princess, and the Canadian newspapers were especially sympathetic to the royal family. The *Montreal Star* said, 'In this country there is no thought but the warm and human feeling that a tour postponed or cancelled would be a tiny price to pay if the continued presence of the daughter would help the father back to health.'

The need for an early decision became imperative. This came the next day, on the 27th: it was known to be the King's wish that the tour should proceed. A bulletin was issued from Buckingham Palace saying that the King was stronger and his appetite improving. Immediately afterwards there came an announcement from Clarence House that Princess Elizabeth and the Duke of Edinburgh would leave London by air for Canada on 7 October, arriving in Montreal on 8 October.

The closeness of the two announcements, first of the postponement, and then, the next day, of the decision to go ahead almost immediately, came as something of a surprise to the Canadians. The statements were not inconsistent, however, and they emphasized the royal desire to proceed as quickly as possible. There was to be a difference of only one week between the original and the new starting dates. The outcome was so much what the Canadians wanted to hear that there was complete satisfaction.

After all the uncertainty of recent weeks, the decision brought not so much a relaxation of tension as a considerable heightening of expectation. It was therefore in a mood of great anticipation that the Canadians were looking forward to the Princess's arrival. Recent events had evoked keen sympathy for her. Pent-up emotions awaited release. So much so that, on the eve of the Princess's departure from England, the chairman of the committee organizing the tour described in a nation-wide broadcast across Canada how he had made a preliminary trip along the route to be taken by the Princess and the Duke, and everywhere found so much enthusiasm for the visit as to suggest it would become 'a month-long national celebration in which all Canadians will share'.

It must be emphasized that the prevailing mood in Canada was different then from now. There was still the hangover from before and during the war, when ties between Canada, Britain and the Monarchy were exceptionally close. The developments that followed as Canada came to terms with its internal divisions of loyalties between the traditionally English-speaking and French-speaking populations, and the overall struggle by Canada to retain its own national culture and identity in the face of enormous pressures from across its southern border – especially by television – from the United States, have in the intervening years created a somewhat different outlook. In 1951, it was the former mood which prevailed and the events recalled here reflect the spirit of that time. Nevertheless the visit was to be for Princess Elizabeth something more than a celebration.

Three

Security Precautions

ONE OF THE CONSEQUENCES of the King's ill-health was that the traditional precise planning of a royal tour now needed to be supplemented by the most exceptional security for the Heiress Presumptive to the Throne. Conditions in Canada had moreover changed so much since the previous royal tour in 1939 that great care had to be taken with unfamiliar arrangements. The improvements in air travel and the youth and fitness of the visitors meant in the meantime that it was possible to plan for greater distances to be covered within the time available. More locations could be included by flying the royal visitors from place to place in many areas, rather than going by sea, train and road, as had been customary. On the other hand, a certain amount of train travel would permit the visitors to see at close hand the beauty and variety of the country they were visiting and enable them to meet more people at little wayside stops.

It was unfortunate that the Princess was inevitably going to start the tour feeling a little tired. The worry about the King's health – which was more serious than had been publicly disclosed – and the on-off uncertainty of the tour with the postponement of its start; the substitution of the planned sea journey across the Atlantic by a long and somewhat tiring air flight; and a midnight departure after a long day of farewells could all be expected to contribute to her general fatigue. Yet there was also the exhilaration of an exciting tour ahead to act as a counter-balance.

Princess Elizabeth did indeed have a long day to cope with on 7 October 1951 before leaving London. She had luncheon with the Queen and Queen Mary, visited the King at Buckingham Palace in the afternoon, and said goodbye in the evening to her two small children. While she was away, Prince Charles was going to celebrate his third birthday, which she would miss by a few days.

It was midnight before the Princess and the Duke of Edinburgh were seen off at London Airport by the Queen and Princess Margaret, the Minister of

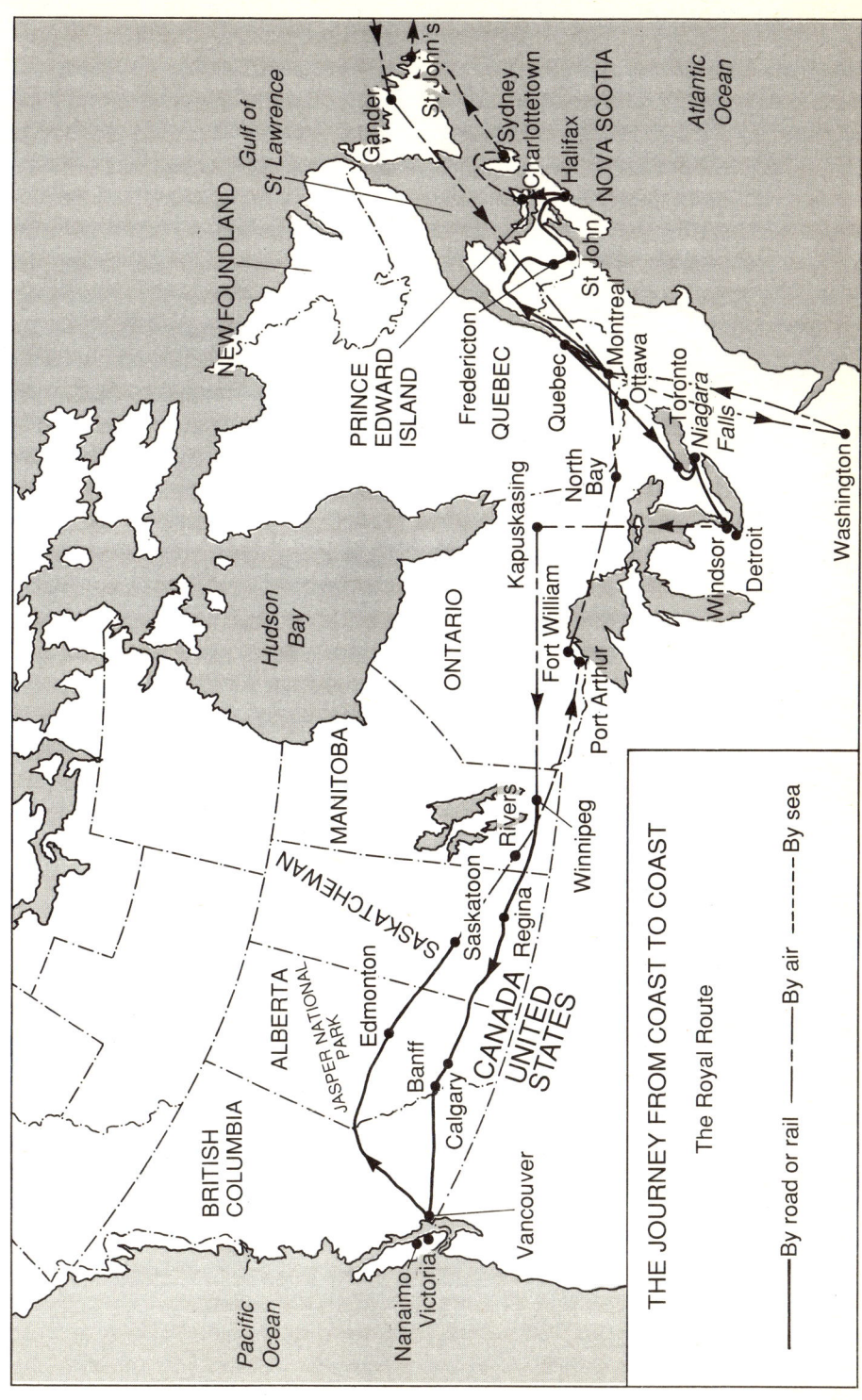

THE JOURNEY FROM COAST TO COAST

The Royal Route

——— By road or rail   ——— By air   ----- By sea

Civil Aviation, the High Commissioner for Canada, the Chairman of British Overseas Airways, and a small crowd held back at a distance of fifty yards from the aircraft. (There was no central International Terminal at Heathrow in those days, only a few small brick buildings and a large number of war-time Nissen huts, all strung out between the Windsor road and the tarmac of the runways.)

The aircraft to carry the royal visitors across the Atlantic was a silver, blue and white four-engined, propellor-driven BOAC Stratocruiser named *Canopus*. It was normally used on the airline's commercial flights, appropriately called the Monarch service. Compared even with modern jumbo jets, it was a plane with some enviable old-fashioned comforts. There were twelve sleeping berths located above the seats, where modern planes now have luggage racks. These could be lowered down when required to form luxurious couchettes, with comfortable mattresses, sheets, blankets, pillows, and a secure curtain drawn across to ensure absolute privacy for those passengers wishing to change into night attire. A breakfast of scrambled eggs, bacon and toast, all cooked in the galley, could be served in bed to those who preferred it that way. The plane was double-decked, with a lounge on the lower deck that had comfortable chairs where first-class passengers could travel at ease – when not in bed!

Such comfort was much appreciated by those able to enjoy it, for the aircraft was very slow. The journey from London to Gander in Newfoundland alone took nearly eleven hours. BOAC's regular service normally left late at night so that passengers could sleep most of the way and, allowing for time-zone changes, arrive at Gander in reasonable time in the early morning. After the refuelling stop and the chance to walk around, the onward flight to Montreal took another four and a half hours. Allowing for further time-zone changes, it was possible for those passengers not on diets to have three breakfasts between London and Montreal (one before Gander, one at Gander and effectively a third between Gander and Montreal), and still arrive in Montreal in good time for lunch.

For the royal flight, the plane took off at 12.30 a.m. (11.30 p.m. GMT), and took ten hours twenty minutes to fly the 2,470 statute miles to Gander – an average speed of 240 m.p.h. It crossed the north Atlantic at a height of 20,000 feet, and at the most northerly point of its great-circle track was flying into a head wind of 54 knots, which gave it a ground speed of only 185 knots.

Elaborate escort and security arrangements were in operation along the route. In the air the crew of *Canopus* maintained ground contact with Britain by radio-telephone until Northern Ireland was behind them. They then switched to wireless telegraphy contact with a number of powerful control stations, with another aircraft, and with ships spaced out across the north Atlantic. During the first part of the journey, contact was maintained with Prestwick transatlantic control, but after passing a position 30 degW this was taken over by Gander control. Listening posts at Goose Bay, Labrador (an alternative landing place in the event of bad weather at Gander), and the RCAF Eastern Command headquarters at Halifax, Nova Scotia, maintained continual 'watch' on emergency frequencies.

Shackleton long-range aircraft of the RAF Coastal Command patrolled the route during the royal flight, flying to about mid-way across the Atlantic, where aircraft of the Royal Canadian Air Force took over. As *Canopus* approached Gander, two Lancasters from the RCAF Search and Rescue base at Greenwood, Nova Scotia, stood by at Gander and at Torbay near St John's, Newfoundland. At sea, the Air Ministry weather ships normally stationed in the Atlantic were placed on alert, while five warships were spaced out along the *Canopus*'s track: the aircraft carrier HMS *Triumph*; two destroyers, HMS *Wizard* and HMS *Scorpion*; and two frigates, HMS *Burghead* and HMCS *La Hulloise*. All maintained contact with distress frequencies as well as with *Canopus* and other vessels.

As they approached Gander, the royal visitors had their first sight of Canada – a view of wild untouched country with countless small lakes and rivers and islands, and with vast stretches of spruce forest. *Canopus* arrived at Gander soon after dawn, and, during the rest and refuelling pause of two and a half hours, the Princess and the Duke were able to stroll in the sunshine in the cool clear morning air. The aircraft then resumed its flight to Montreal, which it reached within the scheduled four and a half hours, just before noon in local time. The whole journey had taken seventeen and a quarter hours, of which about fourteen and three-quarter hours were flying time.

Early-morning clouds and drizzle over Montreal had threatened a dull day, but about an hour before the royal plane was due, the rain suddenly stopped, the clouds lifted and within minutes the warm sun shone brightly, drying up the puddles on the concrete at Dorval Airport. The maple and birch trees just outside the airport boundary were already scarlet and gold in their splendid autumn colours. Still glistening after the recent rain, they provided a beautiful Canadian backdrop to the reception ceremonies.

The plane in fact arrived slightly early and taxied across the tarmac for ten minutes before reaching the section of the airport where a dais had been erected. The official welcome appeared to be smoothly set up for normal procedure and protocol: the decorated dais, the microphones, the VIPs behind and the press to one side, the arrival and greetings and inspection of the Guard of Honour, the speeches of welcome and the courteous reply, the thanks and then the departure. It was all very formal and familiar.

The reception area was located some distance from the airport buildings on the tarmac outside one of the hangers where the royal plane could pull up close by. A smallish crowd was lined up at some remove on the far side of a security fence. They had been standing there patiently for some time in the rain – something Canadian crowds are never keen on doing – awaiting the arrival of the royal visitors.

This occasion, it should be emphasized, was *not* the start of the royal tour. It was the formal welcome of the Princess and the Duke on to Canadian soil by the Governor-General of Canada, the distinguished war-time army commander, Viscount Alexander of Tunis, and the Prime Minister of Canada, Mr St Laurent. Too much ceremony and excitement would pre-empt the official start of the tour in Quebec City on the next day and steal some of its thunder. That had to be avoided at all costs. The greeting ceremony was designed deliberately to be fairly low key.

Although Montreal was the largest city by far in French-speaking Canada, Quebec City was the capital of the province and had prepared a grand opening greeting. Montreal's turn to receive the royal visitors would come later in the tour. As far as the media were concerned, however – especially the photographers – this was the first glimpse of the Princess in Canada and they were out to make the most of it. They were present in force by the score: cameramen, photographers, journalists and broadcasters – all interested in the Princess. It was to be a foretaste for the future.

The arrival went fairly much to plan, with the difference that instead of the photographers remaining in the press area – as they would have done in Britain – they pursued the royal couple in jostling North American fashion, except during the inspection of the Guard of Honour. There were far more of them than normally followed the royal couple at that time. Camera equipment was larger than it is today; they carried bulky camera bags slung over their shoulders; and they were wearing hats and coats against the weather. The royal couple disconcertingly seemed before long to become almost submerged in a struggling sea of attention.

Cameras flashed close to the Princess and then the used bulbs were instantly discarded, for in those days before the development of electronic flash equipment, each flash-bulb – an object like a small light-globe – had to be replaced after every picture exposure. As the Princess and the Duke turned towards the plane to shake hands with the aircraft crew, they had to skirt round an area already littered with discarded bulbs and broken glass. The real problem, however, was yet to emerge.

Out of consideration for the people waving and cheering from behind the fence, it was decided that as the Princess and the Duke were leaving to go to the railway station to board their train for the overnight journey to Quebec, their car should drive close to the boundary fence to give the crowds an opportunity to see the royal couple close-up. This, of course, also gave the photographers, who included a strong international contingent as well as Canadians, their perfect opening. Some wanted good close-up shots of the Princess with the excited faces of the crowd in the background; others wanted to see the Princess's face (not the back of her head) as she smiled and waved. It was a natural and normal professional reaction, and was what the rest of Canada (and the world) wanted to see. In the excitement of the moment, the photographers took their opportunity and streamed across the tarmac towards the fence to await the slow progress of the car towards them.

Preceded by two provincial police on motor-cycles and followed by four Mounties in scarlet tunics riding gleaming motor-cycles, the royal car circled up to one end of the fence and then drove slowly back alongside the fence close to the crowd. The Princess sat on the side of the car nearest the crowd, from where she could acknowledge the enthusiastic greetings.

As the car approached them, the photographers and film cameramen surrounded it and pushed their cameras towards the Princess's face, simultaneously letting off their flash-bulbs in close proximity. These flash-bulbs contained magnesium foil, or a magnesium coil, which generated a very bright flash. But they also had a tendency to explode, and the glass bulb would fragment into tiny splinters of glass. Although safety bulbs had been introduced which had a protective coating over the glass to prevent any slivers scattering, many of the older bulbs were still in circulation. Small powdered slivers of glass were subsequently found in the Princess's fur coat and some half a dozen used bulbs landed on the floor of the royal car.

The discharge of flash-bulbs so close to the Princess must have been unnerving for her, though she never showed it. Even so, a disturbing situation for everyone concerned had arisen before the tour was even begun. An immediate review of press procedures was conducted behind the scenes and prompt preventive action taken officially. From then on in Canada safety flash-bulbs were obligatory, and no photographers, film cameramen or journalists were allowed nearer to the Princess than fifteen feet.

This latter precautionary edict was enforced rigidly for the remainder of the tour by the enormous Mounties who provided the royal escort. Invariably – and sometimes unceremoniously – they always got their man if anyone tried to break ranks, as occasionally happened in small towns along the route when local photographers and reporters temporarily joined the party. These, being unaware of, or unfamiliar with, the directive, would try desperately to obtain good coverage for their local newspapers. Besides coming under the watchful attention of the Mounties, they would also be eyed uneasily by the élite of the international press corps travelling with the tour, who were anxious above all not to be scooped by a local man.

Four

'O Canada'

NOBODY KNOWS FOR CERTAIN how Canada came to receive its name. One popular version has it that early Spanish or Portuguese seafarers visited the country looking for an El Dorado, but finding no gold came to the conclusion: *aca nada* – 'nothing here', and went away. Before that the Norsemen, sailing Canadian waters in their high-prowed long-boats when the Danes were subjugating the Saxons in England, had made some attempts to live in North America, but they also gave up.

The waters of the Gulf of St Lawrence had become familiar, but it was a French fisherman, Jacques Cartier, who discovered the St Lawrence River in 1534 and sailed up it to unlock the doors to the north. He learned the Huron-Iroquois term for an Indian town (or collection of towns), and in his narrative when he returned to France reported: 'Ils appellent une ville – Canada.' From then on the name 'Canada' was adopted for the whole territory and later the whole country. English sovereignty over the neighbouring 'New Found Land' followed some years later and was proclaimed in the name of Queen Elizabeth in 1583, making it Britain's oldest colony, though no effort was made to settle it until 1610.

In the meantime, another Frenchman, Champlain, had arrived in Canada and in 1604 founded the settlement of Port Royal. In 1608, in the 'very beautiful and pleasant bay' where Cartier made his winter quarters, he founded and named Quebec, using an Algonquin Indian name. On the heights of Cape Diamond at Quebec he built a formidable fortress, the Citadel, whose guns could look down on, and command, the passageway of the great St Lawrence River. It came to be known as the Gibraltar of America, or the Gibraltar of the Western Hemisphere, so impregnable did it become. Stormed five times, it was never taken.

Even so, on a gloomy, wet and cold autumnal night in September 1759, during the Seven Years War between England and France, General Wolfe and a British force landed stealthily in the darkness and stole up the cliffs beside the Citadel. On the Plains of Abraham above, they defeated the French forces under Montcalm, though Wolfe himself died in the battle. Montreal fell in the following year and France formally surrendered Canada to the British Crown.

It was at the spot where General Wolfe landed some two hundred years before that the Princess began her tour – also on a gloomy, cloudy and wet autumnal day. The site of that first famous landing was now a railway station set among some customs sheds by the dockside. As the royal train steamed slowly into the station beside the St Lawrence River, the first people to see the train and wave a greeting were several German immigrants lining the deck of a ship that had docked the previous night.

The Princess started the day looking less tired and pale than she had appeared to be on her arrival in Montreal. This was just as well, for she had a long day ahead of her, with many engagements. These included:

§   The formal reception at Wolfe's Cove and inspection of the Guard of Honour.

§   A visit to Parliament Buildings, where she met the members of the Legislative Assembly and their wives.

§   Next, on to Laval University, where she was welcomed by the Catholic Archbishop (who was Vice-Chancellor of the University), and by the Rector, who presented the Deans of the Faculties.

§   Then to the City Hall, to be greeted by the Mayor and Members of the Council and their wives.

With official protocol satisfied, it was now the turn of the general public.

§   A long slow drive by the Princess and the Duke through the crowded streets of the lower town of old Quebec – the only walled city of North America – with its picturesque narrow streets, gabled roofs and dormer windows. Quebec is the capital of French-speaking Canada, and everywhere the red and white Canadian flag was accompanied by the blue and white flag of Quebec with its fleur-de-lis in the corner. Banners strung across the streets said 'Bienvenue'. Huge and excited crowds shouted their greetings in French to *La Princesse*.

§   Then she drove up to the Citadel. Here, at one of the most ancient fortresses in Canada, she reviewed one of the oldest and proudest of the French Canadian regiments, Le Régiment de la Chaudière, of which she was Colonel-in-Chief.

§   Also at the Citadel, she met a long line of mothers and widows wearing silver crosses denoting the loss of a family member in the war. She spent some time speaking with them, mostly in French.

§   As the Princess left the Citadel, a row of trumpeters manned the canon-studded battlements. They stood outlined against the sky, and they sounded a fanfare as the wind rustled the royal-blue banners on their trumpets – the royal-blue colours of Quebec.

And all of that came before luncheon. In the afternoon the Princess went:

§   To the Plains of Abraham, scene of Wolfe's posthumous victory, where she reviewed the 27th Brigade and took the salute at one of the largest military parades in Quebec's history.
§   Then saw a demonstration by schoolchildren at the Municipal Coliseum.
§   Finally, she attended a reception at the Bois de Coulonge given by the Lieutenant-Governor and the Prime Minister of Quebec.

By this time it was 6 p.m. and the Princess was allowed an hour and three quarters to rest briefly and prepare for a full evening of engagements.

The visit to Quebec could up to this point already be described as a huge success. Quebec more than any other Canadian city represented the traditional culture and architecture of Europe. As the busy day went on, the people of Quebec recognized in the young Princess a poise and style with which they could identify, and a beauty they could admire. Her fluent French delighted the *Québécoise*, not only in her speeches but in the readiness with which she used it in speaking with the ordinary people. The word had gone round very quickly after her visit to the Citadel of how concerned she had been with the individual wives and mothers who had lost husbands and sons during the war. She had shown interest and compassion and they recognized and appreciated her sincerity and feeling for them.

It was the Princess's appearance in the evening, however, that was to transform the day into an undoubted triumph. The people of Quebec had a great sense of occasion and the Princess arrived for the state banquet at the Château Frontenac looking radiant despite her long day. She was magnificently attired, wearing a silver and tulle evening dress with a very full skirt, crossed by the blue of the Garter ribbon, with the Garter star, a superb diamond tiara, necklace and ear-rings. Everyone was stunned by the spectacle, and the pictures taken that night sent shock-waves of expectant excitement across Canada. They were to start the myth of the Fairy Princess that was to predominate during the early days of the tour.

When the Prime Minister of Quebec, Mr Duplessis, proposed the toast, he said that most of the people of the Province of Quebec were of French origin but they had, for centuries, been faithful to the Crown, and Quebec was a synonym for loyalty. There was no doubting his sincerity and the support he received from those present when he paid a personal compliment to the Princess, saying that the people of Quebec derived inspiration of high promise from her example and that of her husband. He concluded, to much applause,

'It is of great comfort to have persons in high places capable of preserving the traditions we cherish.'

The state banquet did not mark the end of this extraordinary day, however. The Princess and the Duke then went on to a concert given by the Orchestre Symphonique de Québec, and when they finally arrived back at the railway station to board the royal train, they found another crowd waiting there to greet them. A day originally scheduled to be of nearly thirteen hours' duration had lasted for some fourteen hours and did not finish until after 11.30 p.m.

The train was over an hour late leaving Quebec City for the overnight journey to Ottawa, and when the Princess at last got to bed, however tired she may have felt, she would have been fully aware that the next day was likely to present a similar experience. Her first engagement, at 10 a.m., would be the formal reception in the national capital by the Governor-General and the Prime Minister and the presentation of a large number of Ministers, Diplomats, High Commissioners, the Chief Justice of Canada, Parliamentary Speakers, Members of Parliament, Service Chiefs, members of the Ottawa Board of Control, and their wives. The final engagements for the day would be another state dinner followed by a reception for Heads of Missions and Canadian officials at Government House, which would not start until 10 p.m.

The Princess was not accustomed to this kind of pressure, but it was to continue during the next few days and disclose a problem that only she could overcome.

The crowds were far bigger than anyone had expected, and the Princess confessed later that she had been overwhelmed by their numbers and the welcome she received. In Quebec City it was estimated that some half a million people had turned out to greet her – double the population of the city. On her arrival in Ottawa, there were small boys in the trees and children overflowed from the crowd into the official reception party. More crowds stood four and five deep as the royal couple drove for miles through the beautiful parks of the national capital.

In Toronto two days later, the Princess received a tumultuous ticker-tape welcome as she drove down the concrete canyon of Bay Street, and the next day troops had to be called in to help the police control the crowds as she drove around the city. The Princess was so delayed during the day packed with engagements that she arrived an hour late for the official dinner in the evening. Her speech, which was being broadcast to the nation, had to be delivered before the main course was served in order to catch the radio deadline.

The element of constitutional responsibility also weighed heavily upon the Princess. She was there representing the King and she was nervous and anxious not to make mistakes. The *Ottawa Journal* had emphasized this aspect when it said:

Our impression of this Princess who will one day be Queen is of a young woman trained with great care for the peculiar and exacting duties of a constitutional monarchy – a young woman of integrity and devotion around whom the Commonwealth can maintain in unity its democratic development. That is the spirit in which Canadians will greet Elizabeth and Philip on their first visit to this country; in particular it will be the spirit in Ottawa its capital.

Although she followed the official routines impeccably during those early days in the big cities, a little muscle in the Princess's right cheek was twitching constantly. She kept glancing surreptitiously at Prince Philip to see his reactions and seemed reassured by his almost imperceptible nods of approbation. At times the Duke stood at her elbow, whispering and joking to put her at her ease. In many ways, his confident supporting presence carried her successfully through this initial tentative period.

The Princess found herself caught temporarily between conflicting demands. Many of the official engagements were highly formal and she had to maintain the dignity of the Crown. These formal occasions were carefully choreographed and she needed to concentrate very hard to follow the correct procedures. Away from formality, however, the atmosphere was far more relaxed than anything to which she had previously been accustomed. Yet she did not yet have the experience to switch easily from one mode to the other.

The reception accorded to her by the crowds was warm, friendly and very personal. The people were delighted to see her and showed it enthusiastically with a New World lack of inhibition. But her response was not always what they expected or hoped for. Protocol for royal occasions was less formal overseas than in England, but the Princess was still reacting as she did at home. She was reserved by nature and her normal expression was fairly serious. It became even more so when she was concentrating. Her tense half-smile and formal wave of the hand was an acknowledgement rather than a response. It did not seem to reciprocate the feelings of the crowd. She seemed too formal, too distant, too 'English'.

The press corps saw her in close-up for most of the time and its Canadian and American members were puzzled by her. They were accustomed to film-star reactions, but the Princess was not a film star and had no intention of behaving like one. Even if she had known how, it would have been incongruous. What she still had to discover for herself was her own way of responding to the warmth and emotion being poured upon her, and a manner that would show the crowd she was enjoying herself as much as they were. She was still feeling strange and strained and could not yet relax sufficiently to enjoy herself in the same way.

The occasional adverse comment was made, which puzzled the Princess when she heard about it. 'But my smiling muscles are aching,' she protested.

Many of the major events during the first few days were not 'smiling' occasions. Unfortunately, on those occasions when she really did smile – or laugh – spontaneously, the cameras often were not there to record it.

What all the newspapers were looking for at the start of the tour was a really good human-interest story to offset the formality of the official engagements. Then, when it came on the evening of the third day, the press found itself excluded. The event appeared innocuously on the official programme as 'Buffet Supper' at Government House and the press were told it was private. Late in the evening, a press release and pictures taken by a 'pool' photographer were issued for general distribution. The press corps was dumbfounded.

The Governor-General had also arranged a square dance at Government House for that same evening, but it did not appear on the programme. To provide some relaxation for the royal visitors, this too was kept as a private event. Princess Elizabeth took the floor in country-style attire of brown checked blouse with white Peter Pan collar and cuffs and steel-blue flared skirt with appliqué and beaded embroidery and black shoes. Prince Philip wore jeans and a white checkered shirt and red kerchief. The royal couple thoroughly enjoyed themselves and experienced dancers agreed they did very well at their first attempts at 'Cattle in the Crop', 'Haste to the Wedding', 'Rock Valley', 'Swamp Lake' and 'Farmers' Jamboree'.

The 'pool' pictures of the Princess dancing and looking happy and relaxed were duly released and published around the world. But they, with the pedestrian press release describing the clothes and naming the dances, were viewed askance by the frustrated reporters and photographers of the press corps.

Both these occasions demonstrated the difficulties of trying to reach a compromise between attempting to appease the media and showing consideration to the guests. As happens so often with royalty, a fine line has to be drawn or a compromise arranged between conflicting factors of popularity, privacy, dignity of the Crown, consideration for the individual, or even the physical problems of space and numbers. It was a Catch-22 situation and priority was given to the feelings of the royal visitors. In the long run, it was a wise decision so far as the visitors were concerned, but in the short-term, a golden opportunity for the media had been missed at the square dance, the best human-interest story of the tour till then being covered by only a press release and 'pool' pictures.

There was no time to dwell on disappointments, however. By the stage the tour left Toronto and began to draw breath after six hectic days on the east coast, the very large press corps of over a hundred correspondents, broadcasters, photographers and cameramen travelling with the royal party was growing reconciled to the fact that this was a most unusual tour, that it was unfamiliar and frenetic, and that everyone had to live very much for the moment. Nothing like it had happened before, and considering what a mad competitive scramble it became, it was remarkable what a good-natured relationship was established and maintained between the English, Canadians and Americans who made up the hard-core of journalists and cameramen travelling most of the distance there and back across Canada.

The Canadian press arrangements fortunately were superb, probably the best encountered in my experience. This did not prevent the occasional niggles, but under the Chief Information Officer from the Canadian Government there were ten press officers representing the Navy, the Air Force, the Trans-Canada Airline, the Canadian National and Canadian Pacific Railways, the Canadian Broadcasting Corporation, National Film Board and Department of External Affairs. They were all there to help; no one was trying to sell anything – except the good name of Canada.

The royal train was run conveniently in two sections. The Princess and the Duke travelled in the first section with their very small household group and entourage and various officials and police in attendance. The Princess and the Duke were in the first car, which was normally reserved for the Governor-General.

The second part of the royal train carried the press, among them myself as *The Times*'s representative. We were lucky that the railways had recently taken delivery of some brand-new steel and chrome rolling stock and we were the first occupants. The cars were the last word in comfort and smoothness. The doors between them hissed open automatically as one approached along the corridor. Comfortable seating compartments converted easily into sleeping berths. The dining car had beautiful spotless table linen, polished silverware and gleaming glass; there was a buffet and bar, and the lounge car had comfortable armchairs. It was remarkable how little time we seemed to have in the train to enjoy this luxury, and it is sad now at the start of the 1990s to think how these wonderful trains are ceasing to exist.

The advantage of running the train in two sections was that the press section could be held back until the last moment before moving off. This gave correspondents time to file their stories. The disadvantage from the press point of view was that they were given very limited opportunities to talk to the members of the Royal Household, in particular to Lieutenant-Colonel Martin Charteris, the Princess's Private Secretary, and to Lieutenant Michael Parker, Equerry in Waiting to the Princess and the Duke, and the Duke's Private Secretary. The latter was an Australian and a naval friend of the Duke's.

The biggest problem confronting the British press group, however, was the time factor. Montreal on the east coast of Canada was five hours back from London; Vancouver on the west coast was eight hours back from London. In my case, the deadline for the first edition of *The Times* was 9.30 p.m. in London; and normally about 12.30 a.m. for the last edition, unless some major event occurred suddenly. To meet the first edition of the paper, I had to have my 'copy' in London by 4.30 p.m. local time on the east coast of Canada and by 1.30 p.m. local time on the west coast. Before then, however, the story had to be written, filed from a cable office and transmitted to *The Times* in London. To be on the safe side, I used to allow at least an hour between filing time in Canada and receipt in the office. The dispatches were sometimes quite long and had to be retyped for transmission; and might also have to join a queue of other press messages on such an occasion. This meant that my first dispatch for the day had to be filed by 3.30 p.m. on the east coast and 12.30 p.m. on the west coast. A second dispatch then had to follow within three hours in order to update the previous report for the final edition of the paper.

Any royal activity that happened after these times missed the next day's paper in England and had to form part of the report for the following day. I normally therefore wrote up this late material and held it in draft to form part of the next day's story for the first edition. Then, to keep the story topical, I would cover fairly fully the morning activities and anticipate the afternoon events as being about to happen. This meant a story in three parts: yesterday; this morning; and what was expected to happen in the afternoon and evening. For the final edition, I might rewrite the whole story, or update the afternoon activities with a description of what actually did happen.

It may sound complicated, but it seemed to work quite well. The drawback was that I never had time for any lunch, though I usually managed to get an evening meal before attending the press briefings for the next day. These provided background information on the places to be visited, engagements to be carried out, people to be met and so forth; details of transport arrangements for getting from one place to another; and the issue of the vital official passes. I would then sit down to draft my first-edition catch-up story of that day's events. In other words, we never stopped chasing our tails. As the press briefings were sometimes as late as 11 p.m., sleep became a problem too.

During the first few days of the tour, the unexpectedly large crowds created all kinds of complications for the press, particularly for those of us who had to break away from the programme to write and file stories and then attempt to rejoin the action. The press arrangements went along splendidly provided one stayed with the royal party. Special cars and buses with police escorts ferried us from place to place to arrive at the new location before the Princess and leave again just before she departed; or even to follow in the motorcade procession. But in those circumstances, try breaking away – even worse, try to get back in again.

The sheer physical problem of moving through the crowds in either direction could be almost insuperable. Official press passes were essential – but useless. If you left the party, the only way to rejoin was by leap-frogging by taxi or any other means about two stages ahead of where the action was at that moment, and then waiting patiently for the royal party to catch up. Streets were shut off and traffic blocked, so you had to walk (often quite a long way) from the nearest point which could be reached, then push through the crowds, apologizing and, for what it was worth, waving your pass. Inevitably one missed certain events, but the Canadian journalists, who were not competing with the British reporters, were not only happy but often quite anxious to help with information. National pride was a telling factor in Canada.

All our tribulations were treated philosophically by the various nationalities on the train, among whom were some very high-powered journalists covering the tour, including Canadian newspaper editors, bureau chiefs from New York and big-name columnists of English mass-circulation newspapers. Some of these notables were a little put out at first at having to return to the hurly-burly of street reporting, but soon became caught up in the exhilaration of the experience, and even seemed to enjoy themselves in a masochistic sort of way. The struggle to survive professionally during the first few frantic days established a camaraderie, rather like that during the blitz on London a few years earlier.

Once the tour moved away from the east coast and the appalling frenzy and long hours of the big city events lay behind us, the pace settled down and we began to get to know one another and to sort out and assess the 'goodies' with whom we were respectively not competing, and the 'baddies' who were our competitors. The train became home for days at a time.

Cable facilities, our life-lines to our offices, were always in the centre of the towns, large or small, that we called at, so temporary press facilities were provided for us conveniently in aircraft hangers, hotel rooms, schoolrooms, community halls or wherever. Rows of typewriters of various makes and borrowed from goodness knows where were arranged on desks or benches and sometimes at uncomfortable heights for typing. At one small town we all rushed into the 'Press Room' and fell with joy upon typewriters that we found neatly lined up on proper typing desks. We couldn't believe our luck. Then there came a great howl of dismay. The place was a secretarial training school and all the typewriters had blank keys for teaching touch typing. Despite their ability to type like machine guns using one or two fingers of each hand, most reporters did need to see the letters on the keyboard. The cable companies were appalled to be left clutching bundles of illegible hand-written scrawl to deal with as the press train pulled away into the night.

In my situation I had one important advantage, though it also had its inconveniences. *The Times*, being then a newspaper of record as well as reporting events, favoured length rather than short snappy reports. Writing a really good descriptive *short* piece, getting everything in and protecting yourself against leaving out the one item the other papers all picked on as being the most interesting, was extraordinarily difficult and nerve-racking. It was like the case of the famous general in the past who apologized for the length of his dispatch as he had 'not had time to write a shorter one'. I could just sit down, however, and, within reason, keep going. Furthermore, I sent summaries of all the speeches the Princess and the Duke made in English; but filed in full, as an attachment, the complete text of any speech the Princess made in French – and *The Times* was printing long extracts of the French versions. Because of a log-jam on the penny-a-word press-rate channel, I threw caution – and money – to the winds and began to deal with a commercial cable company that charged sixpence a word. I expected trouble from the office, but if any messages of panic or rebuke (sent at the penny-a-word rate) were ever launched in my direction, I never received them.

The cable costs must have been horrific, for the cable company representative was constantly at my elbow, but there were no delays in dispatch and the messages went straight through to London without hold-ups. This earned me extra writing time, and one further bonus. The cable representative made special arrangements with various small towns down the line when we were travelling by train, whereby he would come to my compartment and collect my dispatches, by day or night, as required. He would then bundle them up in a package and, as we *whoo-whooed* our way through some small station without stopping, would throw the parcel out of the train to someone who had been forewarned and was waiting on the platform. Romantic daydreams about the train being pursued by Indians were replaced by a vision of my precious dispatches being handed in at the station office to a shirt-sleeved clerk with dark eyeshade and black sleeve-protectors, who patiently began to tap them out on a Morse key, a letter at a time, to some big city from where they could be forwarded on to London.

The Canadian journalists on the train could not understand at first what I was up to. When they found out, they thought it hilarious and asked whether I wrote with a quill pen. I explained that there had indeed been a 'leader writer' on *The Times* when I joined it who did use a quill pen and who also wore carpet slippers in the office, but that he had now retired and I had to admit to being the last of a distinguished line.

Among the fringe advantages of travelling on the royal train was the fact that the mail coach was attached to the press section of the train, and that when the special commemorative royal tour postage stamps were issued, all letters home received a 'Royal Train' franking across the stamp.

Travelling in the conditions I have described produced its humorous moments and characters. One of the English correspondents was Gerry, a short stocky middle-aged journalist with a fine professional reputation who had been sent from his Washington bureau to cover the tour. Gerry's great-grandfather had been a Belgian who crossed the Alps with Napoleon, and he was made of pretty stern stuff himself. After the edict was introduced that nobody should approach closer to the Princess than fifteen feet, Gerry often found his view of proceedings being blocked by the broad back of a Mountie.

His efforts to ease around these barriers were sometimes treated in a brusque, not to say cursory, manner. He attempted to solve the problem by buying a little Mountie doll and sticking pins in it every night when he went to bed. Needless to say, this practice had no effect at all, and he continued to jostle good-humouredly with the Mounties for the remainder of the tour.

He was fairly unhappy one night when we stayed in a small town and the press were all somehow squeezed into a small hotel. We were sleeping four or more to a room, and one distinguished bureau chief from New York was bedded down (uncomplaining) in the corridor. During the night I heard a figure bumping his way in the dark to the bathroom and a sleepy muttering: 'What a lucky chap you are, Gerry. You'll only have to file one story a day. Plenty to drink. You'll live in a parlour car on the train, and first-class hotels. What a lucky chap you are, Gerry.' Bump! Grunt! 'Oh, what a lucky chap you are, Gerry!'

Gerry became very popular later on as the train moved westwards. Everywhere we went the day of the visit was proclaimed a public holiday, with the dire result that the bar on the press train invariably ran dry. Efforts to replenish it with private supplies similarly proved unsuccessful. Canadian licensing laws at that time required you to have a licence to buy alcohol. But the licensing offices were closed, and so were the bottle shops. Gloom descended over the press train. Then, one evening, Gerry walked into the lounge car with a bulging coat and a smug look on his face. 'Attention everybody,' he said. 'The wheel has turned full circle. I've just bought some fire-water from the Indians!' And he produced a large unopened bottle of Bourbon. That night there was peace in the camp.

But all of these adventures lay before us down the line. Our long journey westward from Toronto was still only just beginning and we had other more urgent problems to deal with first. After the set-back of the square dancing in Ottawa, the press corps became somewhat reconciled to the thought that good human-interest incidents were going to be few and far between. The sheer size of the programme, the speed at which it was being carried out and the very substantial press coverage of routine events meant that there was little time or occasion for informal or intimate moments. A more intriguing question of greater public interest arose of its own accord. Everyone who had ever met the Princess was asked, 'What is she like?'

The Canadians were just beginning to find the answer, which tantalizingly was divided into two parts: fantasy and fact. It all depended on the individual who had met her, and under what circumstances. Canadians naturally were accustomed to the glamour of Hollywood, the razzle-dazzle of 'tinsel town', with beautiful film stars dressed up as princesses. Here now, however, was something not in their common experience: a beautiful young woman who was the descendant of the line of Henry VIII and Queen Elizabeth I (to go back no more than a few hundred years); who appeared more magnificently attired than any film star; who wore her own jewellery, which was beyond price, blazing and flashing colours in the bright lights; and decorations that had their origins in legend. A Fairy Princess? A romantic myth? Inevitably a spell was woven.

Those who met her in these circumstances all agreed on their reaction: there was substance to the myth. The illusion did not vanish like a dream in the morning as reality met up with fantasy. They retained real and lasting memories of a firm handshake, beautiful eyes that held them in a very direct gaze, and a clear voice that, for the moment, was speaking to them, and to them alone. The fantasy became crystallized in the mind like a jewel, and so it remained.

There were also those who had met her in small groups, at more private moments: patients in hospital, mothers and children, loggers and miners, ordinary people. They, too, had consistent reactions. She talked quietly and sincerely to them. They received her undivided attention, and if necessary her sympathy. She was so popular with patients and staff in the hospitals that additional hospitals were added to her itinerary as the tour proceeded. When a hospital in Winnipeg was inadvertently by-passed, 120 veterans were driven 150 miles to Rivers, Manitoba, to meet her.

These personal contacts with the Princess were to influence the public attitude towards her. To the people in the big crowds, she had been seen from a distance as a slim figure looking beautiful and younger than her twenty-five years, friendly and precise yet rather shy. Today such remoteness would be out of the question. Television now dominates all public events and the Queen can be seen in such revealing close-up that coverage conditions are sometimes imposed on certain events. At that time, though, the distance problem meant that greater 'projection' was required by public figures if they were to put themselves across effectively. It is a technique every actor has to learn, however unnatural it may feel at first.

The Princess was learning it remarkably quickly. After her visits to the big cities on the east coast, she emerged from her baptism of fire elated and with a new-found confidence. She was able to look forward to the next stages of her tour with especial interest and enjoyment. She had become more at ease and her natural personality was also beginning to disclose a romantic interest and human curiosity about Canada. There was much to intrigue her imagination.

Five

'Just Be Yourself'

THE WHOLE TEMPO of the visit changed after Windsor, Ontario, the first turning point of the tour. From there on began the great sweep across the vast forests, prairies, mountains and lakes to the Pacific coast beyond the Rockies, and then back again to the east coast. Although the distances were enormous, the pace of the tour slowed. The people were different: nearer to the raw background of this immense country and still close to the early pioneering days. The crowds and gatherings were smaller; there was more opportunity for ordinary people to meet the Princess and even to talk to her.

Windsor is the most southerly city of Ontario, indeed of Canada, and lies across the water from the great American industrial city of Detroit. On the night of the Princess's arrival in Windsor, the Americans floodlit their skyscrapers in her honour, and on the next day, when she reached a promontory that was the nearest point to Detroit, they fired, uninvited, a salute of guns located on the shore of Lake Michigan. It was for the time being a farewell salute also to the bustle and sophistication of city life. That same afternoon there came a complete contrast when the royal visitors flew to Kapuskasing, the most northerly town in Ontario.

Kapuskasing existed solely as a logging and newspaper-pulp milling town isolated in the vast spruce forests only a few hundred miles from the permanently frozen north. Immediately to the north were only a few trappers hunting beaver, mink and muskrat. Beyond them lay the Hudson Bay, the Northwest Territories and the Arctic Circle. To the south of Kapuskasing there were no towns nearer than the gold mines some eighty miles away.

When Kapuskasing was nominated for an eighteen-hour overnight visit by the Princess, the little town of 5,000 inhabitants was astounded. The local paper reported that, 'There couldn't have been more excitement if gold had been found under the city hall.' The Mayor told the local citizens to spruce up their houses, trim their lawns and get their hair cut. Three miles of road between the airport and the town were relaid, and were said by some to have been polished as well. The town clerk reported that the entire population of the 'north country' had applied for tickets to the local Reception; membership of the Brownie pack soared when it became known that a Brownie was to present a bouquet to the Princess; and stacks of ladies' white gloves were flown up to the local store.

On the great day, some 20,000 people from hundreds of miles around were swelling the town's population. Some had paddled by canoe for over four hundred miles. Every square inch of accommodation was taken up and people were sleeping in their cars. The Mounties of the royal escort slept at the city hall and the aircrew of the royal plane bunked down in the cellars of a hotel. The streets were decorated with coloured lights and red, white and blue bunting had been wrapped around the telegraph poles. Those citizens who did manage to get tickets for the Reception were all carefully instructed – and rehearsed – in how to behave in the presence of the Princess and the Duke, and what to say if spoken to. The Princess had to be called, 'Ma'am', and the Duke, 'Sir'.

The eagerly awaited Reception was held during the evening at the Community Club, after a visit to the mill. I had been sitting in the hotel talking with Mr Lester 'Mike' Pearson, then Secretary of State for External Affairs (and later to be Prime Minister), who was also Member of Parliament for the area embracing Kapuskasing. He had decided to let the local dignitaries have a free run before he himself attended as a guest. After a decent interval, we walked over to the Community Club together. The reception had already started, but we found the door shut, locked and deserted, although the noise of the proceedings going on inside could clearly be heard.

We banged on the door and eventually a Mountie came to the other side. He opened it half an inch and said, 'Go away.' We protested we were there for the Reception and had invitations. The Mountie asked, 'Who are you?' 'I'm Lester Pearson,' said my companion. The Mountie looked at him. 'What do you do?' he asked. Lester Pearson was too surprised to protest and patiently explained who he was to the Mountie – who was totally unimpressed. Then the Mountie asked who I was – and was even less impressed. 'You say you got tickets?' he asked and held out a huge hand. We gave him our invitations. 'Wait here,' he said, and shut the door.

After a long wait the door opened again and an enormous sergeant of the Mounties appeared and glared at us. 'Which one of you is Pearson?' he growled. 'Mike' Pearson said, 'I am' – with a touch of asperity by this time. The sergeant seized him by an arm and pulled him through the doorway. 'You come in,' he said, and his arm went across the door-frame like a great baulk of timber, barring my way. 'You stay out,' he added, and slammed the door in my face.

Somewhat incensed, but also extremely curious, I inquired later what had been going on. It was explained that in that part of the world matters were seldom as orthodox as in the busier cities. Moreover, local resources were sparse not to say inadequate when it came to receiving royal visitors. To put on a good show for the royal couple, the Town Council had borrowed family treasures, cutlery and china from the more well-heeled citizens and these were all on display or in use. Unfortunately, certain of the guests were strangers who came from goodness knows where. As the locals looked around at the great crush present, one or two of the more faint-hearted and mistrustful among them figured that possibly – perhaps probably – their valuables were likely to be 'souvenired' to remote parts where the wolves howl to the lonely sky, and never be seen again. They therefore surreptitiously began slipping their own property into their pockets to ensure its safety.

The Mounties, having noticed items disappearing, then locked the doors so that no one could get away – or anyone else get in – and began methodically inviting all present, one at a time (with a couple of notable exceptions), into a side-room where they could be searched and questioned without disturbing the reception. It was just at this point that I had been trying to gain my entrance.

Despite this irritating diversion, when the royal guests departed they left behind a memory of a most happy occasion. Some of the locals were admitting somewhat sheepishly, yes, they had slapped the 'Dook' on the back, yes, they had called him 'Philip'. One man who had just started a business as a tailor admitted to feeling the lapel of the Duke's jacket and telling him he had got a good suit on. 'Fits well, too,' he told the Duke.

The enjoyment was mutual and the mood had continued in the hotel afterwards during a private dinner at which one of the waiters wore a bow tie that concealed a small electric bulb, powered by a hidden battery and operated from a remote switch. The bulb lit up and flashed and flickered while the surprised guests were being served. It was said that a certain important guest asked where he could get one like it.

In Kapuskasing the royal party slept at the Kapuskasing Inn. All night they heard the thunder of the logging mill across the river and were aware of the inescapable biting scent of pine in the air. After it left Kapuskasing a new element crept into the tour, perhaps semi-consciously at first. It had to do with the haunting beauty of this vast remote country, with the first shrill touch of its bitter winter, with a sense of the latent power and mystery that lay beyond every horizon. Such sentiments began to surface in all the comments the Princess offered, and alongside them came admiring references to the pioneers of Canada who had made such awesome contributions to the opening up of a country whose area of 3,700,000 square miles disappeared northwards into the icy wastes of the Arctic Circle. Something of the romance of Canada, wild, terrible and lonesome, was being expressed, reflecting a tingle of excitement for the unknown and a thrill of enjoyment.

From Kapuskasing the royal couple flew to Winnipeg. The weather and scenery were forever changing as the party moved westwards. All the wonderful gold and red shades of autumn foliage of the Quebec and Ontario maples and birches were left behind as they flew across the pine forests, then west above the flat prairies. The rain that had marred the start of the tour was giving way to menacing skies which threatened snow. The sun still shone when they arrived at Winnipeg, but there was a bitingly cold wind. Later they rejoined the royal train and travelled westward all night as the first light fall of snow came silently. In the morning the golden stubble of the prairies was half-covered with snow and particles of ice were lodged in standing stooks of wheat not yet harvested.

While she was in Winnipeg, the Princess confessed that she had for a long time thought of the city as the tiny settlement established on the Red River to act as a clearing house for the fur traders of Hudson Bay, though it had meanwhile become one of the great grain centres of the world. Huddled figures in black Ukrainian shawls were evidence of the multi-cultural farming communities attracted to this rich land, and from that time on the Princess's imagination was to be fired by increasingly romantic images. She was approaching the heartland of romantic lore. The next day she was to be at Regina, the headquarters and training centre of the Royal Canadian Mounted Police – the 'Mounties' – and the following day in Calgary among Indians and cowboys. Beyond these places lay the mighty Rocky Mountains and the west coast, the gateways to the Gold Rush towns in the ice and snow of the north.

The Mounties with their scarlet tunics and flat-brimmed hats had provided constant escort to the Princess from the beginning of the tour, but so far she had not seen one mounted on a horse. At their headquarters at Regina she was at last to witness their famous 'Musical Ride', held indoors because of the icy conditions. Perhaps of even greater interest, she was to tour their museum where the painting in the foyer showed a desolate frozen waste with grey skies and a lone Mountie muffled against the cold, his husky team beside him. A dog was howling as the Mountie looked down at the body in the snow of the man he had been tracking. The succinct caption to the picture read expressively: 'Beyond the Law'. The relics in the museum of the unremitting battle with rogues of all kinds, where the Mountie always 'got his man', were schoolroom lore around the world: exhibits including the uniform and equipment of Superintendent Walsh, one of the original RCMP officers, who dealt successfully with Chief Sitting Bull when he crossed into Canada after being harried by US troops following the tragedy of the Little Big Horn in Montana; the Maxim Nordenfeldt machine gun mounted in the Yukon during the Gold Rush to combat Soapy Smith and his band of renegades preying on the miners leaving Alaska with their gold; the only map of the Klondike and Indian River goldfields compiled from actual survey; various grisly souvenirs – death masks, execution caps, hangman's ropes and nooses, murder weapons, pictures and pieces of uniform and equipment; and the property found on Albert Johnson, 'The Mad Trapper' (the snowshoes he was wearing when he was killed, the three guns he had been carrying), after he was hunted down inside the Arctic Circle for seven weeks in 1931 in the first manhunt in history to use aeroplane and radio.

These tantalizing fringe contacts with the frozen north accentuated the Princess's regrets that she and the Duke would not be going up to the Yukon and Northwest Territories on this visit. There were local compensations, on the other hand. The original name for Regina was 'Ooskunna Kahstakee', meaning 'great pile of bones'. The town was on the site of the killing ground to which the Cree Indians drove the bison. The buffalo bones had been heaped up in the belief that their presence would ensure good hunting. The Princess met one aged veteran who was present when the first tents of the white men were erected. He described how he had lived through the early pioneer days and seen the pile of bones disappear miraculously when it was learned they could be sold as fertilizer. Such contacts provided reminders of the speed of progress and development over a very short span of time.

The natural resources of the country, including its oil and mineral wealth, became more obvious as the royal couple moved westwards, away from the big cities and man-made industries of the east. The Duke, in his second and final speech, right at the end of the tour, would later refer especially to the forests and wheatfields, the factories and universities, scientists and armed services, the Canadian hopes and fears. These, he said, had all made 'a profound impression which it is impossible to describe'. He was sure everyone would understand what he meant when he said the message he was taking away was that 'Canada is a good investment'.

While the Princess subscribed to this sentiment, it became more and more obvious that, although she was the focus of attention for the crowds, she was, for her part, taking an especially fascinated interest in the people and the scenery and the historical background of the country. Back in Ontario, she had met an Indian chief in all his feathered finery, but he had turned out to be a local businessman with rimless spectacles and an immaculate Canadian accent who explained, tongue in cheek, that he had left his tomahawk 'back on the reservation'. In the west at Calgary, she met Indians who greeted her with tom-toms and bells and showed her round a tepee village constructed for the occasion. She stood laughing and talking with them for some time. They had to apologize for not bringing their Medicine Man with them from their own village, explaining drily that, 'It was too cold for him to come.'

And it was cold – fourteen degrees below freezing. Despite the falling snow, however, the Calgarians were determined to show the visitors their famous 'Stampede' of chuck-wagon racing. They sat the Princess and the Duke in the open, wrapped them up in electric blankets and denied it was snowing.

'That's only confetti!' they said. It was all done with great zest and in good heart and the event was an immense success. Calgary had, in fact, found the answer on how to react to the royal visitors, the lesson of Kapuskasing being well learned. Word had come down the track, and the *Calgary Herald*'s advice to all the people who wanted to know how they should behave in the presence of the Princess was, 'Just be yourself!'

The Calgarians also had the advantage of knowing a bit more about the Princess's personality. It had been noted how, if she met people who were pompous or pretentious, she became formally polite – and moved on. Even in the early days of her public life, she showed a remarkable aptitude for firmly terminating a conversation without giving offence. She was very direct and completely sincere, and never said anything she did not mean. She never spoke if she had nothing to say – unless she was obliged to keep the conversation going. She was even-tempered and hardly ever became annoyed or upset and never once complained on the tour, even in private, about the conditions or things she was asked to do. She watched everything closely and tended to become emotionally involved – but hardly ever showed it.

The Princess was notably happy talking to children, and later, in one rare moment in Vancouver – where the emphasis was laid upon children – she showed just how relaxed she had become. She and the Duke were standing amid a gathering of children, waiting for some young ones to be presented. Their names were called, whereupon it was found that the Princess and the Duke were facing the wrong way and the children were coming up behind them. As soon as she realized what was happening, the Princess swung about on her heels with an air of mock dismay and pulled a funny face for the children as though to say, 'Silly me!' The children were in fits of laughter as this inter-play continued for a short time.

For the Princess to clown in public in this way was hitherto unthinkable. It showed just how much new confidence she had gained, and how much at ease she had become. It was also symptomatic of a change in mood as the tour proceeded.

Six

A New Mood

IT WAS IN A SPIRIT of exhilaration that the Princess and the Duke were
able to spend a few days' holiday on the west coast. They had by this time
acquired a new perspective of Canada. Although they had reached the
turning-point of their journey, they could now sense the Canada that lay to
the north. The ships that sailed out of Vancouver were bound for Alaska; the
logs floating down the great Fraser River followed the same route which
carried the first gold from the north; the fishing boats brought in some of the
most beautiful salmon in the world.

Now the Princess could look forward to confronting the three remaining
high points on the return journey back across this huge country. First came
the Rockies, which had been hidden in mist and falling snow for much of her
journey westward; second came the return to Montreal, where she would
arrive this time with a feeling of much greater confidence than on her arrival
in Canada; and third came the visit to Washington – an unknown quantity,
but likely to be a friendly challenge.

The weather had improved for the return trip through the Rockies, which
now glistened in their first coating of winter snow. During the afternoon the
royal train wound like a small toy up the canyon route of the Fraser River. It
ran along the side of the mountain, above it the great sparkling peaks and
below the white water of the river tumbling in the cleft of the gorge. Through
the darkness of the night the train continued, but stopped in the Jasper
National Park so the royal visitors could wake to the dawn in the middle of
some of the highest ranges in the Rockies.

As if to compensate for some of the bad weather they had experienced up to
then, it was a glorious golden sunrise with the sun glistening on the snow peaks
as they climbed through the famed Yellowhead Pass, the traditional route of
explorers and fur traders on their way to the Pacific. Small wonder that the
Princess was happy to go on the footplate of the engine to drive the train for
fourteen miles with the Duke as her fireman. Now outwardly exuberant, she

astonished passengers on a train that had drawn into a siding at Rosevear to let them pass. For once she turned the tables on the spectators. From the cab of the engine, in contrast to her behaviour in the east, perhaps even out of character, she waved animatedly as she went by to attract their attention – rather than they to her.

At Edmonton, 'the gateway to the north', the farthest north her tour was to take her, she was again fortunate with the weather. Two days previously the temperature had been 40°F below freezing, but a chinook – the warm wind that blows over the Rockies from the Pacific and can change temperatures by as much as 50°F – had come to Edmonton and the temperature on the Princess's arrival was 8°F above freezing. The ground was wet and the trees dripping with melting snow.

A boom town, Edmonton still had its frontier feel. Its oilfields were developing fast. The Princess drove for miles down rutted, muddy roads between wooden buildings that had sprung up along the route. Her gifts from Edmonton and the Alberta Government were evocative of the north: a bearskin rug for herself; an Eskimo doll for Princess Anne; and for Prince Charles, an otter-skin coat.

The Princess commented that, with oil and gold, radium and uranium, and vast tracts of fertile grain-growing and dairy land, 'this must surely be one of the richest areas of the world'. She added wistfully, 'I wish we could see more of this part of Canada, and above all I wish we could visit those people who live and work under pioneer conditions in the north. We would like to see some of those places whose names carry with them the spirit of romance and adventure – Great Slave Lake, Yellowknife, Great Bear Lake and the Peace River country – but that must wait for another time.'

From Edmonton there were two long hauls of travel on the way back to Montreal. The first was an overnight train journey to Saskatoon in Saskatchewan, where more than half a day was spent, before flying to Rivers, Manitoba, to inspect the Canadian Joint Air Training Centre, and thence to the twin cities of Fort William and Port Arthur in Ontario – a journey of some 1,200 miles through four provinces and two time zones in under twenty hours. Even now, these distances are regarded as considerable journeys. In those days they were something of an epic undertaking. The aircraft were propeller-driven and the planes vibrated constantly. Long-distance travel was slow, bumpy, tedious and tiring.

The following morning, with the prospect of another 900 miles of flight ahead and a break at North Bay on Lake Nipissing, the Princess and the Duke awoke on the edge of Lake Superior to the sound of the wind howling across the waters and bringing snow and sleet in its train. The day's programme ahead of the royal couple included fourteen engagements and twenty-nine timed movements. It started at 9 a.m. with a local visit to an enormous grain silo, and finished at 11 p.m. in Montreal, where the crowds in Dominion

Square to greet the arrival of the royal couple in the late afternoon were estimated by the police to be about a quarter of a million – one of the largest gatherings ever seen in Canada. Huge crowds remained in the square all evening to salute the royal couple as they left the hotel to watch an ice hockey match, and then to greet them on their return.

During the course of the evening there had been another splendid banquet, given at the Windsor Hotel by Mayor Houde, a legendary and extremely popular extrovert figure in Montreal. The guests were accommodated in five separate rooms and the royal visitors moved from room to room during the different courses and the liqueurs. A small orchestra played and the mood of the evening was so convivial, the rapport between host and guests so well established, that towards the end of the evening, when the Princess commented to Mayor Houde on the singing in another room of the traditional French Canadian folk-song 'Alouette', it was alleged that he was emboldened to adopt a mock conspiratorial manner and say confidingly that in Montreal the song was also known as 'God Save the King after Midnight'.

The Princess was by this stage completely on top of the big occasions. No longer nervous, she was confident and clearly enjoying herself. A sense of her own pleasure was being conveyed back infectiously to the crowds, who reacted delightedly. She continued to observe everything carefully and with great interest. At McGill University the next day she was highly amused by an unorthodox welcome, the style of which was totally new to her. Led by their cheer-leaders, the students chanted the personal greeting: 'Yea Betty, yea Windsor, yea yea Betty Windsor, Rah! Rah! Rah!'

A short time later she was completely carried away at a stadium full of French-speaking schoolchildren. There she received a spoken address in French delivered by a young schoolgirl who stood on the dais accompanied by two other girls, all dressed in tartan frocks. Every time the leading girl said, 'Votre Altesse Royale', all three little girls curtseyed with one accord. The Princess could not take her eyes off them. Then the whole stadium full of children sang with immense fervour in shrill voices 'God Save the King' and 'O Canada', both in French. It was an immensely moving occasion and when they had finished the Princess remained motionless while everyone waited for her to leave. The Duke of Edinburgh had to speak to her twice before she emerged from her trance.

The Princess was to find that this new friendly, informal, but admiring attitude extended even further when she diverted from Montreal to Washington before returning to Canada to complete the tour. She had never been to the United States before, and so the visit to Washington was something of a 'test piece' for the 'new Princess'. The Americans had a deep mistrust of Monarchy as such – had they not rejected it forceably many years earlier and celebrated the event ever since on the Fourth of July, one of the best-known Independence Days in the world? Nevertheless they had a consuming interest in royalty as individuals, and the visit of the King and Queen in 1939 had been a great success.

All eyes in Washington had been following the tour of Canada with avid interest, and for weeks invitations to the reception to be held at the British Embassy had been among Washington's most sought-after prizes. Once obtained, these were proudly displayed on mantelpieces throughout the national capital. The visit was being treated as a private rather than a state occasion and there were no decorations in the streets. As the royal couple arrived, the crowds lining the royal route was smaller than in Canada and the processional cars drove very fast from point to point for security reasons. The Washington newspapers were, even so, full of pictures and reports. The American press, while receiving its guest as Princess Elizabeth of Canada, got its own back on those Canadians who had been claiming Princess Elizabeth as their representative of 'the largest Empire the world has ever seen' by reminding itself, and everyone else, that the Princess also had claim through her mother's ancestry to being one of the nearest living relatives of George Washington.

From the moment when the Princess stepped from her aircraft in Washington, wearing her favourite robin-red coat trimmed with black velvet and with a black hat, it was clear it was going to be a happy visit. She looked more smilingly at ease than at any time during her tour as she was greeted by President and Mrs Truman and their daughter Margaret. From a small dais draped with red, white and blue erected on the tarmac, President Truman opened his speech by welcoming 'a true fairy Princess'. He said he only wished the Princess and the Duke could travel across the United States as they had done Canada. 'I know the people of this country will be just as happy to see you as the people of Canada have been,' he said. 'I would like you to see all of our country and I would like my countrymen to see you. I am sure that would make our good relations and our strong friendship with the British people even better than they are now.'

On a more personal note, President Truman wished the King a complete and speedy recovery from his illness and recalled his own pleasant meeting with the King back in 1939, and again after the Potsdam Conference. He expressed warm appreciation for the way the royal family and the British people had received and entertained his daughter Margaret on her visit to Britain the previous summer. 'She had a fine time,' he said. 'I hope you will have as nice a time here with us and when you leave you will like us even better than when you came.'

Almost immediately after their arrival, the Princess and the Duke attended a reception given by the Committee of Washington Correspondents, a worldly-wise press corps who were permitted the almost unprecedented opportunity of putting questions to the royal couple on a strictly off-the-record no-quote basis. In view of the relative inexperience of the royal visitors, such a privilege could have turned into a disaster, except that those who allowed the risk clearly knew what they were up to. The correspondents privileged to be present were completely won over by the Princess's frankness. The ease and confidence with which she and the Duke answered questions not only took them by surprise but gained their positive admiration.

The Times's Washington Correspondent, who was among them, quoted one American correspondent as commenting:

'You heard no mutterings from cynics, chauvinists, professional proletarians . . . Royalty would not fit into this country's scheme of things; but how glad you are for the British, with whom we are destined to stand shoulder to shoulder in the uncertain world ahead, that they have a Princess who is so capably being the symbol of British lustre, dignity and strength.'

The President gave a dinner at Blair House that evening and was soon taking the Princess's arm and protectively calling her 'My dear'. And the next day the royal visitors were accompanied by Margaret Truman to wreath-laying ceremonies at George Washington's tomb at Mount Vernon and at the Tomb of the Unknown Soldier at Arlington National Cemetery. Later both the Canadian and British Embassies gave receptions.

Normally the British Embassy could accommodate a maximum of 600 guests, but marquees were erected on the lawns to cope with extra numbers and those waiting to enter the ballroom were, by ingenious routing, led through the Chancery corridors and even through the Ambassador's study so that no one needed to stand waiting outside in the cold and the rain. The Princess shook hands with some 1,574 guests, and even those at the end of the line were impressed to receive a firm handshake and a personal greeting.

One local paper said of the reception at the British Embassy that it was 'the best party Washington ever had!' Much of the success of the party lay not only in the way the guests were handled but also in how the guest list was compiled. As the *Washington Post* pointed out, the guests included

not just the officials who were always present on such occasions, not just the hostesses who always want the limelight, but also representatives of most of the national organizations with offices in Washington. In this way the Princess and her husband were able to meet the labor unions, farm groups, women's clubs, patriotic societies, and many others whose members they could not possibly have met in person . . . It was [the paper concluded] a wise precedent for which someone at the British Embassy deserves American thanks and applause.

The main reason why the party was a triumph, however, was the personality of the Princess herself. The *Washington Star* said:

The Princess ought to be told the simple truth by somebody, and the simple truth is . . . that she has charmed and captivated this city to such an extent that our oldest inhabitants, searching around among their memories, are hard put to recall the name of any past visitor quite comparable to her in terms of good looks and sweetness of personality.

After the extraordinary visits to Montreal and Washington, the remainder of the tour through the Maritimes of eastern Canada to St John's, Newfoundland, inevitably came as something of an anti-climax. Nevertheless there were even in the wind-down some notable moments to contribute to the memories of the tour alongside a new awareness of the Princess's personality.

At Saint John, New Brunswick, the 'Fairy Princess' image, which seemed to have been usurped during the central part of the tour, except for the temporary boost given to it by President Truman, flickered back to life for a moment when the finest outdoor night scene occurred spontaneously. It happened like this: the Princess and the Duke had returned to the railway station after another dinner at which she wore full regalia. She and the Duke stood by the train, talking to officials for a few moments before embarking. In the meantime, a large crowd watching from the distant vantage point of a viaduct had, on seeing the royal couple pause, run down the paths and broken the barrier at the station entrance.

The Princess and the Duke hastily boarded the train, to the disappointment of the crowd, who immediately began calling out for them to reappear. Instead of coming to a window or doorway, the Princess and the Duke suddenly stepped out on to the observation platform at the rear of the train. The Duke then turned on the platform lights and the red and green lamps at the rear of the train and the royal couple stood bathed in a pool of light amid the encircling darkness. The crowd, having managed to get quite close to the platform, could see the Princess looking radiant in a white satin gown and a white ermine wrap, with her jewellery sparkling as she and the Duke smiled and waved to those closest to them. The effect was magical and the observers kept up a continuous roar of cheers.

Eventually the royal couple turned to go back inside, despite friendly cries of disappointment. The Princess went to the door, turned for a final wave and a smile and went in. Prince Philip stayed on the platform a while longer. With elaborate drama, he went round pointedly turning out the lights one after another before pausing in the doorway to wave one last time and then, with a broad grin as he disappeared, shutting the door with a flourish. Good-night!

The crowd, however, was in no mood to go home and was happy to stand and sing popular songs, ending with 'God Save the King' followed by 'O Canada' and finally, amid laughter and cheers, a soulful 'Lulla-Lullaby'. Good-night again!

Seven

End of the Beginning

TWO FURTHER HAPPENINGS, each significant in itself, were to take place before the tour ended. The first occurred during a public occasion at Fredericton, New Brunswick, Canada's smallest provincial capital. The second was an individual incident to which I was privileged to be almost the only witness.

At Fredericton the people gave the Princess and the Duke an especially informal and friendly welcome, and the mood was relaxed at the University of New Brunswick as the royal couple prepared to depart and crossed the campus towards their car. Then, instead of simply getting into the vehicle and being driven away, they turned and began to walk among the students lined up to bid them farewell. After a bemused moment of disbelief, they were surrounded by laughing, excited students to whom they spoke freely as they walked about the campus.

This spontaneous event was one of the first, perhaps the very first, 'walk-abouts' during a royal visit, when informal personal contact was made with people in the crowd. It is true that in the war the King and Queen had made morale-boosting, meet-the-people appearances in blitzed areas of Britain's cities, but while these events had proved very popular, they were prearranged. The casual spontaneity at Fredericton was something entirely new, and naturally it also proved highly popular. Oddly enough, it was not to be repeated for many years, when the Queen again started pausing and talking to people in the crowd during the course of a royal visit. Subsequently the practice has caused much concern on security grounds, but the Queen has persisted and the habit has been adopted by other world leaders including, surprisingly at first, Mr Gorbachev, even on his visits to Western countries.

Only some time later would it be realized how much of a pioneering experience the Canadian tour had been, but the University of New Brunswick occurrence was symptomatic. Another example of innovation was the plastic-domed roof for the royal car, hurriedly made at an aircraft factory near

Toronto over one weekend and flown to Winnipeg and fitted to an open Cadillac so the royal visitors would be protected from the chill weather yet still visible to the crowds. Repeated or developed in plastic or bullet-proof glass in other countries, this device had its apotheosis in the Popemobile and has proved invaluable for television coverage of state and ceremonial occasions.

Indeed, the extensive involvement of television and satellites has been a major influence on royal tours, for the events can be seen 'live' by the whole country in which they are taking place and simultaneously viewed all over the world. Television coverage has been helped by the new style of tour, and in return has helped to develop a form of touring with visually attractive events, but especially with a sharpened concentration on the personality of the visitor. In this latter respect, the Canadian tour was remarkably successful even without much assistance from television.

The biggest innovation in Canada, however, lay in the organization and carrying out of the tour itself. It was the first in a new style of royal tour and it laid the ground rules for those that would follow. Previous tours by the King and Queen had involved relatively leisurely itineraries and little or no air travel. But the royal visitors to Canada were young and healthy. Everyone wanted to see them and the country was huge. By making more extensive use of aircraft and integrating this closely with sea, road and rail travel, it became possible to provide a highly concentrated itinerary full of varied engagements. This became the basic pattern for the future, and the death of the King shortly afterwards meant that there would never be a reason to turn back the clock.

When the Princess and the Duke took over the proposed 1952 tour of Australasia from the King and Queen a few weeks after returning from Canada, some 6,000 miles of air travel and two extra countries were added to the programme. Subsequently the introduction of big jet airliners has meant that the Queen and other representatives of the royal family have been able to travel vast distances more economically in terms of the expenditure of valuable time as well as far less tiringly. As a result, royal visits overseas for even quite short periods have become, as time has gone by, ever more frequent events.

Yet if the Canadian tour produced a fresh format for royal tours, it also produced a 'new Princess' – as the Canadians were very quick and only too pleased to point out. The tour's most important element was indubitably the Princess herself. The tour was, on the one hand, the vehicle that enabled the Canadian people to find out more about her, but also, on the other hand, the means for her to discover herself. It was not so much that she was able to cope with the testing exigencies of her first major overseas tour on her own as that she was now able to retain her true personality in public as much as in private. She displayed determination and courage – qualities always respected – and once she had settled down she relaxed and showed confidence.

Her success could be attributed to the compromise she displayed between her personal feelings, her natural dignity and her sense of responsibility as a representative of the Crown. She managed to combine these elements and to look quite natural and unaffected because she watched and listened and took an intense interest in everything going on. If she was enjoying herself – as she often was – she showed it. If she was bored or tired, no one would have guessed it. It was a wonderful example of self-control and self-discipline. As a result she shaped the course of that most varied tour to an outstandingly successful conclusion and laid the basis for the start of her reign as Queen, which was to begin a few months later.

The reality of first-hand experience had done nothing to diminish the romance of Canada's original image. It had merely served to increase in her mind the wonder of a mighty country with such vast potential. In her farewell broadcast made from one of the small reception rooms in Government House in St John's, Newfoundland, and using the same golden microphone that her father the King had used some twelve years previously, the Princess said, speaking in English and French to the Canadian people, 'No words of mine can express what I would like to tell you.' She thanked the Canadians for the warmth of their welcome and for the opportunities they had given her to see all the beauty and majesty of their land. 'I thank you for having shown me these things, and I am grateful for the glimpse you have given me of the greatness of this nation and the even greater future within its grasp.' It was also natural for her, as the mother of two small children herself, to make a reference to the children who had so obviously impressed her throughout the tour. 'I have seen this future in the eyes of hundreds of thousands of your children, and heard it in their voices,' she said. 'For as long as I live I shall remember and cherish fondly the greetings which came to us each day from these young people. I pray that their lot in this land will always continue to be a happy one.'

In conclusion the Princess said, 'I am well aware that the acclaim you have given us, which has often seemed to me to have the breadth and immensity of the sea, has had a far deeper meaning in it than a personal welcome. This has often made me think of the words spoken by your Governor-General in Ottawa during the first days of our visit. He said then that the link with the Crown was a real and tangible strength, and one of the most important factors in uniting the people of the Commonwealth into one great brotherhood. You have shown me the reality of this, and I thank you for it. Destiny has given me the great privilege of being able to live my life for the service of that brotherhood. In these five weeks you have given me a new strength and inspiration, which I know will always help me in the future. For that I am deeply grateful, and say not goodbye, but *au revoir*.'

The tour was ended and it only remained for the royal visitors to embark the next day by sea for Liverpool. But all was not quite over yet. The weather on the day of departure began badly and became frightful. The liner, the *Empress of Scotland*, on which the royal visitors were to sail from St John's was moored off the coast in the shelter of Bell Island at Conception Bay, about four miles from the village of Portugal Cove, from where the Princess and the Duke were to be taken out in the small ferry *Maneco*. When the royal car came driving down the steep rough road to where the ferry waited, moored bow-in to the coast, the weather was already rough. Great waves rolled into the cove and pounded on the rocks, throwing spray high in the air; dark clouds driven by a strong wind swept in low and obscured the tops of the cliffs.

The Princess and the Duke stepped out of their car into a deluge as a band with raincoats on over bright uniforms played 'God Save the King'. Seamen in oilskins removed sou'westers and stood to attention, rain streaming down their faces, as the royal party were escorted aboard. Then the ferry had to back away from the jetty and turn through 180 degrees against the incoming waves before heading out to sea. I and the other non-sailors on board watched anxiously while our little boat rolled as the waves struck us broadside on and we wondered what was really going through the sailors' minds. Meanwhile the unworried crowd on the jetty sang jaunty local songs.

The *Maneco* pitched and rolled all the way until it gained the shelter of the island and entered calmer waters within the lee of the liner itself. It was no day for standing on deck, but as the *Maneco* pulled in alongside the *Empress of Scotland* I stepped out of the rear saloon in which the press were travelling to watch her tie up alongside. I found myself alone on deck except for the sailors at the bow. In the heaving seas, the *Maneco* was scraping alongside the liner and removing a good deal of white paint from her side. As I stood casually watching the ferry scrape forward and wondering who would have the rotten job of repainting the ship, a figure joined me from the forward saloon, which was being used by the royal party. It was the Princess, muffled up against the weather. She too came and leaned on the rail. We were only a couple of yards apart, and the only ones on deck observing the same scene.

It is – or was then – the function of media correspondents to observe and note everything that goes on, but on no account to react or participate in the events themselves. Nor should they take advantage of the privilege of being close to royalty. It was a training and discipline that could sometimes become an almost unbearable challenge to journalistic instincts. Now I had to resist the overwhelming impulse to speak to the Princess. I had never previously spoken to her except by invitation, but to have an informal comment from her on her personal feelings about the tour now at an end – just one sentence, or two if one was lucky – would be a stone-cold international exclusive. On the other hand, it would also be an intrusion and a clear breach of protocol that could possibly damage future relationships. *The Times* enjoyed a close liaison with Buckingham Palace, and the King's Private Secretary was known to be very touchy about protocol.

I therefore decided to play safe and stick by the rules. It was just as well. At that moment, as we watched together, a man's head suddenly appeared out of a lower porthole ahead in the liner. He was looking forward, watching the sailors at the bow of the ferry waiting to throw a line to the bigger ship. The curve of the ferry's side which was touching the liner was moving slowly towards him from behind. It was obvious that unless he turned and saw the danger in time, he was almost certainly going to get his head knocked off. For half a second, as an observer, I paused instinctively to watch it all happen, but then decided I must shout a warning. Within my split-second of hesitation, however, the Princess was leaning over the rail and calling, 'Mind your head! Mind your head! Look out!' The man turned, saw the danger and jerked his head back inside – in the nick of time.

That man was fortunate. He was able to save his head because the Princess showed how instinctively she was able to keep hers – an ability she has continued to demonstrate ever since.

Part Three

Eight

'We Must Tell – The Queen!'

The king's disappointment at the cancellation of his own visit to Australasia was offset by his pleasure at contemplating the prospect of another wonderful tour by his daughter. As some personal compensation and as part of his convalescence, it was arranged that in March he should go on a cruise to South Africa in the battleship HMS *Vanguard*, with the Queen and Princess Margaret, and stay at Botha House on the south coast at the invitation of Dr Malan, the then South African Prime Minister.

To make the King's life happier, the doctors now lifted their ban on his smoking, and he was permitted to do anything he wanted within reason. By the time Christmas approached, he had put on eight pounds in weight and the doctors protested but gave in when he insisted on recording his Christmas Day broadcast to the Commonwealth. Although he sounded older and tired, the King determinedly made the recording, speaking with difficulty and recording one sentence at a time.

He spent Christmas 1951 at Sandringham, attending Holy Communion at the little church on the estate in the morning and in the afternoon listening to his own broadcast. In this he said, 'I myself have every cause for deep thankfulness, for not only – by the Grace of God and through the faithful skill of my doctors, surgeons and nurses – have I come through my illness, but I have learned again that it is in bad times that we value most highly the support and sympathy of our friends.'

The King really seemed to believe he had recovered, and continued speaking in this vein during January when he was enjoying life in the country. He started shooting again, using a special light gun. He also became enthusiastic about another subject. Small practical matters of detail had always been of absorbing interest to him, and during his illness he had been thinking about the problems of Court dress for formal occasions. The men had to wear silk stockings with knee breeches, and a distinguished few wore the Order of the Garter just below the knee. The dress was traditional, but not always becoming, and not very practical. The King wondered whether it might not perhaps be improved.

During his convalescence he had a pair of slim-fitting long trousers made as an experiment, and when Earl Mountbatten came to visit him at Sandringham, the King showed him the trousers with enthusiasm, elaborating on the virtues of this new attire. 'It is so practical,' he said. Then, straight-faced, he added, 'When people come to the Palace for a formal occasion, afterwards all they have to do is slip the Garter off, and then they can go home by bus!' Lord Mountbatten agreed and equally straight-faced replied, 'But Bertie, don't you think that on such occasions they might afford a taxi?'

When the time came for Princess Elizabeth to leave for Kenya, thence onwards to Australia and New Zealand, the King came up from Sandringham to London to see her off. It was a most important venture, originally planned as the first ever tour of Australia and New Zealand by a reigning King and Queen. A long and impressive itinerary had been worked out for them, with Princess Margaret, but now that Princess Elizabeth had taken it over, the programme was revised. The more leisurely option for the King of going by sea to all the state capitals of Australia and a number of coastal towns – with a train journey to the federal capital of Canberra for the opening of Parliament – was abandoned. The engagements were all left in place, but some 6,000 miles of air travel were introduced and many more items inserted into the itinerary in the time thus saved.

The royal couple would go to Kalgoorlie, reputedly the richest gold-bearing mile in the world; see a huge open-cast coal mine and visit the Snowy Mountain hydro-electric scheme. While Princess Elizabeth attended the opening of a wine festival, Prince Philip would visit the Woomera rocket range. They would both go to the 'Flying Doctor' base at Broken Hill, and visit the Eureka Stockade at Ballarat, scene of the armed rebellion by gold miners in 1854. Surfing and life-saving at Bondi; cricket, racing and tennis; the coral strands of the Great Barrier Reef – all these had already been included in the programme as a matter of course.

The tour was planned to end in New Zealand in June after a final reception with feasting, dancing and singing given by a large gathering of Maoris. But before they even reached Australasia the royal couple were going to be busy, for after Kenya they would travel to Ceylon (now Sri Lanka) and thence to the Cocos Islands in the Indian Ocean, newly acquired by Australia to provide an ocean air link. It was therefore to be a prolonged tour, packed with unusual items and of significant importance for Commonwealth relations at that time.

In Ceylon they were to have a guard of honour of sixty elephants, and spend a short holiday among the lovely mountain scenery and tea gardens of Nuwara Eliya before visiting Kandy, the last capital of the Kandyan kings. In Kandy they would see the famous Buddhist Temple of the Tooth wherein was enshrined the sacred relic of a tooth of the Buddha; and at night would view the spectacular Perahera – the annual temple procession by torchlight with a hundred richly caparisoned elephants and hundreds of dancers.

The family's last evening together was spent at the Theatre Royal, Drury Lane, seeing, appropriately enough, the Rogers and Hammerstein musical *South Pacific*. It was the King's first such outing for months and he was lively company during the evening. The next day, Thursday, 31 January, he stood for over half an hour hatless on the cold wind-blown tarmac to say goodbye to the daughter to whom he was devoted – and who adored him in turn. During the preceding formal proceedings in the VIP lounge at the airport, the King had been animated and laughing, talking not only with Mr Churchill and, of course, with Princess Elizabeth and Prince Philip, but at the first opportunity going out of his way to step round the main official group to speak to the other members of the royal party accompanying the Princess, who waited discreetly in the background.

After the plane door had shut, the King moved up to a roof near the BOAC building and stood, still in the intense cold, to continue watching until the aircraft had totally disappeared from sight. It was the last time he was to see his daughter; it was also his last public appearance. The pictures taken of him at the airport that morning, with haggard, anguished face, shocked and disturbed the nation. Shortly afterwards the King returned to Sandringham House with the Queen, Princess Margaret, and his two small grandchildren, Prince Charles, aged three, and Princess Anne, who was then eighteen months old.

The King was always relaxed and contented at Sandringham. The estate was his personal property; he had been born at York Cottage in the grounds, near the big house; and he loved the Norfolk surroundings. Simply to be in the country at Sandringham seemed tonic enough for him. On Tuesday, 5 February 1952, he was, by all accounts, in exuberant spirits. It was a bitterly cold but sunny day at Sandringham; a fine day for the King to go shooting in the grounds of his Norfolk estate.

The air was crisp and invigorating, with a bracing wind sweeping across the flat landscape from the North Sea. A party of six, including the King, and Lord Fermoy, who lived near by, met at Sandringham at 9.30 a.m. and set out in a Daimler shooting brake for a hare shoot about two miles way. Lord Fermoy recollected, 'The King was in great form and appeared to have enjoyed every minute of the outing. If you had seen the way he had jumped in and out of that brake you would not have believed he was dangerously ill. The King was a marvellous shot and he was in splendid form. He got one pigeon at about eighty to a hundred feet. The King was always bright and cheerful and at lunch he chatted and laughed the whole time. There wasn't a discordant note during the day.'

The shoot broke up at 4 p.m. and the King's last words to Lord Fermoy before going into Sandringham House were, 'We will go out again on Thursday. I shall expect you about nine o'clock.'

Some two months earlier, while he was still at Buckingham Palace, the King had mentioned his love of the country to Mr R.G. Casey (later Lord Casey), the Australian Minister for External Affairs. During their discussion of the forthcoming royal tour of Australia, Lord Casey had thought the King looked thin and that his voice was weak. The King had told Lord Casey, 'I have been through a great deal in recent times, but my main task is getting well. I am going to dedicate myself now to that task. I am a man who likes outdoor life. I love all things that England offers in such wealth out of doors, and one of the things that I don't get is country life. Kingship keeps me in this room through affairs of state constantly, even when I am not quite up to it. I just yearn to get to the country.'

Kingship was the responsibility that this modest and unassuming man had taken on when his brother, King Edward VIII, abdicated in 1938. He suffered a speech impediment that was both an embarrassment and a handicap. Nevertheless, once committed, he assumed the responsibilities with thoroughgoing dedication. In recent years he had aged visibly and begun to look more than his fifty-six years. This had been due to a series of grave illnesses, but it was really only in the last twelve months of his life that he started to show signs of his suffering. As Lord Fermoy said, 'It wasn't so much his step; it wasn't so much his bearing. It was in the drawn look about his face, and the fact that he seemed thinner every time we saw him.'

After his whole day's shooting with Lord Fermoy on the Tuesday, the King was cheerful at dinner. Among the guests was Mr Charles Moore, the King's Racing Manager at the time. But horses were of only secondary interest that night, for Charles Moore had just returned from Treetops Hotel in Kenya's Aberdare forest, where Princess Elizabeth and Prince Philip were at that moment sitting in the little cabin up a giant fig tree, overlooking a waterhole in the jungle and watching elephants and rhino and other big game in the moonlight. Moore was the brother-in-law of Lady Bettie Sherbrooke Walker, who with her husband owned Treetops and who was that evening Princess Elizabeth's hostess.

Charles Moore was able to describe to the King and Queen exactly what it was like at Treetops and what the Princess would be seeing. The King had naturally been following closely the details of his daughter's visit to Kenya. He and the Queen had gone there as Duke and Duchess of York in the second year of their marriage. They spent Christmas at Government House, Nairobi, where Princess Elizabeth had just been staying, and then went on safari in northern Kenya, not far from where the Princess was at that moment. They had fallen in love with the country, and as they discussed it, the King was able to visualize with nostalgic delight what it was like for his daughter to be there. With these thoughts in his mind, the King retired to bed early, still in good spirits. His bedroom was on the ground floor so that he had no steps to climb.

The next morning, his under-valet, James MacDonald, started to draw his bath water as usual at 7.15 a.m. Then he took the King his tea. He wasn't able to rouse the King, so he drew back the curtains to let in a little early-morning light. As he reapproached the bed, he saw that the King was dead. The room was undisturbed; the King had lain quietly in his bed and during the early hours of the morning died peacefully in his sleep. It was learned later that the cause of death was coronary thrombosis; a clot of blood had reached the heart and the reaction would have been almost instantaneous and painless. The King had been dead some hours when his valet found him.

The Queen was told and immediately went to the King's bedroom. It was said she stood for a moment by the bedside, gathering her self-control. Then she leaned forward and gently kissed the King on the forehead. It was reported that, straightening up, she said, 'We must tell Elizabeth.' She paused, and added, 'We must tell - the Queen.' Despite all the resources to hand, this proved to be an extraordinarily difficult thing to do.

A cold grey early-morning mist that was to persist all day hung flatly across the Sandringham estates as the young local doctor, hastily summoned to the royal household, sped up the drive, his overcoat tightly buttoned across his pyjamas. It was already too late, but that did nothing to lessen the urgency or importance of his visit. Nobody on the estate seems to have noticed him, or to have regarded his visit as significant. A little later it was remarked, however, that Pipe Major James MacDonald (namesake of the under-valet) was not playing the bagpipes on the terrace during the King's breakfast time. This was a morning tradition started by Queen Victoria and not one to be easily broken.

For some hours, therefore, all remained outwardly quiet at Sandringham House. Elsewhere frantic efforts were being made - in secret, and unsuccessfully - to contact the new Queen.

Nine

The Princess and Sosiani

AT ABOUT THE SAME TIME as James MacDonald was drawing back the curtains of the King's bedroom to let in the cold morning light, Juma, the Kikuyu bedroom boy, padded softly across Princess Elizabeth's bedroom in the Sagana Lodge on the slopes of Mount Kenya to draw together the printed cotton curtains to keep out the burning glare of the mid-morning sun. Situated on the Equator, the Sagana Lodge had been Kenya's wedding present to the Princess and the Duke, and this was their first opportunity to visit it. They were stopping there for a few days' holiday at the end of the official visit to Kenya before sailing for Ceylon on the next stage of the tour.

The clocks in the lodge were three hours ahead of Sandringham, and Princess Elizabeth had just returned from the night of watching the wild animals at the waterhole in the heart of the jungle. It had been an unusually exciting experience, and one fraught with an unexpected moment of danger for her. She was also eagerly anxious to write home to her parents to tell them all about her 'tremendous experience' while the memory was still fresh. It needed to be done while she had the opportunity, for the next day she and Prince Philip would fly to Mombasa to embark on the SS *Gothic* bound for Ceylon. The letter was going to be a long one and she wanted to get it away before she sailed. She knew her parents had been taking a keen interest in Kenya, and particularly in the visit to the Aberdare forest.

The safari in 1924–5 of the Duke and Duchess of York had been up river and in lion country just north of this area and of Mount Kenya. It was fairly tough going as they covered most of the ground on foot with the assistance of mules. They were plagued with flies, slept in tents, ate in the open off a card table – and thoroughly enjoyed themselves. The party photographed and, in the safari convention of the time, shot big game. On the way home through Uganda, the King hunted elephant on foot at close range and shot one from an unprotected position in some reeds. The tusks were duly mounted and adorned the hall of their home at 145 Piccadilly.

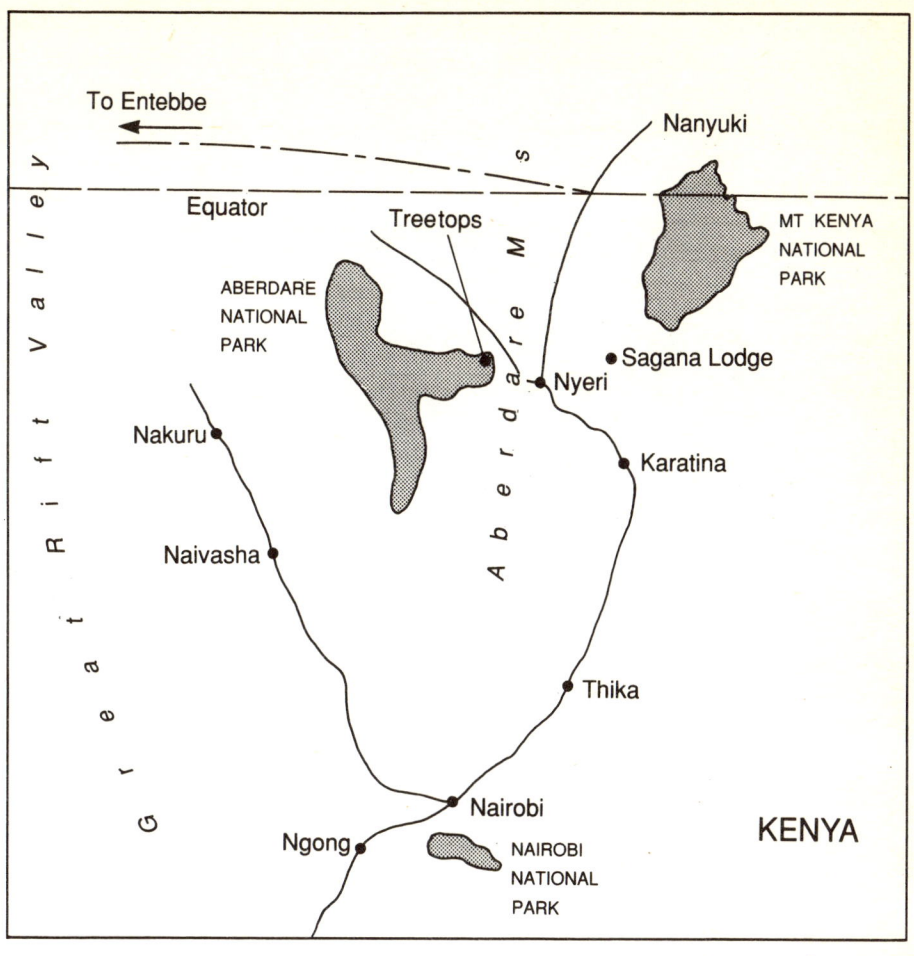

To Entebbe

Equator

Nanyuki

Treetops

MT KENYA
NATIONAL
PARK

ABERDARE
NATIONAL
PARK

Sagana Lodge

Nyeri

Nakuru

Karatina

Naivasha

Thika

Nairobi

KENYA

Ngong

NAIROBI
NATIONAL
PARK

Great Rift Valley

Aberdare Mts

In November 1951, while Princess Elizabeth was still on her Canadian tour, the Queen attended the Royal Command showing in London of the film *Where No Vultures Fly*. The King had not been well enough to go, but the Queen was accompanied by Princess Margaret, the Duke and Duchess of Gloucester (who both knew Kenya, and had stayed at Treetops), and Princess Marina. *Where No Vultures Fly*, made in Kenya by Ealing Studios and directed by Harry Watt, was a dramatized version of the efforts to get national parks established in Kenya to preserve wildlife. Kenya's most magnificent variety and collection of big game, all to be seen in superbly spectacular surroundings, made the country the safari centre of the world. Anthony Steel and Dinah Sheridan were the stars and the film featured, in a dramatized and slightly fictitious way, the efforts of a young accountant turned game-warden named Mervyn Cowie to preserve big game in areas where it could be observed.

Mervyn Cowie, by this time Director of National Parks in Kenya, was flown to London for the Royal Command Performance and afterwards presented to the Queen. If the deceptively quiet and precise Cowie, with carefully brushed military moustache, soft voice and gentle sense of humour, was difficult to identify at first sight with the screen hero of Anthony Steel, there was no mistaking his love of the animals as he spoke about them – or the fighting glint that came into his eye at any suggestion of opposition to his schemes.

The film featured some wonderful scenes of wild animals against a background of rolling golden plains and snow-capped mountains, and the Queen recalled to Cowie her own memories of Kenya, and expressed the hope that Princess Elizabeth would have the opportunity to see some of the many animals depicted in the film. Cowie promised her that the Princess would see many such animals. In particular, he assured her that the Princess would see some of Kenya's lions – of which he was very proud. The royal family had been disappointed when visiting the Kruger National Park during the royal tour of South Africa in 1947 when, despite every effort, no lions could be coaxed into view. The Princess had still not seen a lion outside a circus or a zoo. Cowie promised she would see one in Kenya.

A print of *Where No Vultures Fly* was sent to Canada and the Princess and Prince Philip viewed it during their sea voyage back across the Atlantic. Mervyn Cowie meanwhile returned to Nairobi, only to find to his consternation that the Princess's programme in Kenya would include a visit to Treetops in the Aberdare forest – but to no other national park. Therefore there could be no lions! After some views had been expressed in a crisply unorthodox manner, the Nairobi National Park was added to the itinerary.

But over and above a certain amount of fretting about routine details, Kenya was on the verge of experiencing problems of a more serious nature, none of which were to be allowed to surface during the royal visit. Incredible as it seems in view of its imminence, there was no indication of the seething unrest into which Kenya was about to explode with terrifying violence. There were, it is true, considerable whisperings at the long bar of the New Stanley Hotel, and in the Equator Club, of the extraordinary powers and disturbing activities of the 'witch-doctors', but that old-fashioned term was shortly to be replaced amid horror and shock by a more fearful expression – 'Mau Mau'. This clandestine movement was to originate as a struggle for freedom, but tragically, before independence was obtained, it became identified world-wide with savage terrorism. Kenya – whose capital, Nairobi, had grown within half a century from a swamp where the Masai warriors watered their cattle to the commercial centre of three colonial territories – was about to identify itself as 'God's own country, with the Devil's own problems'.

Even on the brink of this disaster, there was no outward sign of impending trouble. The city itself was never very splendid architecturally, though it had its own distinctive character and some unusual buildings. A mixture of European city and frontier town, it still retained a strong pioneer atmosphere. People still remembered picturesque caravans of camels setting out with trade goods for Abyssinia or passing, laden with ivory, through the town. The Town Hall, built in 1934, stood on a spot used by the natives for the construction of game pits; and the early sentry boxes in Government Road had half-doors with the lower one shut to provide some protection against leopards or lions. The Norfolk, the first hotel in Nairobi, was still the favourite haunt of older residents, and stories were legion of the settlers' pastime of shooting out the paraffin street lamps from the veranda. The original Post Office still stood, the first permanent government building; before the First World War a blue flag being flown there meant a mail ship had left Aden for Mombasa; a red flag, that overseas mail had been received; and a white flag – or a white arc-lamp at night – that mail was ready for collection. Postal arrangements had become more sophisticated since then, but the overseas cable and telephone service still left something to be desired.

Now the streets of Nairobi were gaily decked with bunting; the shop windows decorated; the kerbstones immaculately whitewashed; and all grass lawns trimmed and tidied. Masses of blossom enlivened the rather dull city: bougainvillaea in all its variety of colours, Cape chestnuts, yellow wattle, crimson and pink hibiscus; and the 'yesterday, today and tomorrow' bush – the flowers of which rapidly change from deep to pale mauve and then to white – had just started to bloom.

The Europeans had been on a buying spree for new clothes, and the shops had sent to London for more finery, particularly for more ladies' gloves and men's hats, not normally much worn but *de rigeur* for the Garden Party. The Asians – still a long way from their unhappy nemesis – treated the royal visit in carnival spirit with parties and rejoicing. The Africans, less demonstrative, nevertheless showed keen interest. The Somali newspaper *Pamoja* printed pictures of the royal family and circulated posters explaining, with unconscious prophetic timeliness, that Princess Elizabeth was not only 'Kingy Georgey's Daughter' but the future Queen. Those Africans not normally allowed in the centre of the city now came to see the Princess and lined the streets, standing patiently for hours in the sun for a glimpse of the royal visitors.

The official part of the tour was confined mostly to Friday and Saturday – the first two days of their visit – and was completed uneventfully. In Nairobi it included the conventional events: a drive into the city; visits to the new cathedral and the Scottish kirk, the Town Hall and hospitals; meetings with young people; the opening of the new headquarters of the Kenya Regiment, and the Garden Party at Government House. At the latter – a great white colonial-style building amid gracious trees – the presence of some monkey-skin regalia, leg-bells and bare feet among the white gloves and floppy-brimmed hats on the sweeping shaded lawns had raised a few eyebrows. But Sir Philip Mitchell was known to be a liberal-minded Governor. These particular African chiefs betokened no menace and they were being treated, for good reason, with a special respect just now. Many loyal chiefs were in Nairobi for the occasion. Chief Pelipel of Turkana, who wore ostrich plumes and the breast feathers of pelicans fixed into clay on his head, had come over five hundred miles from the Abyssinia-Sudan border to greet the Princess. Also there was a famous old Kipsigis fighter who took part in the Nandi rising of 1905, together with another old warrior from the same tribe. The colonial government emphasized the loyalty of these elders from the tribes represented.

On the Saturday, their last day in Nairobi before going a hundred miles north to spend four relaxing days in the royal lodge and visiting Treetops, the Princess and Prince Philip attended their final official engagement at a civic luncheon given at the New Stanley Hotel. Here the Lord Mayor presented them with a gift for Prince Charles – a family of toy lions. Then, as they were leaving after the lunch, Prince Philip stopped in the doorway and said, 'I've left my hat.' He was standing with Mr 'Tubby' Block, who was Acting Manager at the time, the Manager himself being on extended sick leave. (Tubby Block later became Chairman of Block Hotels Ltd, the group which subsequently owned not only the New Stanley but also the Norfolk Hotel, the Outspan at Nyeri and Treetops.)

Tubby Block immediately sent someone upstairs to the suite of rooms allocated to the royal couple as rest rooms, to retrieve the hat. As the royal party left, Tubby asked the servant who had fetched the hat, 'Did you find it all right?' 'Oh yes,' was the reply. 'It was on the bed.' There was a gasp from a woman standing near by. 'Oh no! A hat on the bed!' she said. 'That is an omen of bad luck – it means a death in the family.' Nobody gave the matter another thought until four days later.

That afternoon the royal visitors went to the Nairobi National Park, the entrance to which is only five miles from the centre of the city. The park is

A 'Fairy Princess' myth swept across Canada
when pictures like this were taken at the
beginning of the tour

Above The first transparent car canopy, made hurriedly in Toronto over a weekend, because of cold weather in Winnipeg, started a new trend

Below Driving the royal train for fourteen miles through the Rockies

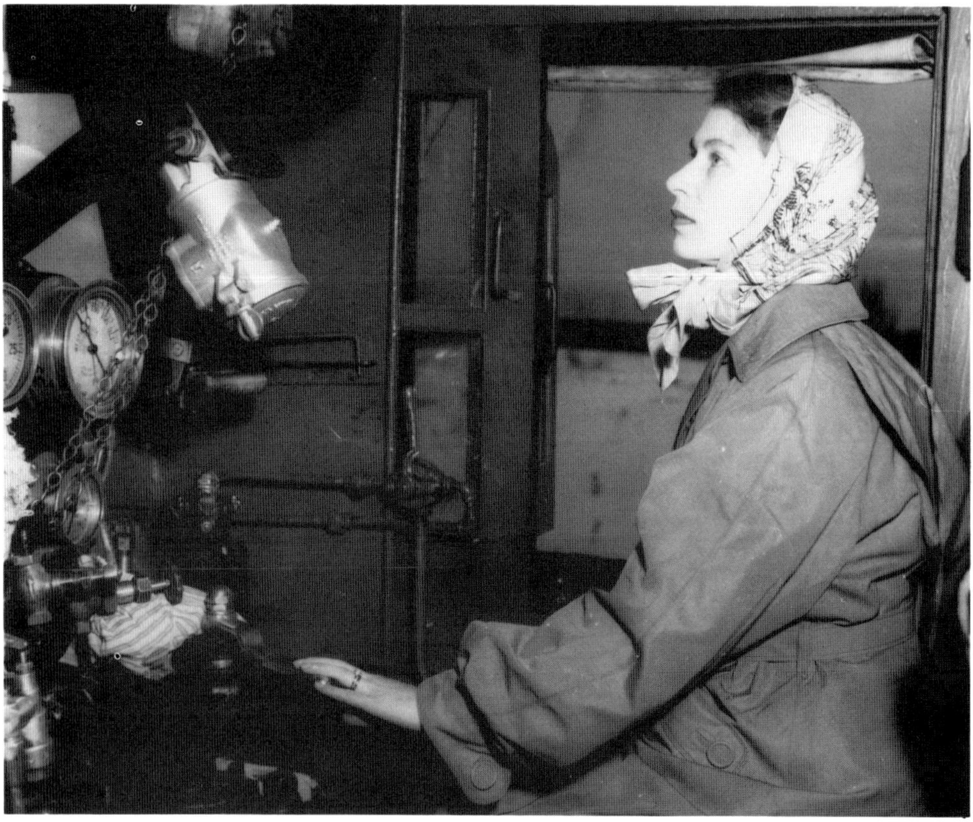

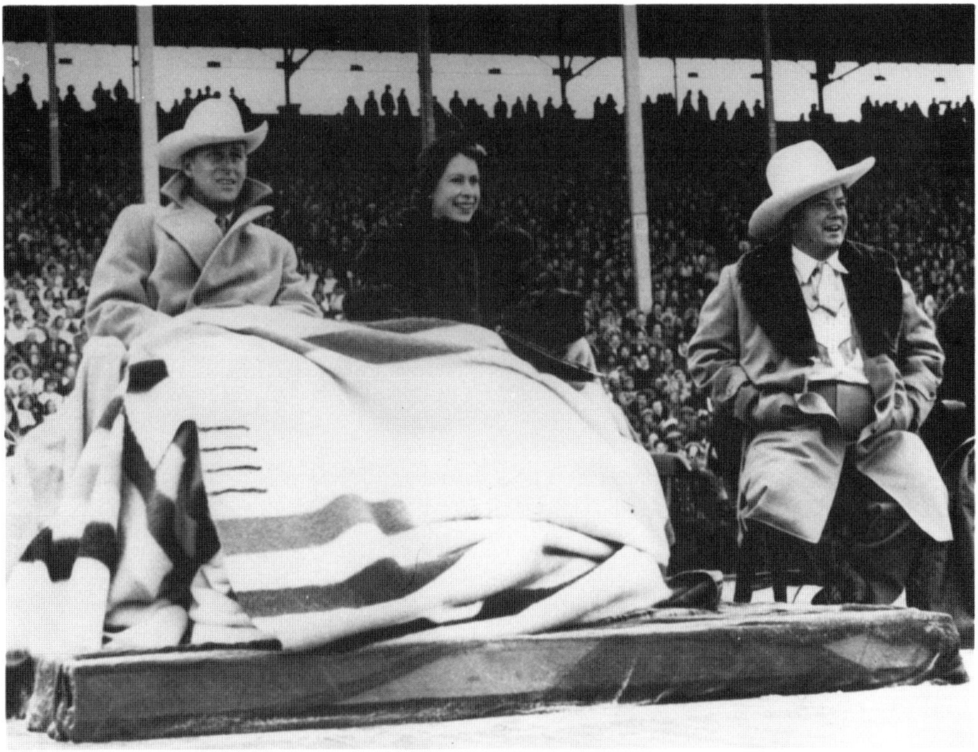

Country style: (*above*) watching the famous Calgary Stampede at 40°F below freezing; (*below left*) the 'Raleigh touch'; (*below right*) square dancing

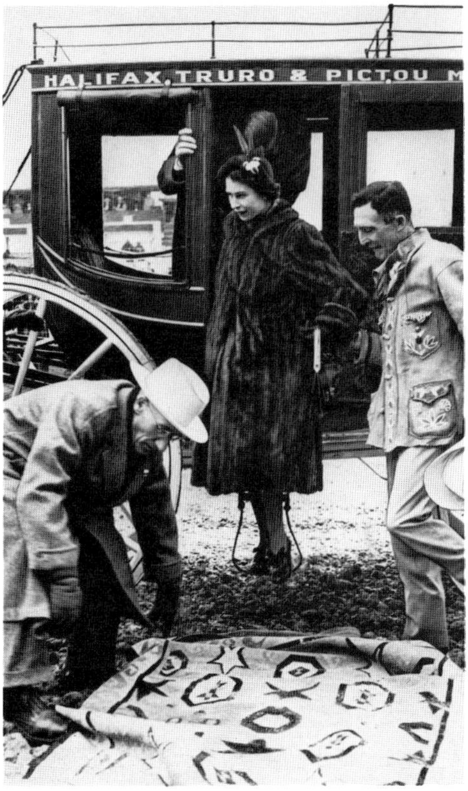
HALIFAX, TRURO & PICTOU

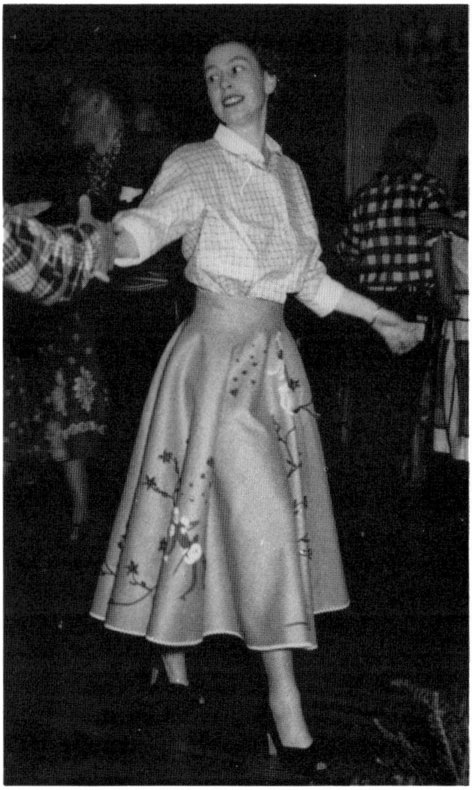

Above Goodwill in Washington as President Truman accepts from the Princess the King's gift of a looking-glass for the renovated White House

Below The Princess's first spontaneous royal 'walk-about' astonished students at the University of New Brunswick in Federicton

As the Princess waved 'good-night' from the
viewing platform of the royal train at Saint
John, New Brunswick, the crowd responded by
singing her a lullaby

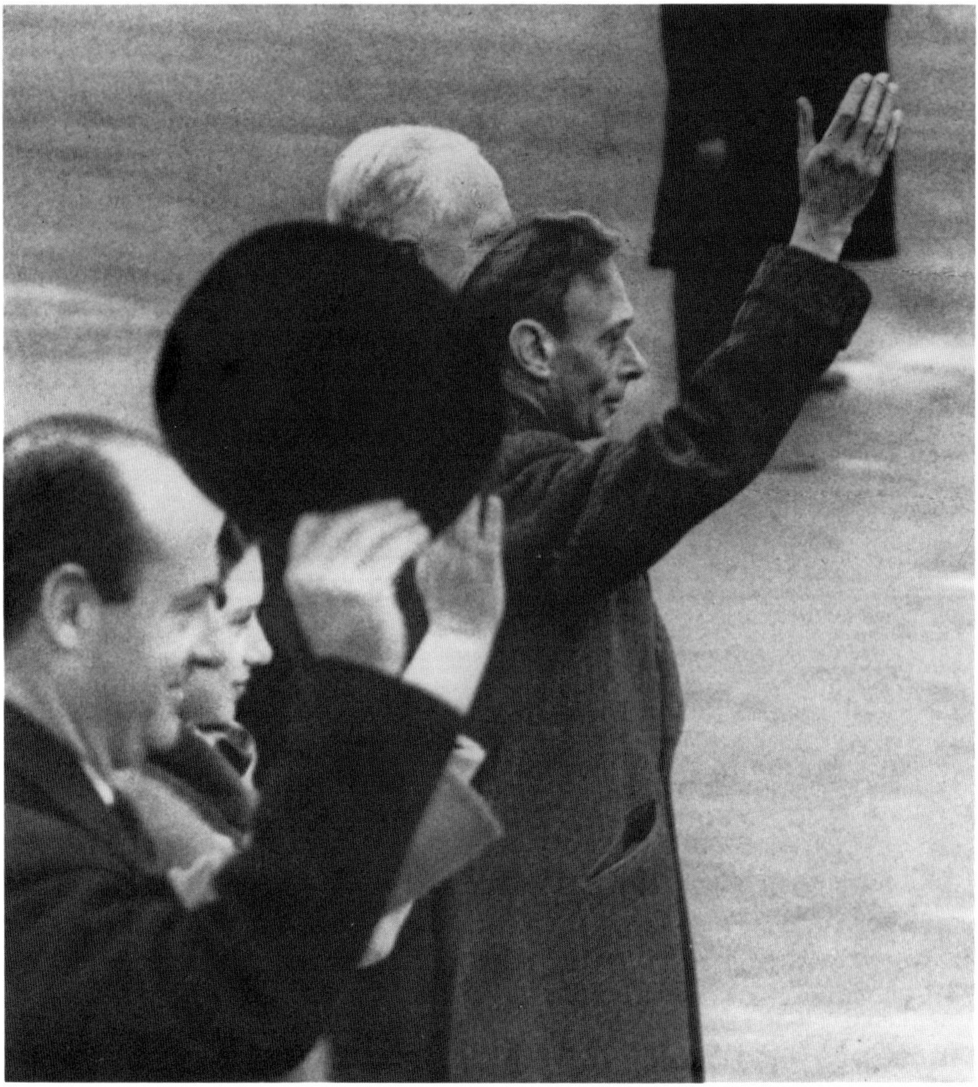

Bareheaded despite a cold wind, the King bade a fond farewell to Princess Elizabeth and Prince Philip at London Airport. It was to be the last time he saw his daughter

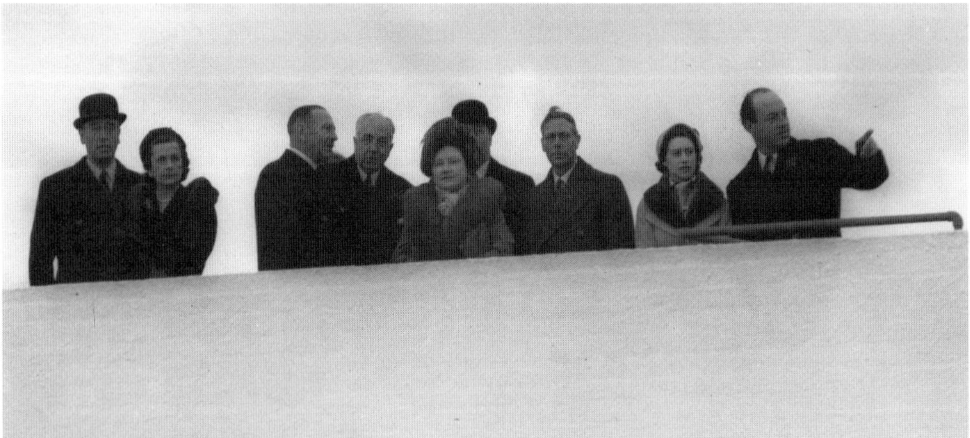

Above Stooping to conquer at a Nairobi ceremony. The little boy was named Prince as he was born on the same day as Prince Charles

Below Prince Philip arrives for a game of polo near Nyeri.
In attendance: Lady Pamela Mountbatten (Lady-in-Waiting)

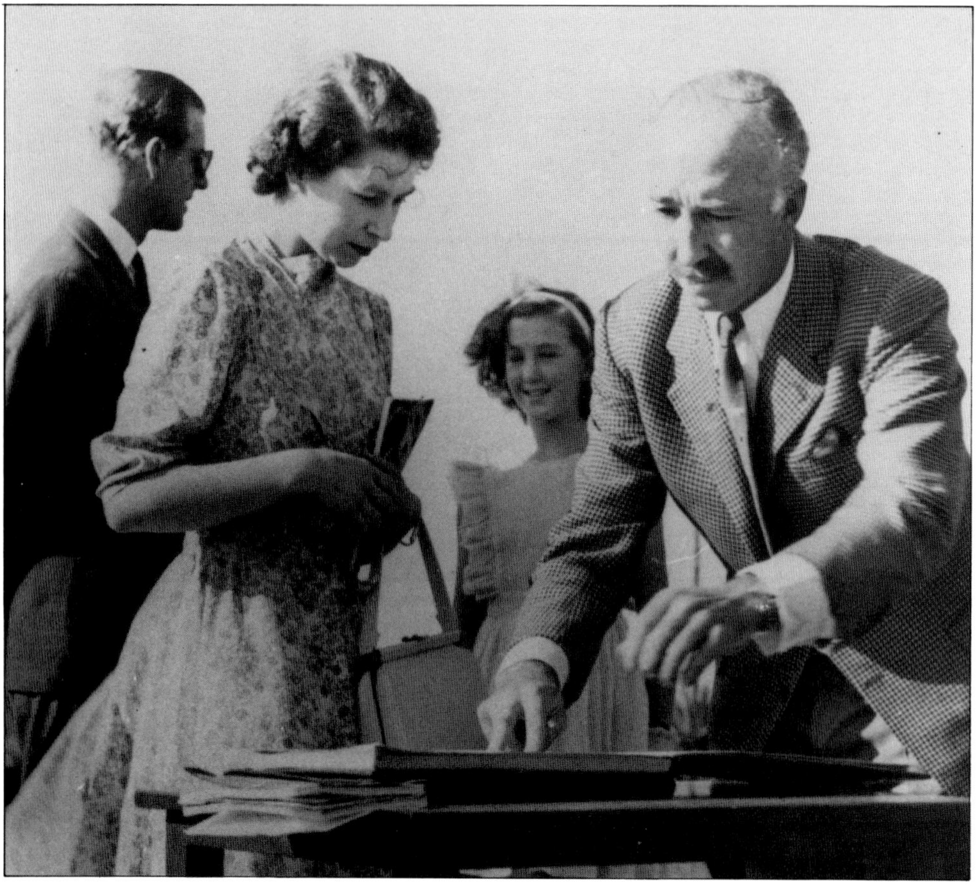

Above Signing the visitors' book at Nairobi National Park, with the Director, Mervyn Cowie

Below 'Wonderful,' said the Princess as Sosiani looked straight into her camera lens

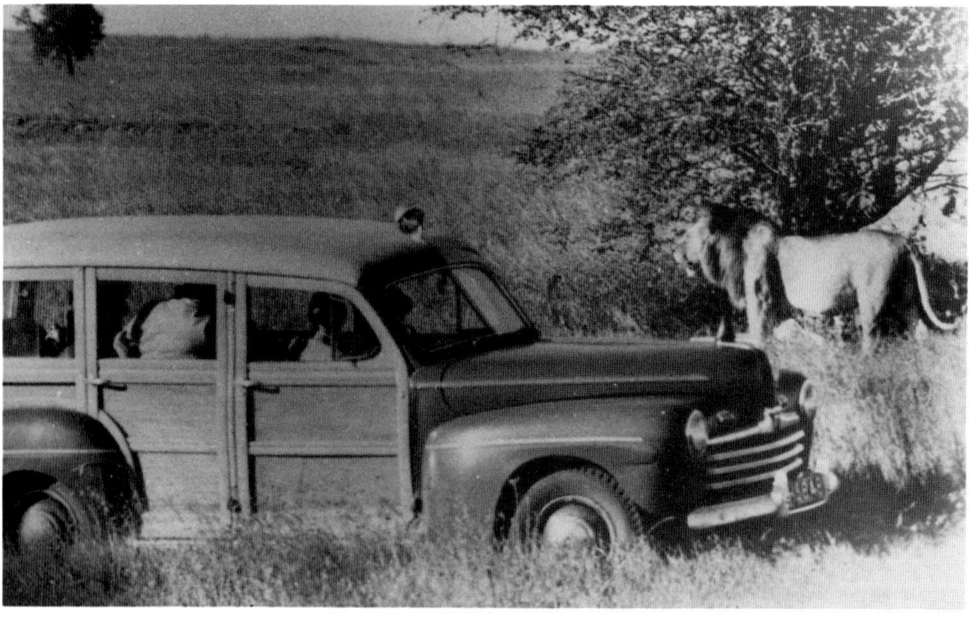

Above Sagana Lodge: Kenya's wedding present to Princess Elizabeth and Prince Philip, where the Princess was to learn she was Queen

Below Major Sharpe shows the royal couple the gardens he created for them out of the forest area at the lodge. Behind (*left*) is the Governor of Kenya, Sir Philip Mitchell, and (*right*) Colonel Martin Charteris, the Princess's Private Secretary

The Queen at Treetops. She went up a Princess
and came down a Queen

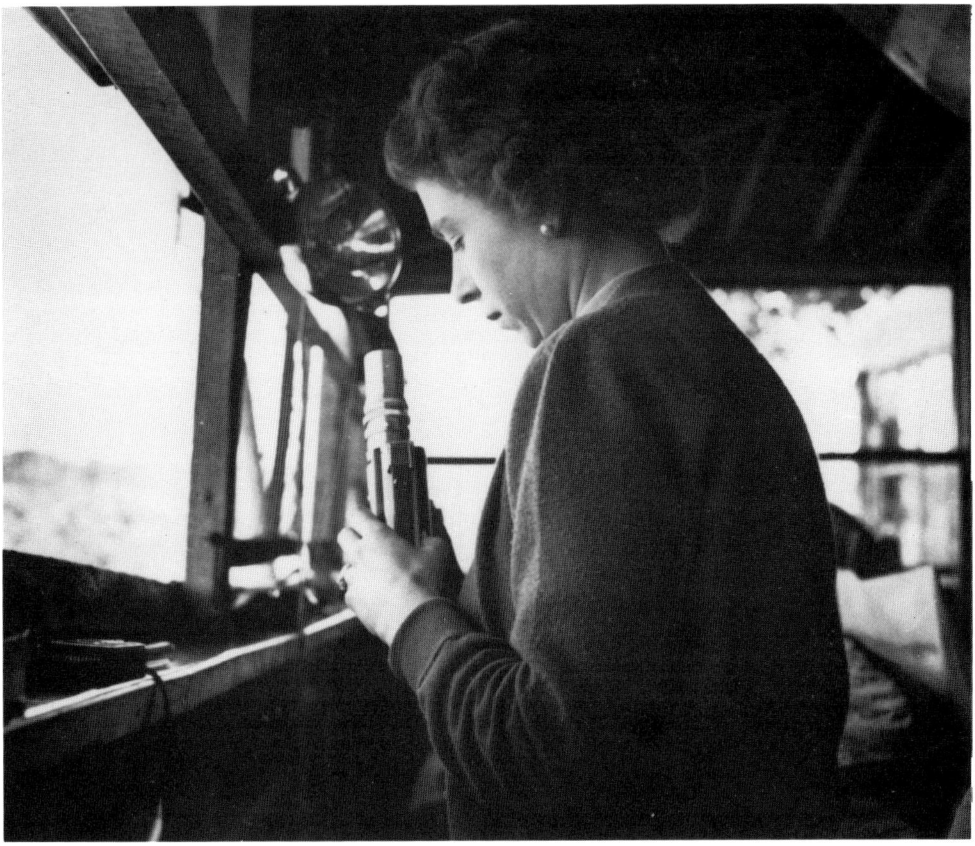

Above A keen photographer, the Queen made her own record at Treetops of 'one of the most wonderful experiences' she had ever known

Below Elephants at Treetops, and the head of the waterbuck the Queen saw killed in a fight at the pool

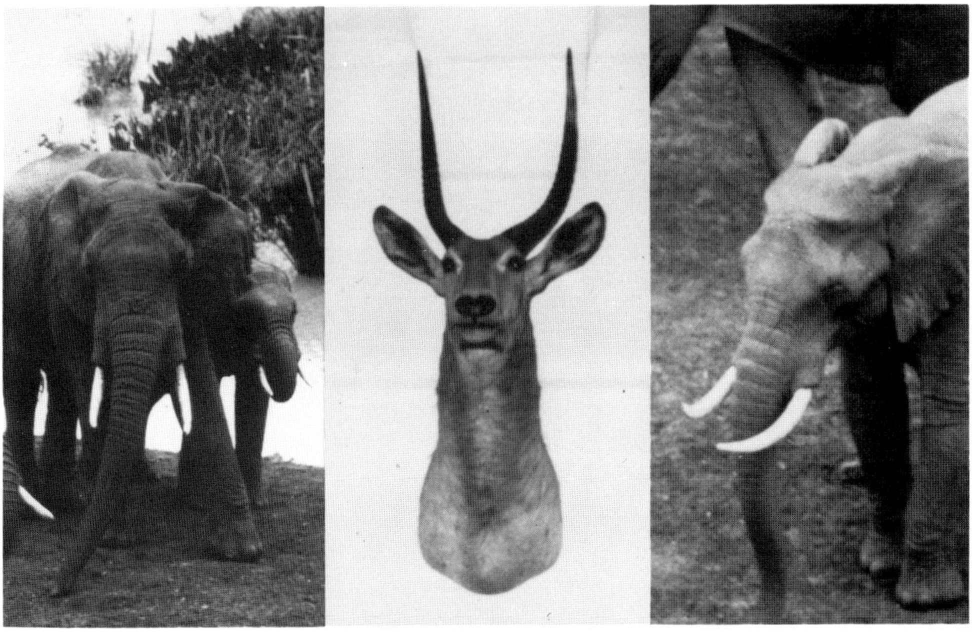

The guardian elephant that the Queen had to approach when she climbed the ladder up to Treetops, stood behind the bushes to the left of the ladder

'Escape' ladders were nailed to trees along the jungle trail that was the only path to and from Treetops

Below The three men who escorted the Queen at Treetops during the night of the royal visit: (*left to right*) Commander Michael Parker, Eric Sherbrooke Walker, Colonel Jim Corbett

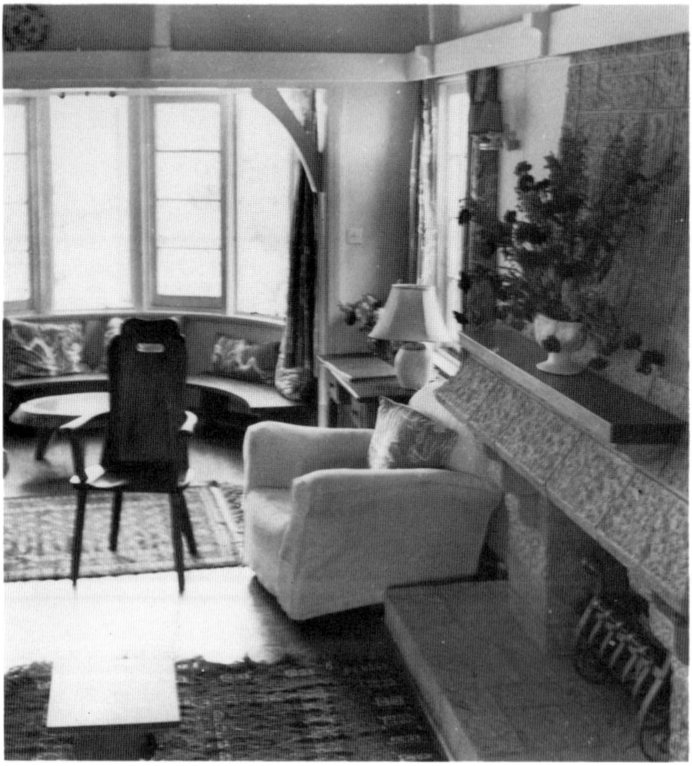

Above On the day before this picture was taken, Princess Elizabeth was writing at the little desk at the Sagana Lodge when she was interrupted to be told that she was Queen

Below Prince Philip was resting in this room when the news of the King's death reached the lodge

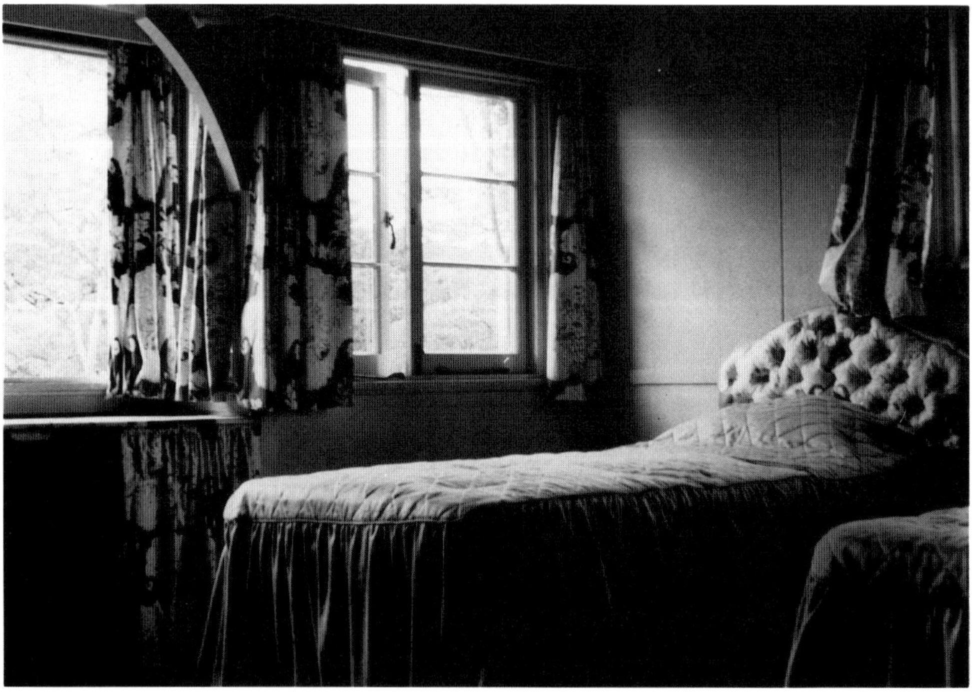

Tired, the Queen arrived back in London to be greeted by
Mr Churchill, Mr Attlee and other VIPs before driving to Clarence
House. It was remarked that she was 'still crying inside'

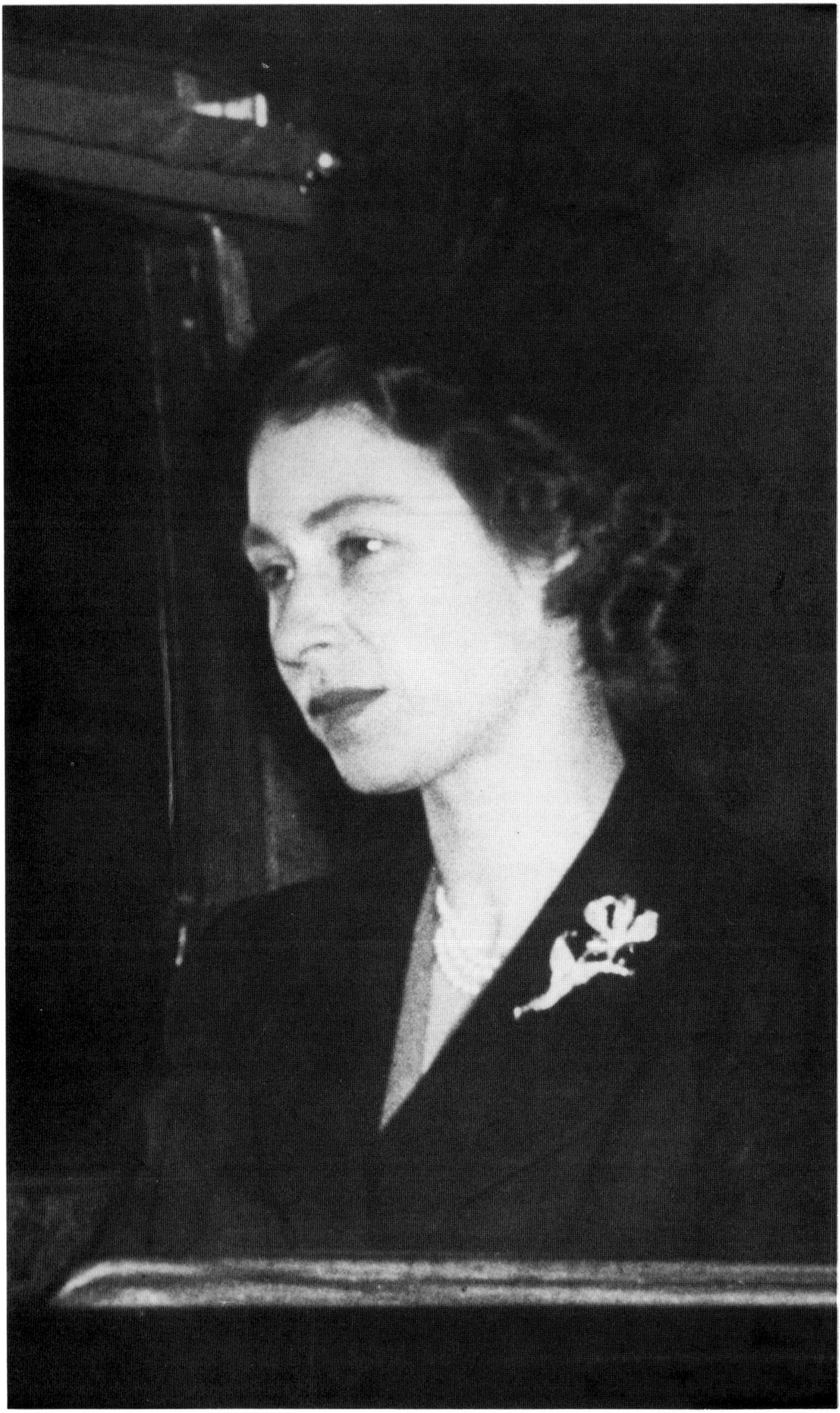

fenced on three sides, but open-ended to the south so the animals may come and go as they please. Mervyn Cowie's love of his wild animals had become a by-word. He had often been heard to say that the fence on the Nairobi side was there not to keep the animals in but the humans out.

In general, the animals within the park lived then and live today entirely natural lives, killing and being killed as they would in any completely wild surroundings. Visitors may drive round any of a large number of dirt tracks in closed cars which the animals have grown used to, and take their chance on whether they light on anything interesting. The park contains a great deal of open grass plain, but also some quite steep gorges with enclosed pools where the animals can make themselves invisible.

Because of the special attraction of the lions, Mervyn Cowie did make some efforts at one time to persuade them into areas where they could be seen. For this purpose he started supplying them with an occasional carcass tied to a tree in an open part of the park. It was a practice, however, that led him into a number of disconcerting escapades with lions, and with some leopards, which also discovered the meat supply. On one occasion, he was on his way to deliver the meat, driving a box-body car, which was an East African cross between a station wagon and a small van. Beside him on the seat were several coils of rope, slats of wood and some tools. Behind him were his two Masai assistants and the greater part of a freshly killed zebra. The tail-board of the car was down, and as he drove slowly to the spot where he intended tying the zebra to a tree, he passed an old lion called Macora, who normally did not get much of a look-in during the initial grabs for the food. Mervyn Cowie thought no more of it until suddenly he felt a jolt at the back of the car. Looking in his driving mirror, he could see his two assistants, but behind them he could also see, to his consternation and horror, Macora, who had sprung aboard, attracted by the scent of the zebra carcass.

Mervyn Cowie reacted instinctively and jammed a foot on the brake. Immediately Macora shot forward inside the car. There was instant confusion as the lion, the two Masai and the dead zebra became intertwined, and all (except the zebra) began giving off noises of extreme dismay. Macora was the first to recover himself, and with the presence of mind to remember why he was there, seized a leg of the zebra and smartly abandoned ship.

For the next couple of hours the two Masai, speaking simultaneously, vociferated their views on feeding the lions. They announced that they had lost their enthusiasm for the job and in future would be looking for something with better long-term prospects. Mervyn Cowie admitted later that, while he understood their natural disturbance of mind in the circumstances, he could not at the time understand their fear of a recurrence, for, after all, would not the lion always go for the dead meat? It was only subsequently that the follow-up thought occurred to him: what if the lions grew used to boarding the car and found no dead carcass aboard? Then he realized that this was exactly what the Masai had been trying tell him so vehemently.

The discontinuation of the practice of feeding the lions cast grave doubts over whether Princess Elizabeth would in fact see any lions when she visited the park, as Mervyn Cowie had promised. This caused the Director of National Parks acute mental anxiety. He discussed with Kenneth Beaton, Warden of the Nairobi Park, and other wardens, how they could ensure that some lions would be visible to order. They considered at great length various schemes, such as putting down a bait, dragging a kill, or trying to drive the lions into open country. Having reconciled their consciences to these artificial methods in consideration of the importance of the visitors, they finally ruled them out on the practical grounds that, whatever you try to do with wild animals, you can never be sure how they will behave. If they fed the lions for a few days before the visit, it might stop them going off on a hunt elsewhere, but equally, it might result in them being so overfed that they would never even emerge from some secluded haunt. In the end, they decided to watch the movements of the lions carefully for some days ahead and trust to providence.

Wardens from other national parks were mustered to act as watchers and there were other observers in aeroplanes. On the day before the royal visit, lions were reported in various sections of the park, and when Mervyn Cowie went home that night to his house bordering the National Park, he was greeted with some heat by his mother, who lived near by. She told him that one of *his* wild lions – of which *he* was so fond – had 'bitten' one of *her* cows, and was even now eating it under a bush. Her fury was undiminished when, in answer to one of her first questions, Mervyn Cowie admitted she would get no compensation – after which she continued to air her opinions of lions (and her son) at some length.

The day of the royal visit dawned bright and clear, though slightly windy, and the small army of observers was out and about early to locate the lions. But now it seemed 'there was not a lion left in Africa'. They searched by ground and from the air without finding any trace of a lion. By 10 a.m. they were truly worried, having given certain optimistic assurances about the lions. Then, later in the morning, a warden turned up at the rendezvous with the news that he had seen four lions on a kill below White Grass Ridge. The news was not, it so happened, greeted with unalloyed sighs of relief. The four lions were a group of large fully grown males that were notorious mischief makers in the district and had become known collectively as 'The Four Hooligans'. The reprobates were now deep in a ravine below the ridge, where it would be impossible to take a car, and where it would be quite out of the question for anyone to approach within viewing distance on foot. Mervyn Cowie, Ken Beaton and other wardens jumped into a truck and set off to assess the situation for themselves.

They found the lions down the ravine with a wildebeest they had just killed but not yet eaten. Ken Beaton suggested to his somewhat startled colleagues that they should drag the kill out of the rocky valley up to a place where it would be more accessible. Everyone agreed that this was an excellent idea, but how would they achieve it? For one thing, the lions were liable to be uncooperative. Devoid of any better idea, the wardens decided to give it a try.

They nosed the truck carefully down the rocky slope till they were as close to the kill as they could get. Then, by using the hooter and flashing the lights of the truck, by banging empty petrol tins and the sides of the truck with sticks, by yelling and shouting, they succeeded in driving the lions away from their kill long enough for two wardens to tie one end of a rope round the wildebeest's leg and the other end to the truck. Fortunately the rope was just long enough. Then they all jumped back hurriedly into the truck.

As the angry lions returned, they were astonished to find their kill suddenly snatched away from them and starting to slide up the hillside. Every time they grabbed hold of it, there was more shouting and hooting and banging, until eventually the wildebeest was out of the ravine and dragged to a lone tree in the long white grass. Again the shouting and banging continued while the kill was tied with wire to the tree. Eventually the truck drove off, leaving the puzzled lions in peace to enjoy their meal.

By 4 p.m. that afternoon Mervyn Cowie and Mr Beaton, in their official capacities, were standing cool and imperturbable, immaculately dressed, awaiting the arrival of the royal visitors. A table had been set out in the road for the Princess to sign the Visitors' Book, which she did, and then, the opening formalities over, Mervyn Cowie began to explain to the Princess what he hoped to show them in the park – including, of course, some lions. At this point Prince Philip said with carefully studied nonchalance, 'We hear you have – er – lost a cow.' News travels fast in Nairobi, and Mervyn Cowie had told the story of his mother's cow to some friends the previous evening, but he had not expected it to reach the royal ears quite so quickly and wondered uneasily how much more they might have heard.

During the tour of the park, Mervyn Cowie drove the safari wagon with the Princess in the front seat beside him and Prince Philip sitting behind with Ken Beaton. The royal visitors were in a relaxed mood, thoroughly enjoying themselves and taking a keen interest in all they saw about them. Almost at once they came across some giraffes, two with their necks intertwined affectionately and another with its nose in a whistling thorn bush, eating. Secretary birds with their quills raised along their backs stepped carefully through the grass looking for snakes, and a flock of guinea fowl scattered at the approach of the vehicle.

Large herds of zebra and wildebeest and Thomson's gazelles divided to let the car pass through, and Grant's gazelles stream-lined ahead against the sky like a frieze, their horns back over their shoulders. Three cock ostriches also strolled by, but of all the birds and animals the royal visitors saw that day, the

Princess was most taken with the little dik-dik, the smallest of the antelopes, no larger than a fox terrier, which moved delicately and nervously through the grass.

Egyptian geese rose and flapped heavily away as the car drove through Lion Valley towards the pool by the Camp of the Birds where vultures came to drink. As they drove up White Grass Ridge to the Embakasi Plain, the two wardens were both trying to conceal their unease. Ahead they could see the lone tree on the hillside where the kill had been tied. Mervyn Cowie looked back at Ken Beaton, the same thought in both their minds: 'Hope to God they are still there.'

From about five hundred yards away they could make out a dark form under the tree, and as he looked in his rear-view mirror, Mervyn Cowie caught Ken Beaton's eye and received a broad reassuring wink of relief. At a range of about three hundred yards, he confidently drew the Princess's attention to the shadow under the tree, and said he thought it was a lion. As they came nearer, he could see it was only one lion, but a magnificent specimen with a big mane, black on top and tawny ginger underneath. He was still eating his dinner. The lion was Sosiani, so named because he had been born near the Sosiani River. Sosiani was also believed to be the lion which had, as a cub, once spent a night in Ken Beaton's house after its mother deserted it. The lioness did not come back on the second night, but on the third night, as Mrs Beaton was feeding the cub with milk from a bottle, she heard the lioness outside, grunting and snarling. She put the cub out with great alacrity. Despite the human scent on the cub, the mother did not reject it this time, but licked it clean, and the youngster grew up to become one of the four biggest nuisances in the district.

The car edged up towards the tree until it was broadside on about ten yards from Sosiani. The Princess impressed both men with the expert way she handled her camera and light meter, and soon she was taking pictures. The lion licked the kill but eyed the truck watchfully. Then he got up and took several paces towards it until the visitors were looking straight into his big yellow eyes. The Princess continued taking pictures of every movement, and muttering under her breath between shots, 'This is wonderful! Oh good.'

The real focus of Sosiani's attention, however, was an accompanying safari truck behind the royal visitors. In this was Len Young, a photographer who was taking pictures of the visit for the National Parks. The truck had stopped with the royal car between it and the lion. Len had opened the roof and was standing with head and shoulders out of the top the better to take pictures as the driver slowly backed them over the stony ground to provide a better view of both the lion and the royal visitors. Sosiani stood there, his ears pricked, his head thrust forward and his nose twitching. Then he took four or five slow, deliberate steps towards the truck, which stopped immediately in response to an urgent signal from Len Young, who ducked back down inside and closed the truck roof. Sosiani paused, yawned hugely, then slowly and reluctantly turned to resume his place in the shade. 'Marvellous!' said the Princess.

Mervyn Cowie's relief at finding a lion and his delight in the performance Sosiani put on was so great at that moment, he said, that he would willingly have jumped out and given the lion a big hug. Despite its unpromising start where lions were concerned, luck was in for the visitors that day. Not long afterwards, as they were driving slowly along, they spotted three lion cubs playing on a grassy mound. As the car drove closer, the cubs promptly disappeared from sight. But as the Princess sat watching patiently, the three little lions were unable to contain their curiosity and before long their heads popped up one after the other above the mound, their eyes round with interest. Reassured, they soon resumed their play. There was no sign of the mother, but as the car remained where it was, the lioness emerged from a patch of long grass some yards away, where she had lain hidden. Slowly she paced forward and positioned herself protectively in the grass between the car and the cubs as they rolled over each other and down the mound.

It was dusk as the car finally drove back to the gates. As Mervyn Cowie recalled, it was the time of day when the hyenas were accustomed to leave the park through a gap in the fence on their nightly 'dustbin patrol', scavenging through the suburban garbage cans in search of scraps. They provided a reminder of how close in this remarkable setting the wild surroundings were to the developed urban areas.

Ten

The Sagana Lodge

FOR THEIR LAST THREE DAYS in Kenya, the Princess and Prince Philip drove up to Nyeri, one hundred miles north of Nairobi and almost directly on the Equator. Here, in the high altitude and exhilarating clear air, they stayed in the Sagana Lodge for the first time. As the lodge was very small, they chose as their only companions for those three days Lady Pamela Mountbatten and Commander Michael Parker, two close friends who were part of their Household.

Lady Pamela was a first cousin to Prince Philip and, like the Princess, a great-great-granddaughter of Queen Victoria. Though she was younger than the Princess – she was only twenty-one – they knew each other well and she had been one of the Princess's bridesmaids. A quiet, sympathetic personality, she could be relied upon, in the role of Lady-in-Waiting during a long tour, to maintain a lively sense of fun. In any case, the Mountbatten family had a long experience of accompanying the royal family on tours, for in particular her father, Earl Mountbatten, had been a close friend of Edward VIII when he was Prince of Wales, and often accompanied him on overseas visits.

Lieutenant-Commander Michael Parker had been a friend and colleague of Prince Philip's in the Royal Navy, during the war and afterwards. This companionship continued after the Duke's marriage with his appointment in 1947 as the Duke's Private Secretary and Equerry-in-Waiting to Princess Elizabeth. An Australian and, like his father, a career officer in the Royal Navy, educated at an independent boys' college in Melbourne and at Dartmouth Naval College, Commander 'Mike' Parker defied his exclusive upbringing with a fresh, bustling opposition to pomposity and stuffiness. His cheerful effervescence, restless energy and down-to-earth practicality were not always in tune with the surroundings in which he found himself, but he had proved a lively companion and a valuable aide, whether his duties involved urgently improvised logistics of travel, problems of sailing, or smoothing down – and keeping at bay – ruffled press photographers.

This was therefore the small party that occupied the Sagana Lodge, and the same companions only would also accompany the royal couple up to Treetops where they were due to spend a night observing big game from the small cabin overlooking the waterhole in the Aberdare forest. It was also to be the same group in Kenya, with one addition, upon which the Princess would lean shortly afterwards, when the news came through that she had become Queen.

The addition was Lieutenant-Colonel the Hon. Martin Charteris, who was not staying at the Sagana Lodge, but was conveniently accessible near by in the Outspan Hotel. Colonel Charteris was Princess Elizabeth's Private Secretary (later to be the Queen's Private Secretary; he was subsequently granted a Peerage and was for some years Provost of Eton College). In Kenya he was temporarily the Princess's Assistant Private Secretary, for Sir Michael Adeane had been appointed Acting Private Secretary for the duration of the tour. Sir Michael was normally Assistant Private Secretary to the King, but as he had been involved with many of the arrangements for the tour made on behalf of the King, and because of his seniority and experience, he was temporarily seconded to the Princess's Household. Sir Michael Adeane, however, was then at Mombasa, whither he had gone direct, ready to sail on the SS *Gothic* for Ceylon when the remainder of the royal party joined the ship after the end of the Kenya visit. With him in Mombasa were General Sir Frederick 'Boy' Browning, Daphne du Maurier's husband, Comptroller of the Princess's Household, and the other Lady-in-Waiting, Lady Palmer. Charteris had been involved in an unpleasant adventure on his way to Kenya for he was in one of two BOAC aircraft held at Cairo Airport when mobs took over the city, burned down the famous Shepheard's Hotel and killed a number of Europeans.

Colonel Charteris could scarcely have provided the Princess with more able support. A master of protocol and procedure, with an incredible capacity for dealing with detail, he also possessed the zest and freshness of outlook that both the Princess and Prince Philip sought in their own approach to their official duties. Grandson of the Earl of Wemyss, a product of Eton and Sandhurst with sculpting and wildfowling as his hobbies, he also had an easy informality which enabled him to deal with anybody, and cope with anything, with suave good humour and immaculate efficiency.

Going northwards from Nairobi, like the arms of a 'V' with the city near the junction point, are two immense valleys. Dividing them is the spine of the Aberdare mountain range, rising to 13,000 feet just below the snowline. To the west of the Aberdares lies the great Rift Valley, which extends for 4,000 miles from the Jordan Valley in Israel to the coast at Mozambique. To the north-west of Nairobi it is seen at its most dramatic: a great cleft in the earth's structure lined by escarpments and dotted with old volcanoes. Farther north near Lake Rudolph at Olduvai Gorge, this fault in the earth's crust has disclosed some of the most ancient anthropological findings of early man, discovered by Dr Louis Leakey.

On the Rift Valley side of the Aberdares there were, too, the European farms of the White Highlands, set in rolling countryside reminiscent of the English downlands. They stretched to the papyrus swamps of Lake Naivasha; and the neighbouring Lake Nakuru, where the innumerable pink-legged flamingos provide one of the most staggering spectacles of bird life to be seen anywhere in the world.

On the other side of the Aberdares – to the east – the second great valley, forty miles wide, extends to the slopes of Mount Kenya, whose icy peak reaches to over 17,000 feet – higher than Mont Blanc. From the Aberdares the land falls sharply away from the high ranges into deep valleys where waterfalls drop huge distances. Lower down are the forests and bamboo where the pretty little colobus monkeys, never seen in the lowlands, fly through the branches with long white hair streaming out like wings. This is the main tribal area of the Kikuyu, the largest tribe in Kenya, whose towns and villages stretch from Nairobi all the way up this valley and line the undulating, hilly, fertile slopes of the Aberdares. It was the Kikuyu who were to provide the main hard-core support for the impending uprising.

In the heart of the area lay the important town of Nyeri; nearly twenty miles to the east of Nyeri, on the slopes of Mount Kenya, was the Sagana Lodge; and ten miles to the west, on a promontory of the Aberdare National Park, was Treetops. On the outskirts of Nyeri itself was the Outspan Hotel, where the remaining members of the Royal Household were staying with other officials and the press members accredited to the royal tour. This fine hotel had its own interesting history, for it was here, in a little cottage in the grounds built especially for him, that Lord Baden-Powell, the Chief Scout, spent his declining years. 'The nearer to Nyeri, the nearer to bliss,' he wrote when he was eighty-one.

On their way to the Sagana Lodge from Nairobi on Sunday, Princess Elizabeth and Prince Philip stopped at Karatina, a main township in the heart of the Kikuyu territory. Several thousand Africans in full ceremonial paint, with ostrich feathers stuck in the clay in their hair, were gathered in this market town for the occasion. A number of warriors had black ostrich feather bobbles stuck on the end of their spears to denote they came in peace. The reception was notable for the almost total lack of reaction on the part of the Kikuyu. Never demonstrative, they stood passively throughout the visit, some openly sullen, while armed British soldiers and local askaris patrolled vigilantly. Then the big black cars drove off in a cloud of dust towards the Sagana Lodge at its location on a remote hillside on the forest slopes.

Some years before the royal visit, the Governor, Sir Philip Mitchell, had decided it would be a good idea to give Princess Elizabeth and Prince Philip a game lodge as their wedding present from the people of Kenya. Sir Philip had earned a reputation as one of the most capable Governors to serve in East Africa. He was a professional colonial servant who had spent all his working life there up to the war. When the war started, he co-ordinated the East African war effort from Nairobi. Later he served in the South-East Asia Command and returned to Kenya after the Japanese surrender.

He was tall, dressed immaculately, spoke perfect Swahili and was, as an administrator, far-sighted, businesslike and a perfectionist who did not suffer fools gladly.

The idea of making the royal couple the gift of a game lodge was attractive, and in the end it was Sir Philip Mitchell who chose the site, though initially he sent for Mervyn Cowie and asked him to pick a place and build a game lodge in one of the National Parks. The instruction brief was that 'it will have to be in the style of one of your safari lodges, accessible, healthy and in a game area'.

In his book *Fly, Vulture* (published in 1961), Mervyn Cowie described how he set about this task. All the low country below 6,000 feet was ruled out because of the mosquitoes, ticks and tsetse flies, while most of the high country was thickly forested and inaccessible. The lodge must have a good water source and easy security arrangements; it also needed to enjoy a view of typical African scenery. After a lot of thought, Cowie chose the southern promontory of the Ngong Hills, south-west of Nairobi, which was the traditional headquarters of the Masai. It was near here that Karen Blixen (Isak Dinesen) had her farm in the 1920s. In her book *Out of Africa* she described the area, saying, 'The views were immensely wide. Everything that you saw made for greatness and freedom, and unequalled nobility.'

Cowie wrote:

Here, I thought, we could build a delightful rondavel style of cottage, remote yet accessible, safe yet surrounded by buffaloes, lions, rhinos and giraffes, and all kinds of wild animals; cool and healthy at an altitude of 7,000 feet and only twenty miles from Nairobi. The site was once described by General Smuts as the most inspiring view in Africa. To the west is the Great Rift Valley, fifty miles across and 5,000 feet down. To the south is the snow-capped dome of Kilimanjaro and other volcanoes. To the east is an endless panorama of golden rolling plains framed by a range of blue hills, and to the north are thousands of square miles ranging from altitudes of 2,000 feet to 19,600 feet and from arid thorn-bush to the rich forests of the Aberdares. Yes, this was the place.

The Governor approved, the Masai agreed, and Mervyn Cowie and Ken Beaton built a rough track up to the site.

I could think of nothing more delightful to offer our Royal couple [said

Cowie] than a cosy house from which to watch the sun rise over Donyo Sabuk, or to see the brilliant hues of a sunset over the western wall of the Rift Valley, and at night to listen to the grunts of the wildebeest from the plains below, the wail of the hyena and the roar of a lion. Yes, this would truly be a Game Lodge.

Plans proceeded and, with architectural advice, a cottage was designed on paper. There was still a road to construct, water to be supplied and staff quarters to be built. Then the Governor sent for Mervyn Cowie and Ken Beaton. 'Gentlemen,' he told them, 'I have changed my mind.' He said the site selected was unsuitable. He had been there the day before with this wife and it was too full of burrs. He was still wearing the same suit, he said, and to prove his point he picked some grass seed and burrs from the turn-ups of his trousers and laid them on the shiny table. He then went on to explain that he now favoured a location on the slopes of Mount Kenya. It was arranged that they should meet a few days later on the Sagana River on Mount Kenya to discuss the new site.

When Cowie went to keep his appointment with Sir Philip, he arrived ahead of the Governor and noticed that there was an unusual number of buffalo flies about. These were large black flies which had a sting though they were not dangerous. Cowie caught some of the flies and put them in a matchbox. When the Governor arrived, Cowie solemnly announced, 'I am sorry, sir, this place won't do.' When the Governor asked why not, Cowie replied, 'Because it's full of flies,' and pulled out the matchbox and threw the flies on to the ground one at a time.

The gesture was not appreciated, and after a lot of discussion and walking through the forest, the Director of the Royal National Parks was obliged to concede that the site would make a good fishing lodge. His disappointment was tinged with regrets that the lodge would not be in a National Park, nor would it be a game lodge. There was also something in his reaction of a plainsman's natural aversion to forests. It would be dangerous to walk near because of rhinos and elephants; there was no view of Mount Kenya; there were no lions, giraffes or plains game; and finally, it would be cold and damp. Sadly, Cowie asked leave to withdraw from the scheme, and the lodge was duly constructed by the Public Works Department and completed just before the royal visitors were due.

Cowie says in his book that he never did find out why the Governor changed his mind, though he was sure Sir Philip had a good reason. Later consideration led him to believe that the Governor must have been influenced by the knowledge that members of the royal family were very keen on fishing and therefore decided in favour of a fishing lodge. In his less charitable moments, he reflected that since the Governor himself liked fishing, a fishing lodge conveniently available could be seen as providing a motive for his decision.

The road from Nairobi to the Sagana Lodge was unmade dirt surface for considerable distances, climbing up winding hillsides and through small villages, banana plantations and open bush. When the royal party arrived at the lodge, the Governor was there to greet them. He took one look at the Princess as she stepped out of the car and said, apologetically and with English understatement, 'I'm afraid you've had rather a dusty journey.' The Princess spread out both arms expressively towards him and laughingly said, 'Just look at me!'

The key to the lodge was handed to the Princess so she could formally and ceremoniously open the iron-studded door. Unfortunately the lock was very stiff and she could not turn the key. In the end Sir Philip himself had to coax it to open. The Princess entered the lodge and embarked with the Duke on a twenty-five minute inspection of the house and gardens. As they went in they found themselves in a tiled entranceway, then went down two steps between upright timbers forming an arch into the main living-room, which was about thirty feet long. Polished red-cedar floor-boards were covered with Persian rugs. The walls were plain cream with a white-painted timbered ceiling above. A high shelf displayed coloured plates. A big grey stone fireplace with wrought-iron grate filled with logs took up most of the right-hand wall; a large soft comfortable sofa with beige loose covers was placed opposite the fireplace. Four large easy chairs to match the sofa stood in each corner. It was a light, comfortable room, full of bowls of flowers; and containing no indication whatever of special royal use, except possibly a large red-backed volume of *Debrett's Peerage* that stood conspicuously out of place among the magazines and novels.

They walked through the room to the rear, where a big bow window overlooked the terrace and a river valley. Beside the window was a small writing desk, soon to have its own small place in history, though no one could know it yet. As they progressed, some of the story of the building of the lodge and the creation of the gardens was explained to them. They were told of the great care that had been taken in the siting of the lodge in an area of primeval jungle, thick with trees and undergrowth, on the side of a hill overlooking a little river valley. Major H.B. Sharpe, the Keeper of Parks and Gardens, had come along two years earlier to lay out the garden.

The landscaping could hardly have been in better hands. 'Sharpie' was one of those inspired gardeners who can literally make deserts bloom. Elspeth Huxley in her book *Out in the Midday Sun* described how much he loved colour and how he had become famous in Kenya for creating beautiful gardens in the areas in which he was formerly stationed as a District Officer. He had originally trained as a botanist at Kew Gardens and started life in the Colonial Service in Kenya as a Plant Inspector. This did not stand very high in the colonial hierarchy, but he had risen to the rank of major in the First World War, which gave him greater status in Kenya later.

As a District Officer, Sharpie had been highly successful, but his somewhat rebellious attitude towards authority caused him to be regarded with cautious suspicion. Nevertheless it helped him to achieve his objectives. When he came to the Sagana Lodge, he found the setting perfectly suited to his taste. The trees obscured the distant view, however, and when he wanted to cut some of them down and open up the perspective, he was told that the Governor had forbidden any clearance.

Sharpie insisted that, to start with, he must get rid of a Cape chestnut that was overhanging the house. The builder protested that he had had the utmost difficulty in fitting the building in between that tree and another farther along the hillside. Sharpie then pointed out that the roots had been half cut away to achieve this and the tree would most likely fall on the house anyway. The builder gave in and the tree was removed.

As for the larger problem, it was agreed that the Governor should be approached and the difficulties explained. Sir Philip then consented to some clearance of trees, but was adamant that this should be minimal and that great care should be taken not to spoil the natural beauty of the setting. Seen from the rear terrace, a line of blue gums on the ridge across the valley waved gracefully against the sky; but some of these were sacrificed to open up a view of the Aberdare Mountains to one side. Farther over some more were removed to reveal an aspect of Mount Kenya, though maybe one effect of an over-cautious reaction to the Governor's instructions was to leave the snow peaks tantalizingly part-obscured.

The river itself, only fifteen feet wide, had been hidden by undergrowth. This was cleared to disclose arum lilies growing to the water's edge and wild banana trees lining the bank. Now, additionally, giant salmon-coloured cannas were planted along the bank in time to be in bloom for the royal visit. Some of the silver-stemmed albizzias at the river bottom were removed to enhance the beauty of others which surrounded and shaded a level patch of ground, which was duly transformed into a green lawn, half-encircled by a loop in the river. Multi-coloured plants of all varieties on the hillside and in the dark red soil of the flower beds around the terrace were gifts from private gardens all over Kenya.

The Princess, entranced by the garden, bubbled with enthusiasm, delighted in the warmth of the sunshine after the cold weather in England and commented freely on the charm and the scent of the flowers now in bloom. Her attention was drawn to a large fig tree to one side of the terrace. It was alive with fruit-eating birds, including a pair of golden orioles, with vivid yellow plumes, that were in residence in the tree. After that she made her way slowly down the hillside to the river, cool, clear and sparkling – the melted snows of Mount Kenya tumbling downhill over waterfalls and through pools harbouring fat trout. There, on the patch of lawn beside the water, the royal visitors each planted a tree to mark their visit.

The moment she arrived at the lodge, the Princess had met Turk, and inevitably they immediately became firm friends. Turk was a small wire-haired fox terrier belonging to Mr J. L. Richardson, the Assistant Superintendent of Police, who had the lodge under his care. Besides being a guard dog, Turk knew his ceremonial; he was used to parading with the police, when he would take the salute with both paws. His real fame came, however, from a recent three-quarter-hour battle with a rhino which Mr Richardson encountered unexpectedly one night when taking an evening stroll down the road. It was one of the hazards of this approach road that it was frequented at night by elephant, rhino and buffalo, which used it like any other trail and were inclined to resent disturbance.

On their first evening, the Princess and her husband went back down the road to the little church at Nyeri to attend Evensong. The windows of the church were left open so that people who could not get in could still hear the service. The next day, Monday, the first full day of their stay at the lodge, the royal couple resisted the temptation to spend a lazy morning, but instead rode over for breakfast with Mr and Mrs Edward Windley at the Provincial Commissioner's house near by.

As Provincial Commissioner, Mr Windley was their official host while they were in the Nyeri area. A tall, elegant and gifted young man still in his thirties, he was already marked out for distinction. He was a fund of local knowledge – not all of which could be imparted to his guests during breakfast. Mr and Mrs Windley talked about the whole of this very lovely area and about the royal lodge. They spoke of how the workers had been interrupted from time to time by the unannounced arrival of curious rhinos; of how baboons had eaten the wallpaper; of how elephants had broken through the forest patrols a few days earlier and threatened to ruin the gardens; of the care taken to preserve the trees on the hillside, yet to open up the view. The Princess said then, as she was to say again later, how much she thought her father would like it there, and how she hoped he too would visit the Sagana Lodge.

Back at the lodge later in the morning, they found that the ever-practical Mike Parker had already been down to the fishing area beside the stream and had caught four fine trout for lunch. The fish were to prove such good eating that, in the cool of the evening, the Princess and Prince Philip also went down to the stream and between them caught about a dozen more trout. It provided a pleasant relaxation for Prince Philip who had, in the heat of the afternoon, played four chukkas of polo at Nyeri – two chukkas for the local Nyeri team and two for the opponents from Nanyuki.

Earlier, at midday, when there was a report of a herd of elephants about six miles away, the royal visitors got into their car, accompanied by the local game wardens, and came upon the elephants, about thirty altogether, walking along a track. They were able to film them from about half a mile away. Some of the elephants had been rolling in red mud at a waterhole, which inevitably enabled the local humourists to point out, perfectly truthfully, that the royal couple had seen pink elephants. What was more, they had film to prove it!

The elephants on this occasion were something of a bonus, for it was planned that the real opportunity to see big game at close quarters would be provided on the next night at the world-famous Treetops Hotel.

Eleven

Beware – Elephants!

TREETOPS HOTEL achieved fame before the war as the only hotel of its kind to be built in a tree. It overlooked a waterhole where a large variety of big game came nightly to drink. Under superb natural conditions, observers could watch animals ranging from elephant and rhino to the shy impala and the rare bongo. Although the range varied from night to night, there were always sufficient animals to excite and to vary the interest. It was an idea which immediately caught the imagination and soon Treetops became known world-wide.

Treetops and the Outspan Hotel were the creations of Eric and Lady Bettie Sherbrooke Walker. Eric Sherbrooke Walker had read theology at Oxford but did not proceed to Ordination. Instead he met Lord Baden-Powell, who, in 1908, appointed him his first Scout Commissioner, and he remained Baden-Powell's private secretary until the First World War, when he joined the Royal Flying Corps, was shot down and captured. 'BP', however, sent him some wire cutters disguised as a ham bone and he cut his way to freedom.

After the war he had an adventurous time in Russia; and also on board ship in the West Indies, helping to relieve the suffering of those enduring Prohibition in the United States. Later he wrote a book called *Confessions of a Rum Runner*. He married Lady Bettie Feilding, daughter of the Earl of Denbigh, and they went to East Africa, looking for inspiration and a future life together.

At Nyeri in Kenya, they found a site they believed to be the loveliest in all East Africa. In one direction it overlooked Mount Kenya; in another the Aberdare Mountains; and, on a third side, the land sloped down a steep green gorge to the River Chania. Loch Leven trout had been introduced into Kenya in 1905 by the famous Colonel Ewart Grogan, who once walked from the Cape to Cairo. The Chania River, like many others in the area, was, as a result of the Colonel's enterprise, well stocked with both rainbow and brown trout.

The whole area was at that time largely uninhabited. By 1926, Nyeri had a European population of nine, with government offices and a sawmill, but it had already become the meeting place for ranchers and planters from many miles around and had an eighteen-hole golf course and a small hotel called the White Rhino – 'that charges at sight'. When the Sherbrooke Walkers built their hotel, the lady owner of the near-by sawmill won a bottle of champagne in a name competition by suggesting it be called 'The Outspan' – a South African term meaning 'where, at the end of the day's journey, the traveller outspans the weary oxen'. One of the features of the hotel to distinguish it from all others thereabouts at the time was that, despite its remote situation and difficulty of access during the rainy season, every bedroom had a private bathroom and lavatory, so providing expatriate guests with luxury and nostalgic memories every time they flushed the water-closet.

'BP' first visited Kenya in 1906, but did not return there until 1935, when he was inspecting Scout rallies throughout the country. He renewed his acquaintance with Eric Sherbrooke Walker at the Outspan and fell in love with 'the wonderful views over the plains to the bold snow peak of Mount Kenya'. When in the winter of 1937 his doctor in England ordered him to rest, there was one place to which 'BP' looked. 'I am coming to spend the rest of my life at the Outspan,' he wrote, and he did. Using some of the funds collected by Scouts and Guides from all over the world to celebrate the Baden-Powells' silver wedding anniversary, Sherbrooke Walker built a cottage in the grounds of the Outspan, and in 1938 the couple came to live there. They had a large sitting room with veranda, two bedrooms, two bathrooms and two fireplaces, and their own private garden with a view across to Mount Kenya. As his home at Bentley in Hampshire had been called Pax Hill, 'BP' wanted this new one to be called Pax too – or Pax Two – and when he learned that in Kiswahili *Pax tu* meant 'completely and utterly Pax', the cottage was immediately named Paxtu.

In 1938 Lady Baden-Powell wrote home to her children, 'We are utterly and supremely happy,' and there they stayed while 'BP' sketched and wrote in his declining years. And there, in 1941, at the age of eighty-four, he died. He was laid to rest in the little hillside churchyard at Nyeri, and on the headstone of his grave was inscribed the insignia ☉ which is the Scout trail sign meaning, 'I have gone home.' Today his grave is a Mecca for Scouts and Guides from all over the world.

By 1931 the Outspan was receiving guests who wanted to photograph big game rather than shoot it, and after one or two encounters on foot with wild animals, particularly rhino, the Sherbrooke Walkers started to search for a more satisfactory and safer way of getting closer. Lady Bettie recalled how, when she was a small girl at home, she and her brothers and sisters had a small house in a tree. They also started to think about the Swiss Family Robinson and, inevitably, Peter Pan. Thus, in 1932, the idea was born and the

Sherbrooke Walkers began to look for somewhere to put their little tree-house. The eventual site was suggested to them by Captain Alfred 'Ugly' Sheldrick, a retired Indian Army Cavalry officer who had a coffee plantation at Mwliga on the edge of the forest near Nyeri. He knew of the waterhole, which, he claimed feelingly, was used by animals that trampled on his coffee trees. It was beside a track along which the elephants passed on their way from the Aberdare forests to the slopes of Mount Kenya. The track ran directly beneath a giant mgumu, or wild fig tree, standing by the pool. As soon as they saw it, the Sherbrooke Walkers realized it was exactly what they were after.

The tree was immense and spooky, like something in a picture from a child's fairy-tale book illustrated by Arthur Rackham. It was of vast girth and its gnarled trunk rose for twenty feet without a branch protruding. Then it burst diagonally outwards, fanning in all directions with long, thick convoluted branches intertwined and seemingly providing room for unlimited platforms. Thirty-five feet up in this great tree, 'Ugly' Sheldrick built the Sherbrooke Walkers a little two-roomed house with a veranda facing the pool. A very tall chimney carried away the smoke from a small wood stove, and supplies were lifted up by hand. It made a perfect little Wendy house. The tree top was as soft as velvet, the air was filled with the singing of birds, and at night the sky was bejewelled with innumerable stars. (Only one thing was lacking – virtually the only creature that could *not* be seen from this vantage point was a crocodile, with or without an alarm clock in its stomach.)

The surroundings to Treetops were wild and unspoiled. The final approach to it was uphill through the forest for just over a quarter of a mile. Since it was a forest highway, safety ladders were nailed to the larger trees, right up the whole path. The track ran diagonally to the left along the hillside, then cut back again until it reached a small glade. At the far side of this clearing, opposite the path, was the giant fig tree. It stood on the edge of the grass and mud that bordered an oval-shaped pool. The forest surrounded the pool on three sides, with many Cape chestnuts. Treetops was on the eastern side of the waterhole with its back to Mount Kenya, and looked westwards across the pool to more open country.

The first Treetops was small, with only four bunks in the two rooms. Visitors had the option of being left there on their own, or the Sherbrooke Walkers would stay as hosts and look after them. During the early period, the reactions of visitors in this intimate and lonely environment could be almost as interesting as the behaviour of the animals. Some, left alone, confessed afterwards to feeling apprehensive, even a bit frightened; most were intrigued and fascinated by a totally new and often unexpected experience. Formality fell away and everyone became relaxed. Among the first visitors were the Duke and Duchess of Gloucester. After dinner, instead of sitting on the balcony while the Sherbrooke Walkers cleared up, the Duchess of Gloucester rolled up her sleeves and helped to wash the dishes.

Not all the visitors grew so relaxed, however, or were even seriously interested in watching the animals. One bright young thing of the time spent a night of her honeymoon at Treetops – so she could write her new name on an elephant's back. She even brought a billiard cue and chalk to help her do it. But when her chance came, with an elephant right below her, she couldn't reach, so insisted on being lowered over the balcony on a rope tied round her waist, despite her husband's protestations. The attempt ended in confusion and blushes when she reached forward and suddenly tipped head-downwards with her legs in the air and her skirts around her neck. Her squeals mingled with those of the startled elephant as it took off in alarm.

Fortunately it was more usually the animals, not the visitors, that provided the spectacle. But it was not the visual scene alone that was so impressive. Visitors were almost as keenly aware of the invisible 'atmosphere' of the jungle about them. The forest was full of unfamiliar smells and sounds. The snufflings and snortings; the whistles, grunts and screams; the rustling and movement; even the sound of unidentified breathing in these unusual surroundings, all were creepily eerie to the inexperienced. Nevertheless it would have been very disappointing not to be able to see what was happening on the ground below, for the animals mostly came to the waterhole late in the afternoon, used it extensively during the night, and disappeared with the dawn.

The best time to go to Treetops was during the full moon, when the animals could be watched around the pool after darkness fell. So, visits to Treetops were normally arranged only on the few days spanning the full moon. A number of experiments with a floodlamp had proved not very successful as it scared the animals away. The visit of Princess Elizabeth to Treetops, however, was scheduled to take place when the moon would be only half-full, so the Warden of the Aberdare National Park, Mr John Hayward, had been consulted. After some careful thought, he rigged up a floodlamp at the top of a tree on the side of the glade from which the moon normally rose, and this gave a diffused light over the waterhole. It was an ingenious arrangement powered by car batteries and controlled by an improvised dimmer consisting of a jar of salt water and two terminals, one of which was wound up and down noiselessly by a trout reel. The artificial moon worked perfectly and illuminated the pool with a steadily strengthening light that caused no disturbance or fright to even the most timid animal.

By the time of the royal visit, Treetops had been rebuilt several times and now had accommodation for nine or ten guests, with separate dining room and kitchen, an observation balcony across the whole of the side of the hut overlooking the waterhole, and a little look-out post built on a separate platform right at the top of the tree. The hut was reached from the glade by a steep fixed wooden staircase with handrails that had two platforms at intervals on the way up. It was here, in this remote and fascinating spot, that Princess Elizabeth was to spend the historic night of 6 February 1952.

If Mervyn Cowie had been anxious to show the Princess some lions in the Nairobi National Park, the Sherbrooke Walkers were, as her hosts at Treetops, equally keen that she should see some elephants in the Aberdares. It so happened that this was the dry time of the year when the elephants tended to move higher up the mountain into the cooler, moister area of the bamboo forests. The game wardens had been watching the movements of all elephants in the neighbourhood for some weeks beforehand, and extra supplies of salt had been laid at the waterhole to attract them to stay on the lower slopes. For several nights prior to the royal visit there were, even so, disappointingly few elephants at the pool.

On the other hand, the problem caused by a lack of elephants was to be counterbalanced by one caused by their presence. For the last few hundred yards, the approach to Treetops lay across unprotected ground. The path was also used by elephants and rhino, and the density of the jungle obscured any view of Treetops or the waterhole until visitors were almost there. African elephants are notoriously unpredictable, and can be extremely dangerous; what is more, the elephants in the forests and on the mountain slopes are smaller and more aggressive than those on the plains.

Since there was no means of telling from the approach path what might be happening at the waterhole, special warning arrangements were set up with Lady Bettie Walker and her older daughter Honor, who would be going up to Treetops in advance at midday to take the supplies. With them would go Colonel Jim Corbett, a remarkably lively septuagenarian who had been a legend in India and who was now living in retirement in Kenya in the Baden-Powells' former house. Jim Corbett's exploits as a hunter of man-eating tigers and leopards in the foothills of the Himalayas had made him famous. He was a keen naturalist, an excellent story-teller, and his books on his adventures in India, such as *Man-Eaters of Kumaon*, were well-known. As an honorary game warden, he was invited to assist the Sherbrooke Walkers in looking after the royal visitors.

A system of warning signals was worked out. Jim Corbett would be posted on one of the platforms of the ladder up the tree, where he could be viewed immediately the glade was reached. But, before then, any advance warning could be given by Lady Bettie, for the roof of Treetops could be seen through the trees from farther back down the path. If there was danger, or reason for care because of events at the waterhole, she would hang a white pillow case on the roof of the tree house. Sherbrooke Walker and Edward Windley would escort the royal party, and both were to be armed.

But there were others besides them who were concerned with the safety of the royal party. Mervyn Cowie, as Director of National Parks, and John Hayward, as Warden of the Aberdare National Park, both felt they had a strong responsibility over the visit and had been hard at work preparing detailed arrangements to protect the Princess while she was in the park. Cowie then went to discuss these arrangements with Edward Windley, and was dumbfounded to be told by the Provincial Commissioner that he and Hayward would not have any concern with the visit. Cowie's relations with the Governor had been fairly cool for some time, but he had hardly expected to be given instructions by the government to keep away.

Once again the Cowie blood was up. He relates his feelings in his book, *Fly, Vulture*:

Windley told me that he and Sherbrooke Walker would escort the Royal Party up the four-hundred-yard footpath through the forest to Treetops. I had the greatest regard for the Provincial Commissioner, but not as a hunter. I also had tremendous respect for Sherbrooke Walker, and bowed to the lifelong experience he had had with conducting and sending people to Treetops. But was this enough? Here was the heir to the throne of England and her consort, the most important visitors who had ever been to Treetops, requiring extra precautions for their safety.

It was not only the danger of wild animals on the path, but Mau Mau was rumbling through the villages of Kikuyu country. Having grown up with the Kikuyu, I did not share the official Government view that all was well, and I believed that a sinister and desperate rebellion was about to break across the alleged peaceful scene of Kenya. What would happen if a band of terrorists tried to attack the Royal Party on the way to Treetops? I asked. This risk must not be overlooked. At best it may so happen that some inquisitive Kikuyu fanatics may sneak up to the glade merely to see the Princess and by so doing spoil any chances of wild animals coming to the pool.

I was not satisfied and protested to Windley. He was most willing to listen, but there were difficulties. I then heard that Jim Corbett, famous for his amazing adventures with tigers and leopards in the Indian jungle, had been invited to join the Royal Party at Treetops. I conferred with Jim Corbett and received the most encouraging and understanding sympathy. I said, 'I am going to patrol the path before the party arrives,' and he gave me his immediate approval. As a great man of the wilds, he seemed to understand at once and required no convincing of the dangers involved. We shared a profound respect for the Royal Family and our beloved Princess, and we had a mutual knowledge of the unexpected tricks of wild animals. Jim Corbett said he would stay on the platform beneath the tree-house throughout the night, as he was not happy about the easy access of the ladder for a leopard or perhaps a terrorist.

Fortified by this complete concord of outlook and encouraged by a man who was pre-eminent in the lore of the wilds, I returned to the Provincial

Commissioner and informed him that Hayward and I would undoubtedly have to patrol the pathway. 'It is a National Park,' I said, 'and we have a very definite responsibility.' I believed he agreed, but I gave him no opportunity of doing so. All he said was, 'Don't show yourselves to the Royal Party,' which I accepted.

I felt so sure I was right. Jim Corbett agreed. It was not a case of belittling the prowess of Windley or of Sherbrooke Walker. It was just plain common sense in this set of circumstances. Two men were not enough to deal with the situation if something really went wrong. I was not so concerned with the rank discourtesy of being told to keep out of my own province, nor did I wish to interfere with any arrangements made by the Walkers for the royal visit. I did not attempt to join the party at Treetops itself, much as I would have liked to do so. All I really tried to achieve was the safe conduct of the party through the dangerous part of the forest. I was more than thankful that Jim Corbett would be on guard on the platform well before they arrived.

The royal party left the Sagana Lodge early on the Tuesday afternoon, though a bit later than had been planned – which subsequently proved to be a fortunate circumstance for the Princess's safety. They were all appropriately dressed for the occasion. Princess Elizabeth and Lady Pamela wore khaki slacks and bush shirts; Prince Philip and Commander Parker wore light khaki safari suits. It had been intended that they should drive to the Nyeri polo ground and there change to a safari wagon for the last part of the journey over a rough and often slippery dirt track up to the forest. At the same time an opportunity would be given to press photographers to take pictures. But as there had been no rain, the dirt road was dry and clear of mud. It was therefore decided to drive all the way in the Humber limousines – so the Nyeri polo ground was by-passed and the photographers disappointed. There were to be no informal photographs of the Princess and Lady Pamela in slacks and bush shirts!

As arranged, Lady Bettie Walker, Honor Walker and Jim Corbett had already taken up their positions at Treetops, where they awaited the arrival of the royal party, which was due soon after 2 p.m. To their delight an hour or so before the estimated time of arrival, a herd of about forty elephants with many calves slowly gathered at the salt-lick. The area of the waterhole and salt-lick formed an oval about two hundred yards wide and one hundred yards across, of which two-thirds was water interspersed with tufts of grass and weeds. The remainder was salt-lick, which extended right up to the foot of the giant fig tree. It was on this side of the pool below Treetops that the elephants had congregated in a leisurely manner after first grazing over the grass among the bushes on the far side of the waterhole away from Treetops.

For the most part, the elephants idled peaceably. But in one small group there were signs of trouble developing. Three of the bulls, including the leader, were beginning to quarrel. To the obvious annoyance of the older bull, the two younger bulls were paying too much attention to the females. They ignored a number of warnings from their leader and refused to leave the cows alone. The friction and tension built up until eventually, screaming with rage, the older bull charged the younger bulls. All three elephants, trumpeting angrily, then crashed through the trees and off on one side into the forest. Jim Corbett, sitting up at Treetops, anxiously tried to trace the course of the animals from the crashing and trumpeting noises coming from the trees. The quarrel took them in a wide arc away from the salt-lick, but gradually their battling course curved back in a line that brought them right across the path up which the royal party was shortly to walk.

Meanwhile, about ten miles from Nyeri, the royal cars were turning off the road and up a rough track that led through long grass and stunted shrubs towards a line of low hills. The track twisted up and down through the hills and dipped into little valleys, following the contours of the land as the denseness of the trees increased. Finally the track ended abruptly at the foot of a hill which presented a solid wall of primeval forest, green and dark – the edge of the jungle itself. Here the cars drew up in a clearing where Eric Sherbrooke Walker was waiting. A white-haired, white-moustached figure in safari suit, he stood knee-deep in the long grass. Over his shoulder was slung a double-barrelled Holland & Holland heavy calibre rifle loaded with hard-nosed bullets – sufficient to stop a charging rhino or elephant dead in its tracks.

There was a general atmosphere of light-heartedness and excitement among the royal party. Sherbrooke Walker nevertheless insisted on having their attention as he stated the instructions with which he briefed every party of visitors going up to Treetops. He explained that the waterhole was just over a quarter of a mile into the living jungle and the only means of approach was along a forest track. This track had been made by wild animals and was used by them every day. He emphasized that there were many dangerous animals in the neighbourhood, elephants, rhino and buffaloes in particular. The visitors must be as quiet as possible so as not to frighten the animals away from the waterhole: or worse still, he said significantly, so as not to attract the animals towards the party on the path. Do not tread on twigs, do not scuffle the leaves. Do not speak unless it is necessary, and then only in whispers. Keep quiet and move carefully.

He pointed out that rough ladders had been nailed to the stoutest trees at intervals of about fifty yards along the path. If danger was imminent, they should not wait upon the order of their departure but climb the nearest ladder as fast as possible. The safe height was eight to ten feet for a rhino or buffalo, or eighteen to twenty feet for an elephant. He assured them that no one had ever been hurt on that path. He did not tell them of how many occasions there had been when the ladders were used in a hurry.

As the party formed up, there was some jocular banter at the thought of being 'shaken out of the bushes'. Prince Philip and Edward Windley both carried rifles, but Sherbrooke Walker thoughtfully provided the Princess with a long stick like a shepherd's crook to help her up the hilly slopes. They were ready to enter the forest.

While the royal cars had been still on their way from Nyeri, and even as Jim Corbett was nervously cocking an ear to trace the fighting bull elephants' movements away from the path, Mervyn Cowie and John Hayward were tiptoeing into the forest. Since their presence was to remain unknown to the royal party, it was agreed that Hayward should patrol the first two hundred yards of the path, keeping out of sight in the forest, while Cowie did the same for the latter portion, up to the tree house. As Mervyn Cowie reached the top of the rise nearing the pool, he could hear bursts of squeals and trumpeting. Elephants were obviously in possession of the pool. He crept to within range of the platform, and spied Jim Corbett standing there watching. Cowie attracted Jim's attention with a flick of a white handkerchief and received an acknowledging wave. 'Never had I known of so many elephants at Treetops at this early hour of the day,' said Cowie. His account continued:

There seemed to be at least fifty. Some bulls were very cantankerous and kept lunging at each other and rushing off into the forest. It was superb, I thought, that the Princess would be greeted by so many elephants, but it was also very dangerous. The fighting bulls were in a bad mood.

I moved back down the path knowing that there was at least half an hour before the party could arrive. I sat quietly underneath a bower of dense undergrowth thinking.

As he sat there in a patient and watchful reverie, he was abruptly brought back to earth by the crack of a twig close by. He said:

I stood up quickly, released the safety catch of my gun, and listened. Not a sound came through, apart from the spasmodic squeals and rumbling of the elephants at the pool. I crawled forward and round the thick undergrowth, and peered into the forest. There, to my utter astonishment, was an elephant standing quite motionless, bleeding slightly from his left shoulder, and only ten yards from the pathway to Treetops, the pathway that the Princess would come along within the next twenty minutes.

This seemed to be the most unfortunate development. The wind was by no means steady, but for the moment it was blowing gently towards me from the elephant and across the path. Anyone going quietly along would probably not be detected by the elephant, but a party of several people was sure to be heard. The wind might change. I must have passed this elephant twice when I went up to and back from the glade, without having any idea that he was near.

My first thought was to run back to within reach of Hayward, ask him to go back to the beginning of the path and stop the Royal Party advancing until we could be sure that the elephant had moved. But this I rejected as a bad plan, because once out of sight of the elephant I would not know where he had gone. We would then have to comb the forest to make sure the approach to Treetops was clear. That might cause the entire herd to stampede.

Next I thought I would make a slight noise to let the elephant know I was there. He had been hurt in a fight, and he may easily become aggressive. What then, I wondered? The last thing in the world to do was to provoke a situation where I would have to shoot; the whole visit to Treetops would be spoilt, and the Princess would see nothing but the carcass of a proud ruler of the forest. I wanted to go and ask Jim Corbett for advice but there was no chance. While I was away, assuming I got past the elephant successfully, the Royal Party may come up the path. I was in a bad predicament. My mind was in a whirl of conflicting thoughts.

'Don't show yourself to the Royal Party.' Keep off the grass! My own grass, which was now under the full control of an elephant. The wind may change. What the hell?

Meanwhile the elephant was standing quite motionless and silent. He appeared to be drowsing and his eyes were shut. I fixed on a plan. I went over it several times, and tried to imagine every kind of consequence. The plan was to give him my scent and trust that he would either charge upwind or downwind, but not sideways. Sideways would mean straight along the path. I searched for a pebble, not an easy thing to find in a forest, but where the pathways had been levelled, there were some small stones. I picked up a round one about the size of a small plum and rubbed it well into my armpits. Disgusting on a hot day, I thought, but I knew it to be the most effective way of obtaining some powerful human scent. It had been successful on other occasions. I took my unsavoury pebble and threw it just beyond the elephant and to windward of him. The noise of it falling through the branches alerted him, and out went his huge ears. The wind remained steady and the plan worked.

Suddenly his trunk went forward to sniff the air, and then down into a tight curl, and he took off as if he had been pricked in the backside, straight towards the scent and on through the forest. I kept a careful check of the direction as he crashed through the undergrowth. When charging or stampeding, elephants are no longer like silent phantoms gliding along, but huge clumsy animals busting through like a bulldozer. I came up the path just far enough and in time to see the elephant join the herd, being certain of his identity by the fresh blood on his left shoulder.

All was well, I retreated down the path to the first bend. After a few moments and before I really had time to get my breath I heard the party approaching. Very quietly I pushed into the undergrowth and watched the Princess and the Duke go past within a few feet. Better, I thought, that I and not the elephant was hiding in the bushes. I wondered what would have happened if he had not been removed. Perhaps nothing, or perhaps he would have charged. At such short range there would have been a tragedy, a most horrible tragedy. The elephant went straight towards the scent when he took off, which convinced me that he was in a very aggressive mood. He was sore from fighting with another bull and may well have vented his spite on the first person he saw. I shivered at the thought, and came back to reality when I saw Hayward coming up the path.

Together the two men followed the royal party up the path, keeping their distance and out of sight, and then moved off discreetly to one side to another little clearing from where they had a clear view of the foot of the ladder leading up to the tree-house.

The Princess explained later that almost from the moment when they started along the path, their ears were assailed with the angry trumpeting and crashing sounds of 'rampaging elephants'. Yet they could see nothing as they went up the narrow path in single file. Apart from the density of the trees, which created patches of dappled sunlight, the elephant grass growing waist-high on either side also restricted visibility. They trod cautiously, making only slight rustling sounds as they moved slowly up the hillside towards the waterhole.

They were still some way from the Treetops clearing when they came to where they could just see the top of the cabin through the trees – and there was the white pillow case on the roof, fluttering in the breeze. Danger at the pool! A decision had to be taken immediately. To go ahead? Or to turn back? Sherbrooke Walker consulted Prince Philip, who whispered, 'Go ahead!'

With no knowledge of what was going on at the waterhole, Sherbrooke Walker considered it prudent to split the party at this point. He asked Lady Pamela and Commander Parker to stay behind on the path while the Princess and the Duke went ahead with him. Before they went on, Mike Parker said to Sherbrooke Walker, in an attempt to relieve the tension somewhat, 'You promised us a show of elephants – but aren't you overdoing it a bit?' In reply Sherbrooke Walker sternly advised those remaining to climb the ladders along the path at the slightest sign of danger. Still effervescent, Mike Parker whispered to Lady Pamela as the main party departed, 'If you have to go up one of these things in a hurry, watch out when you're half-way up – it may be me overtaking you on the same ladder.' As a diversion for her benefit, and to show her how quickly it could be done, Parker then scrambled half-way up the ladder closest to them. Little was he to know that two days later four of the trees along the path, complete with their attached ladders, would be uprooted by elephants!

By now the vanguard group with the Princess had reached the clearing and was cautiously surveying the scene. Thirty to forty yards ahead across open ground was the giant fig tree. High up, like a child's outsized tree-house, was the wooden hut, lodged above the fork and straddling several of the main branches, half-concealed in the foliage but jutting out over the waterhole. It was solid enough, but its supporting framework of poles, long and slender like yacht masts and reaching up to the hut from the ground, lent an impression of fragility to the structure as a whole.

The ladder up to the hut was on the side of the tree nearest them. To the left of the tree, a thicket of thorn bushes formed a low screen of dead branches several feet high between the clearing and the salt-lick. Spread out between the trees and the pool was the herd of elephants. And, most ominously, standing guard over the herd was an enormous cow elephant which had taken up her position near the base of the tree just the other side of the thicket. She was looking watchfully towards the path, tiny eyes gleaming, big ears flapping nervously.

Since the wind was blowing across the clearing, no scent was being carried towards the elephants, but Cowie and Hayward surveyed the scene with alarm from their discreet vantage point. There are few animals more dangerous or more formidable than a female elephant protecting her young. It only needed one baby elephant to scream in fright, or a startled sign of alarm from one of the adults, and the vast bulk of the cow elephant could be launched through the thorn bushes as though they were non-existent. The two men estimated that the huge guard elephant was only about thirty feet from the foot of the ladder. They moved to a better position and lined their rifles up on the elephant's brain pan. As Cowie's later comment expressed it, 'the suspense was long, the danger was great'. At the time he whispered to Hayward, 'We shoot if she crosses the fence, but not before.' They held their breath and waited.

Nobody in the royal party moved. Nobody cared to speak.

The babies in the herd were quiet and the other cows seemed unperturbed by the noise of the quarrelsome bulls. The guardian cow elephant was vigilant but not uneasy. After a long silence, the Princess turned to Sherbrooke Walker and whispered, 'Is this it?' He nodded. She whispered again, 'Do we go up that ladder?' He whispered in return that they did. But still he hesitated.

To his astonishment the Princess then whispered, 'Well, shall we go up now?' Sherbrooke Walker paused and looked at her for a moment. Then he nodded ageement. He was sure in his mind that, at the slightest sign of any threatening movement on the part of the elephant, he would shoot. He said afterwards that the reason why he didn't speak to the Princess was because he was so overcome by her coolness that he was speechless with admiration.

Up in the tree, Lady Bettie Walker and Jim Corbett could be no more than fascinated spectators of events in the glade. Corbett was later to describe the Princess's next action as 'one of the most courageous acts' he ever saw. After receiving the silent and cautious go-ahead, the Princess began to walk slowly across the glade. Sherbrooke Walker accompanied her step by step with his rifle pointed towards the elephant, and Windley stood by, also aiming his rifle at the head of the guardian cow.

The Princess moved carefully, still meticulously following the advice not to tread on any twigs or leaves that might snap or rustle and not to make sudden movements that might attract attention. Steadily and without hesitation, she crossed the clearing, heading straight for the ladder – and also going directly towards the giant elephant. At the foot of the ladder she paused. At that moment she and the elephant were only about eleven yards apart.

Jim Corbett had watched from above with anxiety as the party came up the path. As the Princess started to cross the glade, he went down the ladder to meet her. She smiled a greeting and carefully handed him her camera and handbag. Then, still with unhurried movements, she grasped both handrails and started to climb steadily up the ladder. Half-way up was a small platform, where Lady Bettie waited, also concerned. Again there was a quiet smile of greeting and together they went up to the balcony above.

Prince Philip followed, and then Sherbrooke Walker and Windley returned to escort Lady Pamela and Mike Parker. When they returned, the big elephant was still near the tree, with many others gathering beside the pool. Lady Pamela, in true Mountbatten spirit, also crossed the glade, acutely conscious of all the things she had been told about keeping quiet and not attracting attention. She safely made the ladder and was climbing it steadily, when, 'Trust me,' she recollected later, 'I sneezed!' There were immediate 'shushes' from above and below. 'I felt that every elephant eye was on me,' she said. Rapidly she crept up the remainder of the steps in mortified but amused confusion.

When Princess Elizabeth reached the balcony, she had been greeted by her hostess, but at that moment had no time to spare to examine the tree-top hotel. Instead, she took her camera and excitedly began to film the scene below. After her apparent calm, she now showed tremendous elation. When Lady Pamela and Mike Parker arrived on the balcony, they found the Princess highly animated, her eyes sparkling with delight. She asked them how they had got on; what it had been like being left behind on the path; whether they had been all right. She started pointing out incidents below, and all the tension that had been bottled up inside her was released in a response of euphoria to this totally unfamiliar and challenging experience. It was probably a landmark in her life, for had she not faced up to and overcome an unusual situation that was potentially dangerous indeed? In doing so, she undoubtedly added a further layer to the self-confidence that was soon to be of such importance.

The next day, within an hour of the Princess and the Duke leaving Treetops, a small group of correspondents attached to the royal party – of which I was one – was conducted up to the hotel after having spoken first to Lady Pamela Mountbatten and Mike Parker on the edge of the jungle. I found myself standing at the foot of the ladder with Sherbrooke Walker, and under his supervision paced out the distance from the ladder to the thicket beyond which the elephant had stood. It measured precisely four paces, and the elephant was only another six or seven yards away on the other side. 'Just look how close the elephant was,' said Sherbrooke Walker wonderingly. 'Princess Elizabeth had never been in a jungle before, yet she walked right up to that huge elephant – and it was facing her!' (Sherbrooke Walker later himself paced the distance from the ladder to the prints of the forefeet of that elephant, and he wrote to the Governor, Sir Philip Mitchell, to record that he made the distance eleven yards.)

'Did she appear scared, or tensed up?' I asked.

Reflectively, and with emphasis, he replied slowly, 'She is absolutely fearless.' After a moment's pause he added, 'She gave no indication of fear, but showed herself entirely prepared to do what she was advised.'

It may have helped that the Princess had always been passionately fond of animals and had no natural fear of them, even though the circumstances here were entirely different and utterly undomestic. Some of the most experienced white hunters in Kenya at that time were convinced that the response of wild animals to human beings was conditioned by man's reaction to them. If you showed no fear, you had less to fear. The problem if you are afraid has always been how not to show it. If she felt any fear, the Princess revealed not a sign. What was more, she had placed complete confidence in her escort. She was undoubtedly in experienced hands and could rightly assume that the situation was not unfamiliar to them. She had no idea of the presence of Cowie and Hayward, also with their rifles lined up on the elephant's head. Even if she had, she might not have been too reassured to have known Cowie's reactions. His comment later to Sherbrooke Walker was, 'That cow elephant under the tree made me sweat blood.'

Twelve

Treetops

THE ELEPHANTS STAYED beside the pool for another hour and a half after the arrival of royal party. The mothers were suckling the babies and instructing them in behaviour in the water. Sometimes they deliberately ignored the frightened pleas for help until their young had learned for themselves how to wade safely through the deep areas; then came the tender consolation. The cows continued to ignore the quarrelsome bulls even after they returned to the herd from the forest, the younger bulls, looking somewhat chastened, following the leader back to the waterhole. The leader was for his part still fussily irritated by their behaviour and chivvied them around to show who was boss.

Prince Philip watched this play with interest and then drew the Princess's attention as one of the young bulls, to create a diversion, mischievously eyed some doves that had settled on the salt-lick. Thoughtfully he sucked up some dust into his trunk before slowly stalking the doves. When he was near enough, he straightened his trunk and fired a charge of dust straight at them. His aim was excellent and there was a great flurry of wings and feathers as the startled doves, in consternation, took to flight to settle indignantly a few yards away. The elephant seemed surprised and delighted with his own invention and hastened to repeat the game until the birds finally flew off to a spot where they would suffer less indignity.

The Princess was so absorbed with the elephants that when she was told tea was prepared, she asked if she could have hers on the balcony so she should not miss anything. She had just finished her tea and was looking at some photographs when all at once two waterbuck dashed out of the forest at top speed and entered the pool with a mighty splash. The Princess was so astonished, she dropped the photographs with an exclamation and hastily reached for her film camera.

One buck was in fierce pursuit of another – which already had a bleeding gash in his flank. The two animals continued to leap and splash their way through the water until the leading buck stumbled. The pursuer, head down, was on him in a flash. One horn entered the first buck's buttock; the other went between his legs and pierced his stomach. The stricken buck dragged its attacker for several yards before getting free of the horns; then turned and plunged into deeper water until he reached the security of some weeds and grass. There he lay, panting. The victor withdrew to the bank and watched his victim for a time before he turned and disappeared into the forest.

The Princess, having filmed the incident, was greatly concerned for the wounded animal. The water around it had started to darken. 'Is that blood?' she asked. 'Do you think it will die?' An elephant approached, sniffed the water and quickly went away. The Princess felt sure the buck was dead by now, but after a time it slowly started to work its way towards the security of another clump of grass in shallower water and thence up the bank and disappeared into some bushes. Later, when darkness started to fall, the pool became temporarily deserted and Mike Parker went down with Jim Corbett to see if the buck was dead – but the body was gone. When daylight came next morning, it was found behind some bushes near by – half-eaten by leopards.

(The head of the buck, which was undamaged, was mounted and set in a place of honour high in the hallway of the Outspan Hotel. From there it gazes serenely down on the reception office, where visitors on their way to Treetops each sign a form indemnifying the hotel management against any hurt or injury that might occur to *them* at the waterhole.)

Shortly after this incident, the elephants also moved away, and until darkness fell the afternoon passed more peaceably with family groups of smaller animals. An ugly old male baboon named Kraa – a familiar figure at Treetops – now appeared on the scene with his family. The previous week the baboons had broken into the hotel, eaten the lampshades and stolen all the toilet rolls. Unrepentant, they now lazily sunned themselves on the salt-lick and in the boughs of the fig tree waiting to see what fresh opportunity might present itself.

One of the baby baboons was already happily teasing a young doe bush-buck that had arrived at the pool with a family of wart-hogs. The little menace was busily, but unsuccessfully, trying to climb the doe's back leg to grab hold of her stumpy tail. The doe was far too quick for the young baboon and always skipped nimbly away at the last moment. But she seemed quite willing to play this game with the baby ape, to the absorbed enjoyment of the watchers above.

So the final daylight hours passed until the sun set and darkness fell with remarkable suddenness. In the early evening all was still in the forest. The hush and magic of the tropical night hung heavily in the trees. The prowling night animals were still stretching and rousing themselves after the heat of the day. The pool was deserted and all was quiet except for the sound of frogs and the occasional call of a hyena. The party on the balcony sat in the soft light of the half-moon and talked in whispers.

Gradually the conversation with the Princess became more personal, more intimate. Speaking gently, she started to talk about her father. She recalled with intense pride his battle to regain his health. She said how pleased the family had been one day when the King had put a walking stick to his shoulder and said, 'I believe I could shoot now.' They knew then that he was getting better. He had indeed started shooting again – and looked happier for it. The Princess said she was in close contact with her father and knew where he had been shooting that day, and where he would be shooting the next.

It was not until dinner was announced that the party left the balcony to go into the small dining room. On this occasion the folk tradition of the British always dressing for dinner – even in the jungle – was not observed, not even by royalty! The table was of unpolished wood and the guests sat on wooden benches. Cushions had been supplied for the ladies and for Prince Philip, but the Princess invited the veteran Colonel Corbett to sit between herself and her husband, perhaps in deference to his age, and perhaps also because of his reputation as a raconteur. Prince Philip insisted on Jim Corbett keeping the cushion while he himself sat on the hard bench. Inevitably the discussion included much talk about wild animals, including the unknown, for Prince Philip displayed special interest in the older man's views on the Abominable Snowman.

The meal, though limited somewhat by space restrictions in the kitchen, was more than adequate for the occasion. Under such circumstances, even a simple dinner of hot soup, creamed chicken and mushrooms, and cold sweet, may have its dramas. As coffee was being prepared on the table, the spirit stove on which it was percolating suddenly burst into flames and was knocked on to the rush-matted floor in the ensuing scramble. Amid the subsequent confusion and frantic stamping, the African boy appeared from the kitchen, unconcernedly dropped a wet cloth over the conflagration and removed the stove to the kitchen. He returned a few moments later with the burner working normally and calmly restored the stove to the table and order to the room.

It was just as dinner was finishing that a first whisper of 'rhino' came from the balcony. The Princess crept outside to her seat, and there below her in the moonlight she could see a mother rhino with her calf standing quietly in the water. As she watched, she was able to count another half-dozen rhino either in the water or on the salt-lick.

Jim Corbett had meanwhile started operating the contraption controlling the artificial moon, though it gave a bit of trouble at first. After a little tinkering and nursing, it functioned satisfactorily enough, and Mike Parker went to sit with him. At the slightest sight or sound of movement by the pool, they slowly filtered a soft light over the scene. By this time, the two men had struck up an accord, and later still, when all was quiet and nothing much happening at the pool and the other occupants of the hut were trying to snatch some rest, Parker and Jim Corbett crept down the ladder to sit together at the foot of the tree, where they could talk quietly without disturbing the others.

Mike Parker had read all the older man's adventure stories about man-eating tigers and leopards in India. He knew of him as an amazingly quick and accurate shot with a rifle, a man who had become a legendary figure on the lower slopes of the Himalayas in the Kumaon area of India. His first man-eating tiger had killed no fewer that 456 people. Shortly afterwards he shot another which had terrorized an area of hundreds of square miles for five years, killing 64 people. He knew so much about jungle lore that he became a phenomenon. He was even forced to explain that, although it was true he had dressed up in a sari and posed as an Indian woman picking leaves or cutting grass in an endeavour to attract the man-eater within range, it was not his practice to hack tigers to pieces with a sickle when they attacked him! Rather did he use his great knowledge of nature and the animals he was hunting to track them down, get within range and then shoot them.

Sometimes he was almost too successful in his methods. His last man-eater – the Thak tigress – he located during the mating season. He heard her about a mile away across a valley. Instead of going in search of her in the undergrowth, he decided to lure her to him, and perched himself on a rock on the ridge on his side of the valley. He was awkwardly placed, but he had a good view of the track up which he hoped to draw the tigress. Then, giving the mating call of a male tiger, he lured her, in an exchange of calls, across the valley and through the dense forest in his direction.

He gave one last call as she moved close, but instead of coming down the track above which he had carefully positioned himself, she unexpectedly approached from a side-angle. Having had difficulty in locating her 'mate' in the undergrowth, she was now in an excited and frustrated frame of mind. Her last call came from the other side of some bushes to Jim Corbett's right, and he received a full-throated blast of hot air on the side of the head, which, he said, would have blown his hat off had he been wearing one.

Corbett was by this stage clinging to the rock with his left hand and holding his rifle in his right, wondering desperately if he would be able to swing the heavy weapon round if the tigress came at him from the side. Fortunately, in her over-eagerness, she stepped round the bushes on his right and continued for several paces across the front of the rock. She turned her head and looked Jim Corbett straight in the eye from close range. Several things then happened at once. The tigress paused momentarily in astonishment – and leaped: Jim Corbett without hesitation fired both barrels one-handed in her face. One bullet went under her right eye; the other, fired as the rifle started to kick, caught her in the throat – just as the butt of the flying rifle struck Jim

Corbett under the chin. In the excitement of the moment, Corbett fell backwards off the rock on to two goats which he had tethered at the bottom of the rock behind him as an alternative lure; and the tigress dropped dead on to the rock itself.

Jim Corbett was sixty-three at the time, and although this was to be his last man-eater, it was by no means the end of his active life, for his immense knowledge of jungle lore was deployed in training troops in jungle fighting during the war. In his later years, he much preferred the photographing of big game to the shooting of it. The unique film footage that he took of wildlife in India is today preserved in the archives of the Natural History Museum in London.

Parker was intrigued by Jim Corbett's apparently extra-sensory perception of danger, which he knew had saved his life from lurking tigers and leopards on more than one occasion. He asked about this awareness of danger, and the older man, whose senses were still acutely alert, told Parker how, feeling uneasy, he had decided earlier in the night to keep guard with his rifle at the top of the ladder. Casually holding on to a rope that dropped down to the ground and was used for hauling up baggage, he suddenly felt it vibrate. He waited, and a moment later the same thing happened. He was convinced that a leopard was pacing backwards and forwards at the foot of the steps, trying to decide whether to climb up to the hut – which it could have done easily.

Corbett had then transferred his hand to the wooden steps. He knew he would hear nothing, but he hoped to feel some movement on the ladder if the leopard did decide to come up. Nothing happened, however, and the leopard went away. As Mike Parker continued to ask him about his 'feel' for danger, Jim Corbett unself-consciously began to talk about the previous day, when he had gone with his sister Maggie to the Nyeri polo ground where Prince Philip was playing.

With dignity, and something of an old-world manner, he took pains to explain that the fact that they did not watch the game was not due to any discourtesy to the royal visitors. On the contrary, they were uneasy for the safety of the Princess. Three sides of the polo ground were surrounded by forest. The fourth side was bounded by a ravine with scrub-covered sides – ideal concealment for anyone crawling up towards the ground. There was a bridge across the ravine and he and Maggie had sat all afternoon by the bridge with their backs to the game, self-appointed sentinels watching the ravine. (This was at great risk to themselves, for if any attack had been attempted, they were in an exposed position and would certainly have been killed.)

Such a statement coming from anyone else might have appeared ludicrous. What on earth were they watching out for? But Parker had his suspicions and took Jim Corbett seriously. Yet he became increasingly incredulous as the older man talked in greater detail about his fear. In a guarded whisper, so that what he said should not penetrate upwards into the tree where the royal visitors were resting, Corbett told Parker of the activities of the new African organization of revolt known as the Mau Mau. He said witch-doctors were agitating the Kikuyu tribes and secret rites of initiation and oath-taking had been introduced. The whole movement of rebellion and civil disturbance was being carefully organized and the leader was already known. Training camps had been set up in the Rift Valley not far from where they were now seated, and calculated acts of terrorism were being prepared.

The royal party had heard nothing of this before leaving England, and only a few guarded whispers since. The Provincial Commissioners in Kenya had all, in confidence, advised the cancellation of the royal visit, but the Governor had consistently overruled them. For some reason, perhaps tiredness after the war during which he had had no leave for seven years, and at the end of his career, his judgement let him down. (Sadly, even after the uprising became violent, Sir Philip failed to take positive action against it and was replaced as Governor.) Although the Governor had played down all suggestions of danger, extra security precautions were being taken. All indications of unrest were now being hushed up by the officials with the co-operation of the local press, so that no general alarm should be felt by the Princess or by the public on her behalf.

Suddenly various unexplained incidents began to drop into place for Mike Parker. When they had arrived at the royal lodge a couple of days previously, he had been puzzled at the number of troops in the area when the military guard post only provided for a much smaller number. He had made discreet inquiries and had been told that a battalion of the King's African Rifles was deployed in the area, with a whole company concealed in defence positions in the forest around the lodge. Parker had been struck by the atmosphere in the market town of Karatina too, where the coldly negative reception of the royal visitors seemed totally out of keeping with the goodwill intent of the visit.

Jim Corbett explained that within the past few days there had been a number of acts of arson in the Nyeri area where African chiefs and leaders refusing to take the Mau Mau oath were being intimidated by having their huts surrounded at night, the doors tied up and the thatched roofs set alight with petrol. Mercifully nobody had yet been killed, but it was clear that heavy trouble was only just starting. Mike Parker confessed later that he had been stunned by these revelations, and deeply concerned. He had immediately questioned whether it would be wise or safe for the Princess and Prince Philip to return to the Sagana Lodge, which was so isolated in the bush. Jim Corbett said he thought the Mau Mau would think twice before attacking the Princess, especially as there was a unit of the King's African Rifles guarding the area. Even so, Parker continued to be uneasy. He reflected that they would only be there for less than two more days; nevertheless he made a mental note to consult Edward Windley at the first opportunity. Subsequent events overtook that necessity.

Jim Corbett's sense of danger, which he passed on to a deeply thoughtful Mike Parker, was not ill-founded. Neither of them, however, realized how great the threat was to be, nor how close to it they were at that moment. The royal party was situated in the heart of Mau Mau territory with the rebellion about to erupt. Treetops Hotel would itself be burned down by Mau Mau sometime afterwards; and the kitchen boy who had put out the spirit-stove fire was to disappear. The acts of arson at Nyeri that week had in fact been the first acts of the Mau Mau uprising. Nyeri was the Kikuyu 'capital', and for the next four years two main armies of 'freedom fighters' were to centre their activities across the whole area. One would operate in the Aberdare forest – where the royal party was at present; and the other was to be loosed in the forests on the slopes of Mount Kenya – where the Sagana Lodge was located.

Within a month, nearly fifty acts of intimidation were to take place around Nyeri; and within a further three months, the first deaths were to occur. It was not until the new Governor, Sir Evelyn Baring, arrived in Kenya some months later that incisive action was taken. Within days of his taking up his office, the State of Emergency was declared. In the four years of bitter fighting many thousands of Africans lost their lives in the struggle for independence.

The uprising was put down eventually, but from it emerged a word new to the outside world: *Uhuru*, meaning 'Liberty'. The world came to appreciate better the incentive for the uprising and to treat it with increasing sympathy.

The battle for liberty was eventually won, and in 1963 Prince Philip returned to Nairobi and handed to the new President, Jomo Kenyatta, the Constitutional Instruments of Independence. Amid scenes of the wildest enthusiasm, he attended the celebrations as Kenya became an independent republic within the British Commonwealth. At a midnight ceremony held before a quarter of a million people, and amid much rejoicing and huge showers of fireworks, the Union Jack was lowered and the national flag of Kenya was raised in its place.

As an Independence gift to Kenya, the Queen gave back to the new republic the now historic Sagana Lodge, which had been her own wedding present from the people of the country.

Thirteen

The Dawn – of a Reign

THROUGHOUT THE NIGHT at Treetops, the Princess intermittently watched rhino by the light of the artificial moon and lay on her narrow bed, fully dressed and wrapped in a blanket for warmth. At 7,000 feet the nights can be cold, and she tried to get some rest until a fresh whisper of 'rhino' brought her creeping out on to the balcony again. She had been told that an African dawn, and particularly the rapid and spectacular sunrise here on the Equator, was a moment of splendour she should not miss. Eagerly she had declared she wanted to see it.

Some time around 6.30 a.m., just before the dawn, Parker called her, and together they climbed the boughs of the tree above the hut to another little wooden platform, high up and clear of all obstructing branches. From there they had a clear view of the eastern sky over the tops of the neighbouring trees on the slopes below. Behind them to the west lay the pool and the distant Aberdare Mountains. The Princess held her camera and light meter in her hand as she gazed eastwards into the darkness in the direction of the path up which she had walked the day before, and way beyond that towards Mount Kenya.

Almost imperceptibly the sky started to lighten, then, discernibly, there was a patch of pale blue, which widened slowly across the horizon and spread upwards. The sky became lighter and bars of yellow appeared. The great mass of Mount Kenya loomed darkly, and as the sun rose vertically almost behind it, the yellow turned to orange and tinged the undersides of a few lingering clouds with gold and red. The high peaks became outlined against the sky, and when the sun finally burst brilliantly above the horizon, its rays lit up the twin snow-caps. As the sun grew in strength, a rose light suffused the mountain and the glaciers glowed pink against the pale-blue sky.

The blinding splendour of this magnificent dawn, with the grandeur of the towering mountain, subdued and awed the watchers. But as the Princess sat overwhelmed, there was another phenomenon. As the sun cleared the horizon, it created a rare trick of the light which is peculiar to the East African dawn. For about five minutes as the light grew stronger, all the surroundings took on a translucent quality that affected everything within sight. The branches of the forest trees became iridescent; and the leaves appeared to be luminous. The sky was shimmering with a pale-blue light and the whole atmosphere around the Princess was vibrant and tinged with magic. It was breathtaking – and eerie.

For the Princess it was to be more than the majestic start to a new day – it was the dawn of her reign. She was already Queen. It was now about 7 a.m. The doctors were to estimate that the King had probably died between 1 and 2 a.m. in Sandringham – or between 4 and 5 a.m. in Kenya time, and therefore well before the dawn.

As the Queen who did not yet know she was Queen sat in silent wonderment at the very top of the wild fig tree, a whole new era was dawning. Suddenly, in retrospect it seemed symbolically, a huge and magnificent bird appeared silently in the sky above her. Very quietly it slowly circled above her with dark spread pinions, losing height until its magnificent snowy-plumed breast and legs and fierce white head could be seen clearly. It was a fish eagle, a familiar species on the other side of the Aberdares where they nested at Lake Naivasha in the dead trees among the papyrus and lilies above the crystal-clear waters of the lake. This beautiful great bird seemed to have come out of nowhere, and it hovered and swung for a time with superb dignity and grace above the pool and over the Queen's head. Finally it dipped as though in salute, and as quietly and as abruptly as it had arrived, disappeared from sight. Not a word was whispered while it was there, but it had been observed the whole time with fascination and a kind of numinous awe. To Mike Parker the experience seemed uncanny at the time. It was to grow into a memory that would haunt him ever afterwards.

By now it was quite light. As the Queen looked down into the pool, directly below she saw an enormous bull rhino standing motionless by himself in the water. He was not alone long, for shortly afterwards another great bull of equal size, but slightly younger, came up. It was soon evident that they were old enemies and had clashed before, but though they now grunted, snorted and charged each other with occasional massive impact, the skirmish was mainly a show of strength and enmity rather than a pitched battle. When honour was satisfied, they separated and disappeared by different ways into the forest, leaving the pool to a family of baby dabchicks.

The royal party's night at Treetops had been a unique and exciting adventure and all their most ambitious hopes over what they might see had been realized. Lady Pamela commented at the time, 'We were all delirious with excitement.' Breakfast that morning was in itself a luxuriant, exhilarating experience. The cool clear sweet air at this altitude was now being warmed by a brilliant sun and everyone felt very hungry. In the little dining room, the

100

794ᵗʰ Visit   Feb 5/6   1952

H.R.H. the Princess Elizabeth
H.R.H. the Duke of Edinburgh
The Lady Pamela Mountbatten
Commander Michael Parker
Lady Bettie Walker
Mr E. Sherbrooke Walker
Colonel Jim Corbett
Honor Walker
animals seen:-
Elephant on arrival (about 40)   2.30 pm
Water buck (many) and a fight between two stags
Baboon
Herd of elephant 5.30 pm (about 50)
Rhino all night (3 at a time)
           in the morning - two bulls fighting.

Elizabeth   *Philip*

Pamela Mountbatten   *Michael Parker*

Bettie Walker   *Honor Walker*

Jim Corbett

Eric Sherbrooke Walker

open windows of which gave a view towards the Aberdare Mountains, a breakfast of piping hot scrambled eggs and bacon, toast and marmalade and coffee was served with an abundance of fresh fruit. All the senses of pleasure – and taste – activated on such an occasion were fully satisfied. And there was no need to hurry.

The party was due to depart from Treetops at 8 a.m., but they drifted out on to the balcony again to cast one last hopeful look down at the waterhole where a solitary white heron stood on the edge of the pool and the family of little dabchicks still paddled busily across the smooth water. Then the irrepressible baboons returned, led by the reprobate Kraa. This time they all came up to the balcony to demand attention – and food. A bag of sweet potatoes was found, and instead of leaving, the royal couple stayed to hand-feed the baboons, forgetful of time. After the sweet potatoes had gone, the cupboards were ransacked for all remaining fruit and other left-overs. Only then did the royal party turn to leave, and for the last time in her life the Queen signed her name as Princess Elizabeth in the visitors' book. Uneventfully the royal party returned down the track through the jungle that had been so fraught with potential incident the previous day.

As he said goodbye to the Princess, Sherbrooke Walker stated firmly, 'If you have the same courage, Ma'am, in facing whatever the future sends you as you have shown in facing an elephant at ten yards, we are going to be very fortunate.' The Princess smiled, Prince Philip laughed and they got in their car and left.

Later Jim Corbett was to write in the visitors' book, 'For the first time in the history of the world, a young girl climbed into a tree one day a Princess and after having what she described as her most thrilling experience she climbed down from the tree next day a Queen – God bless her.' It was a valediction from a very brave and romantic old man who in 1955, when he was nearing eighty, published *Tree Tops*, a short book of tribute about that night in the tree. It was also the year of his death. Jim Corbett was buried in the same small cemetery at Nyeri as 'BP'; and in the Kumaon area of India his name is commemorated in a world-famous national park where tigers may be viewed in the wild.

(His devoted sister Maggie lived on alone in Nyeri. It was her custom every night to feel under her bed before getting into it – in case of intruders. One night she had a tremendous shock. Someone was there! She bent down indomitably, however, and made the man come out. He was a robber who had been surprised by her entry. He assured her in Swahili that he meant no harm. In Swahili she admonished him and gave him a lecture on the evils of his way of life. She concluded by asking him what he intended doing about it. He showed her by jumping out of the window and disappearing into the night. This wonderful old lady survived to the ripe age of ninety-three.)

In Kenya it was now nearly 9.30 a.m., and in Sandringham House, where the day's routines would soon be starting, it was nearly 6.30 a.m. On the edge of the Aberdare forest, the morning was already hot and sunny and the first of the new Queen's subjects to greet her all unwittingly were waiting a mile or so away beside the deserted dirt road where it was joined by the track from the forest. There was a small group of us: a handful of journalists, all dressed somewhat casually, waiting to go up to Treetops after the Princess's departure. We were due to meet Lady Pamela Mountbatten and Mike Parker, with Eric and Lady Bettie Sherbrooke Walker, to hear a first-hand account of what had happened during the hours spent at Treetops. In addition to the correspondents, there was a score of Africans who had been passengers on a dilapidated old bus that was now pulled off at the side. It had been trundling along in the same direction up the narrow dirt road that the royal car was to go. The police escort had halted it so that the Princess's car would not be delayed or have to travel behind it for miles absorbing its dust.

The royal party was by now well over an hour late. The journalists stood in the sun in the middle of the road, talked and looked at their watches. The Africans sat passively – or morosely – on the shadeless bank. Some were wrapped in blankets; a number of women in shapeless cotton dresses walked slowly up and down to rock the babies slung across their backs.

At last we saw a dust trail rising in the distance, outlined against the dark trees of the forest. Eventually the cause resolved itself into a big black gleaming limousine that the chauffeur must have been polishing even on the fringe of the jungle. Now, the epitome of ceremonial splendour, its royal standard flying, it came with power and dignity through the parched scrub as though sweeping down the Mall. It approached fast, considering the nature of the ground, but slowed as it reached the road where we had gathered: the Africans, half-curious, half-bewildered; the rest of us professionally anxious to see the Princess in the enclosed car, but unhappy about crowding too near to the track for fear of appearing intrusively rude. We still had several months of the tour to go, and half the world to cover, and good relations needed to be preserved. The Duke was known to hold strong views about the Princess being embarrassed, so we kept to a discreet distance, prepared to lean forward smartly at the last minute to peer into the car as it passed.

What we got was a surprise. Unlike her mother, the Princess never seemed to be aware of the existence of photographers unless they flashed their lights directly in her face. The present Queen Mother always had a remarkable facility, without ever seeing a photographer, of happening to turn her head at the correct angle, and to smile at the right moment, so that the photographers invariably got the shot they were looking for. Invariably!

We had expected to see the Princess looking somewhat tired. Instead she looked radiant. Her eyes sparkled with excitement and a magnificent flush heightened her superb complexion. She was a picture of happiness and unusually relaxed. As the car slowly scrunched up to the road, she looked out of her window and smiled warmly and searched out each one of us with recognition. This was no longer a formal acknowledgement. Out there, in the middle of nowhere, it became an intimate personal gesture, expressive of a shared understanding. Spontaneously she waved to us individually in a cheery way, and immediately our routine arm-waving changed into informal flutters of reciprocal warmth. All at once we felt awfully good. And why not? She was clearly overwhelmed with happiness and wanted to share it. We were delighted to see it and to be included. And then she was gone, on her way back to the Sagana Lodge.

In our fellow-mood of exhilaration we drove up the track to where Lady Pamela, Mike Parker and Eric Sherbrooke Walker waited for us on the edge of the forest to tell us how it had been before we too went up to have our small share of the Treetops experience.

Two days later, on 8 February, Commander Parker was to write to Eric Sherbrooke Walker from Clarence House, London:

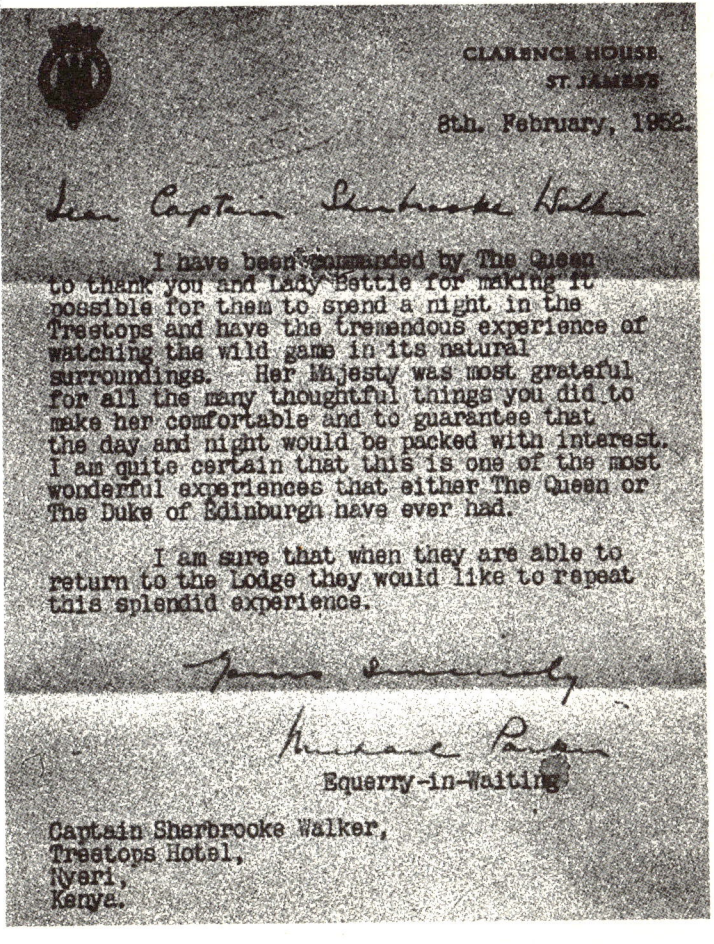

CLARENCE HOUSE.
ST. JAMES'S

8th. February, 1952.

Dear Captain Sherbrooke Walker,

I have been commanded by The Queen to thank you and Lady Bettie for making it possible for them to spend a night in the Treetops and have the tremendous experience of watching the wild game in its natural surroundings. Her Majesty was most grateful for all the many thoughtful things you did to make her comfortable and to guarantee that the day and night would be packed with interest. I am quite certain that this is one of the most wonderful experiences that either The Queen or The Duke of Edinburgh have ever had.

I am sure that when they are able to return to the Lodge they would like to repeat this splendid experience.

Yours sincerely,

Michael Parker
Equerry-in-Waiting

Captain Sherbrooke Walker,
Treetops Hotel,
Nyeri,
Kenya.

Fourteen

Breaking the News

THE MAIN BEDROOM of the Sagana Lodge was cool on a hot day: the walls and bedspreads were a subdued mushroom colour; chintz curtains at the windows overlooking the shaded lawns and river valley were pale and dark blue; and sheepskin rugs covered the red-cedar floor.

Immediately on her return from Treetops, the Queen went to this room, changed out of her khaki clothing and had a bath in the pink and white bathroom. Then the curtains were drawn and for a time she lay and rested on one of the twin beds. She was up again, refreshed, by lunchtime, wearing a cool, flowered cotton dress, though the morning sunshine had gone and the clouds were banking up for a sharp and heavy tropical thunderstorm that broke during lunch.

By this time it was known in London that the King was dead, though it had not yet been publicly announced. No word had yet reached Kenya, however, and the royal couple sat in the living room, discussing their plans for the remainder of the day. The storm ceased as suddenly as it began and the sun sparkled on the wet leaves and the raindrops dripping from the trees. They decided they would go fishing in the stream below later in the afternoon; in the cool of the evening they would perhaps go for a ride. But first Prince Philip decided that he too needed a short rest, and went to lie down in the bedroom. The Queen, still thrilling to the memories of her vigil by the salt-lick, was anxious to get her letter written to tell her father and mother all about it. She sat at the little desk by the bow window in the living room and began writing.

Mike Parker had some paperwork to do in preparation for their departure, but first yielded to the temptation of the river and took a rod and went down on to the lawn by the river bank. There he caught three large trout in no time at all and afterwards, feeling a great deal more like work, sat down in the room next to the one where the Queen was busily writing her long letter. Both doors into the corridor outside the two rooms were open. Parker had just started to sort through his lists when the telephone rang. He took the call, spoke briefly, keeping his voice down, and then sat thunderstruck. The next three hours were filled with conflicting emotions and frenzied activity.

The procedural routine of Monarchy is highly regulated and has the backing of all the resources of the State. It has been evolved over centuries and traditionally works on the well-known basis of, 'The King is dead – long live the King!' The moment of transference of such power and authority is potentially dangerous and politically sensitive. It is therefore protected by carefully worked-out procedures and is a climactic moment in the life of any new Monarch. How astonishing, then, when part of the sophisticated machinery of running a highly organized society breaks down at a critical moment. Everyone is taken by surprise.

The following day I stood in the room in which the Queen had been sitting when the telephone first rang in the next room. With me was Edward Windley, summoned to the lodge during the previous afternoon, who had been an awed spectator of most of the subsequent comings and goings. The lodge was just as it had been left the previous day after the Queen's hurried departure. The servants had carried out a quick tidy round, looking for forgotten items, and discovered a pair of glasses and one of Prince Philip's spurs; otherwise nothing had been touched. I walked across the room and sat at the small desk below the little window overlooking the garden.

At this point, for about the first and only time in a journalistic career, I was overtaken by an obsessional feeling that this was all 'history'. I had grown up only a few miles from the ancient gnarled tree at Hatfield House under which Queen Elizabeth I heard that she had become Queen. For days she had waited at Hatfield for the news. Then, at daybreak on a cold bleak morning in November, Queen Mary died at last, and Sir Thomas Throgmorton took the black and gold betrothal ring that was not to leave her hand until she was dead, and hurried to Hatfield as he had been bidden, bearing the proof. But he was passed on the road by the Lords of the Council, galloping flat out to be the first to tell the news to the Queen. They found her in the park in the early morning, and she knelt on the grass beneath a leafless oak, exclaiming in relief and satisfaction, 'A domino factum est et mirabile in oculis nostris,' from the 118th Psalm: 'This is the Lord's doing: and it is marvellous in our eyes.' The stump of *that* tree is still there, marked with a plaque.

Equally impressive I had always found to be Mary Gow's famous watercolour of Queen Victoria in her night-attire – a cotton dressing gown over her nightdress, her long brown hair streaming loose down her back – as the Lord Chamberlain, the Archbishop of Canterbury and the King's Physician broke the news to her at 6 a.m. at Kensington Palace, and kissed her hand, having woken her up and got her out of bed to do so.

For Queen Elizabeth II, who also became Queen in the early hours of the morning, there was no such rush to break the news. Quite the contrary. No one knew which way to rush.

I had been sitting at another desk the previous day – at the Outspan Hotel in Nyeri – trying to complete the Kenya chapter for my commission to write the official book of the whole tour. The thunderstorm was over and I too could again see the snow peak of Mount Kenya from my window, glistening in the sun. Then my door burst open and Stanley Devon, the *Sunday Times* photographer, shouted to me the news, 'The King is dead. The Queen is going back to England.'

I jumped up and hurried to the lounge where I found Granville Roberts of the *East African Standard*, who was one of the most experienced journalists in Africa, and Colonel Charteris in the centre of a turmoil of inquiring correspondents. Roberts was flushed, Charteris deathly pale. I asked what had happened.

'We don't know,' Martin Charteris replied. 'All we've heard is that the King is dead.'

'What is happening now?'

'I presume the lady we must now know as Queen will be flying back to England as soon as possible.'

I asked how the Queen had been told. Charteris said that that was really Granville Roberts's story, and he ought to be the one to tell it. Slowly and clearly, pausing occasionally to search his memory for the exact words and sometimes corrected by Charteris, Granville Roberts told how he and Charteris broke the news to the royal lodge.

At five minutes past two, a telephone bell in the hotel had rung sharply. It was a call for Granville Roberts from his paper in Nairobi. As Roberts listened on the phone, an urgent voice from the *East African Standard* said, 'We've just had a Reuters flash from London. It says, "The King died peacefully in his sleep early this morning." ' Roberts stood rigid and motionless for a moment, then flung open the phone-box door and called to the girl at the reception desk asking her to fetch Colonel Charteris, who was on the terrace finishing his lunch. Charteris came hurrying to the phone box, a little astonished to be dragged from his meal. He was dressed in sports shirt and trousers as he was due to spend that night at Treetops.

Granville Roberts wasted no time, but bluntly told him the message he had just received. Charteris was clearly shaken. He took several seconds to recover before he said, 'You phone the lodge, use any name you like.'

Using Charteris's name for priority, Roberts called the lodge. Commander Parker answered and Roberts said, 'There is awful news about the King' – there was a gasp – 'Charteris wants to speak to you.' He handed over the phone.

Charteris spoke slowly and deliberately: 'Mike.'

'Yes.'

'Our employer's father is dead.'

'Good God!'

'Yes, I know. It's too awful for words. I suggest you do not tell the lady – at least until we have got this confirmed.' Then he rang off.

Following a brief consultation, Roberts rang Government House in Nairobi and spoke to the Private Secretary, Mr John Irving Bell, saying he had Charteris with him. Bell said he had heard the news but had had no official confirmation. He asked what Charteris thought they ought to do and added that he was in touch with the Deputy Governor, Mr C.H. Thornley, because the Governor, Sir Philip Mitchell, was even then on the train for Mombasa, so as to be there to say farewell to the Princess and Prince Philip when they left Kenya in the SS *Gothic* the next day. Roberts then asked Charteris what Government House ought to do. Charteris said, 'Tell them to put in a priority radio telephone call to Buckingham Palace and get the news confirmed from either Sir Alan Lascelles or Colville' (these being the King's Private Secretary and Press Secretary respectively). This message was relayed to Bell, who replied, 'I will do that straight away,' and went off to try.

Charteris and Roberts then tried to get through to the SS *Gothic* in Mombasa harbour but the line to the Post Office from the hotel was so poor that they gave up and drove instead to the Post Office in a press car. It was now about 2.30. The Postmaster had all phone lines cleared and Charteris was put through immediately to the *Gothic*, where he spoke to General Browning, Comptroller of the Princess's Household. General Browning had not heard the news and his startled reaction was identical to that of Commander Parker. Charteris then asked General Browning what he thought would be the best thing to do and they began to discuss ways and means of getting hold of an aircraft to fly the Queen back to England.

After receiving Colonel Charteris's terrible news, Mike Parker had put down the phone and sat wondering what to do next. It was ten minutes past two. He decided it would be inadvisable to go and wake Prince Philip with an unconfirmed report in case his movement and unusual action attracted the Queen's attention – which he would not be able to explain. He sat feeling helpless, but already turning over in his mind all the things that needed to be done and the logistical problems confronting them. Before him lay the lists of gifts from the people of Kenya, which were so numerous that an additional plane had been provided to take them to Mombasa. Parker recalled that this plane, a Dakota, was already at Nanyuki Airport, some fifty miles away, if it should be required. But still Parker felt he ought to be doing something more to check the news. Then, in the corner of the room on a shelf behind his chair, he saw a small wireless set that he had not noticed before. He examined it and found it to be a short-wave radio. Very softly he moved over to the door leading into the living room where the Queen was sitting and quietly pushed it to. He did not dare to latch it in case the noise attracted her notice and curiosity, but closed it as far as he could. Then he sat down by the radio and, with the volume turned low, played with the tuning dial, searching for the

BBC Overseas Service from London. When he found it he heard the sonorous tolling of bells from St Paul's Cathedral followed by solemn music. Though it now seemed certain that the news of the King's death was true, Parker still hesitated before waking Prince Philip. He decided to wait a few moments longer, hoping for an announcement that would provide more positive information which he could pass on to the Duke. Almost immediately there was a break in the music and he heard the BBC introduction and then the formal statement: 'It was announced from Sandringham at 10.45 a.m. today, 6 February 1952, that the King, who retired to rest last night in his usual health, passed peacefully away in his sleep early this morning.'

Parker switched off the radio and stood up. He quietly went into the room where Prince Philip was asleep and gently shook him awake. Briefly he told him the news. Prince Philip was clearly shaken. 'Oh God,' he said, 'this will be a tremendous blow.' He quickly got up, paused a moment to collect his thoughts and then went into the sitting room. Parker returned to his office. As he did so the phone rang again. It was Charteris speaking from Nyeri. He had failed to get any telephone confirmation of the news, but had heard the announcement on Kenya radio and said he was on his way to the royal lodge.

The Queen's love for her father did not stop short of adoration. She loved him deeply not only for his gentleness and kindness and normal paternal affection, but she also respected him for the way he had accepted his unwished-for responsibilities of Kingship. She admired his courage in overcoming the voice impediment that so limited his public work. She was anxious about the way he was wearing himself out in his efforts to do his duty as he saw it.

It was only six days since the King had stood bareheaded on the tarmac at London Airport in the teeth of the icy-cold wind that blew his hair over his eyes as he waved goodbye to the daughter whom he loved so dearly and of whom he was so inordinately proud. 'That is like him,' the Princess had said on arrival in Kenya. 'He never thinks of himself.' The King had defied his illness, though the marks of pain and suffering were written in his face – and were startlingly evident in the press pictures taken at the airport – to stand there desperately in the open and wish her God-speed on a journey she had undertaken for him because he was too ill to carry it out. As he stood there in anguish, did the King realize he would never see his daughter again? Many people believe he did, that this was his last fond farewell: so public, yet so personal and touching, that conjecture started even before the fatal news was known.

It is unlikely that the Princess shared this foreboding, although she knew that after his last operation his life hung by a thread. Lord Casey, the Australian Minister for External Affairs, had met her some weeks before Christmas and had gone back and said to his wife, 'I am not sure that Elizabeth doesn't know that practically at any moment she may become

Queen of us all. She has such a serious demeanour that I think she was warned, or has some instinctive knowledge that at any time she might have this burden thrust upon her.' Lord Casey also mentioned his impression to Mr Churchill, who replied, 'Yes, there is too much care on that young brow.'

Since then, however, the King had put on half a stone in weight. Though still frail, he seemed to be progressing and there was nothing to suggest a sudden decline in his condition. The Princess had spoken so much and so freely about her father, even in this room. She told Edward Windley on a number of occasions how 'Papa would like it here'. She said her father might like to come out to stay in the lodge during the next winter. She thought the warm climate would be good for his health and the accommodation would be suitable for him, even though the small lodge had only a sitting room and three bedrooms. She pointed out all the time little things about the place that the King would like. With Prince Philip and Edward Windley, she had stood on the terrace looking at the blue gums across the valley. It was suggested that more of these trees should be cut down to open up a better view of Mount Kenya, but that other trees should be added for variety. Never once did the Princess give any sign or make any suggestion that she thought the King might soon die, that she might never see him again. She hoped his forthcoming convalescent voyage to South Africa would do him good. Only the previous evening she had said she hoped to find him completely recovered upon her return.

Prince Philip carried a heavy burden as he entered the room where the Queen sat alone. At that moment she was writing to her parents. How would she take the news? This was no ordinary message of sad tidings, as he well knew.

'Responsibility' had been an obsession with her father, and with her grandfather King George V. Queen Mary had drilled it into her grandchild ever since the curly-haired little girl had been able to understand the meaning of words. But, in a gentler way, her mother's influence had been even more telling. Duty involved responsibility, and in the example of her parents it also meant dedication. Prince Philip could anticipate what other feelings would also soon be going through the Princess's mind.

The sunlight poured in through the bay window of that historic room, slanted along the cream walls and struck the two enormous bowls of flowers on either side of the room, the red carnations and gladioli over the huge grey-stone fireplace and the white arum lilies so prominently placed among the roses and gladioli opposite. Prince Philip decided not to break the news in a room which was so public in such a small lodge. Instead, he led her outside into the garden and down towards the valley where they could be private. There, in the dappled sunlight, against the soft background sound of the rippling stream, she learned of her father's death and that she was now Queen. She had been Queen for some hours, and here she was, suddenly terribly isolated without warning in an African jungle with her husband and a few personal staff, and a very long way from the rest of her family.

Her reaction was unusual and significant. Perhaps, to those who knew her tough strength of spirit, it was not unexpected. She did not burst into tears. She did not become inconsolably grief-stricken. She did not stand staring into space. The shock, as Prince Philip had foreseen, was tremendous. She went very, very pale. She became very tense, very strained – but very clear-sighted and very realistic. Prince Philip said they must be prepared to return to England as soon as they could, and without hesitation the Queen turned and started to climb the hill back to the lodge. It was 2.45 p.m. local time; and 11.45 a.m. in London – exactly one hour after the first Reuters 'flash'.

In the meantime, Mike Parker had broken the news to Lady Pamela Mountbatten, the only other woman present apart from the servants. Lady Pamela's reaction had been two-fold as a cousin of the Princess who had known the King since her childhood. The first part was a deeply personal response on behalf of the Princess: 'Her father is dead – how awful for her.' Then had come the second, overwhelming realization: 'My God – it's the King!'

She and Parker went straight to the sitting room to await the Queen's return. As the Queen entered the room from the terrace, Lady Pamela did not curtsey then, though she naturally did so later. Her immediate reaction was completely personal. She went towards the Queen impulsively as a cousin, embraced her 'and gave her a little hug'. Sympathetically she said to the Queen, 'What can one say?'

The Queen gave a little shrug, as though indicating her fatalistic acceptance of the situation, and sadly replied, 'It's one of those things.' She acknowledged Lady Pamela's sympathy and went into her room by herself. She was alone for only a short time and when she reappeared there was no sign that she had broken down.

'Tears at such a moment would have been an indulgence,' said Lady Pamela. 'There was no time for such indulgence, there was too much to do. In any case, it would have been quite unlike her to give way like that. She has incredible self-control – like her mother. She was devoted to her father and she was crying all right. But she was crying inside – my God she was.'

(At Sandringham, too, her mother was reacting in similar fashion. The Queen Mother maintained such iron self-control that it was feared she would suffer by reaction at some later stage.)

In the Sagana Lodge, the Queen's small staff were faced with a quite monumental and totally unprecedented problem. They had to get the royal party out of the forest and back to England as fast as possible, with no regular transportation facilities readily available. Michael Parker was short-cutting his way through all the travel problems; Lady Pamela and the Queen's maid were 'throwing clothes into cases'. No one had to be told what to do. Parker said later, 'I have never ceased to admire the Queen's team that day: the Queen's maid, Prince Philip's valet, an orderly, the chauffeurs and staff, plus the KAR, went to work and we were ready for departure within one hour – absolutely incredible!'

As far as the constitutional procedures were concerned, Martin Charteris was already on his way to the lodge. Knowledgeable, thoughtful and unfussy, he could be relied upon to grasp the procedural problems confidently and effectively. In the background, already trying to telephone Buckingham Palace on a priority line from his own house near by before coming up to the lodge, was Edward Windley. It was a varied and unusual group of quiet authority and extreme efficiency. In any case, they had available a special set of documents and instructions giving all the procedures for an Accession. These were prepared originally for the Canadian tour when the King's health seemed, so soon after his operation, to be less certain than it had more recently.

As a team, they expected to deal urgently with the present emergency while allowing the Queen privacy to prepare herself for the journey home. To their surprise – and awe – it did not work that way at all. For the Queen now took command of the situation. The years and years of training and talk of her Princess's 'duty' crystallized at that moment into positive action. It was now the most important requirement in her life. Her own emotions, her own grief and heartbreak became frozen deep within her, subordinated utterly to her 'royal duty'. Later back in England, when she did give way to her personal feelings, not even a thick black veil could conceal the depth of her sorrow. But now her heart had stopped and only her brain was working. She seemed to be inspired. Dry-eyed, she took complete control inside the lodge.

Edward Windley, who arrived some time after this moment, spoke of it the following day. He still seemed haunted by his vision of the previous afternoon and kept running his long fingers through his hair and repeating in a dazed fashion, 'She was very pale. She was like ice; just like ice.' When asked how the Queen had received the news, he replied, 'She took it like – a Queen!'

Prince Philip could have taken over the making of arrangements in the lodge, but he understood the situation immediately. With great restraint, he did very little himself. Instead, he remained a tower of strength to the Queen in this emotional crisis, though he himself had also been greatly shocked. He did not show it, but he had realized for the first time that his present life had stopped in one moment and that a new and unknown one with great responsibilities was coming up over the horizon. Relieved to see the Queen occupied for the time being, he contented himself with ensuring that all her requests and instructions were carried out.

Messages needed to be sent all round the world, and in this she was assisted by Charteris, who had arrived from the Outspan Hotel still wearing his sports clothes. She looked up from her desk, said, 'Australia must be told,' and wrote a message to the Governor-General, Sir William McKell. This stated in simple personal terms: 'Owing to the sudden death of my father I have to return home immediately. I regret that for the present my visit to Australia will have to be postponed.'

Similar messages were sent to the Governments of New Zealand and Ceylon. Next she thought of the Government of Kenya and the people who had welcomed and entertained her on this visit. A telegram of thanks was dispatched to the Governor. She also needed to authorize the Privy Council in London to meet after she had been declared Queen. As part of the procedural formality, Charteris had to ask her by what name she wished to be known as Queen. 'Why, Elizabeth, of course,' she replied. The formal and official business was carried out meticulously. Nor did the Queen forget the officials and staff of the lodge. She had with her a number of photographs of herself and her family. These few photographs, together with the official documents signed that day, were to carry the first use of her new signature, 'Elizabeth R'.

About an hour after Parker first heard the news of the King's death, and while all the urgent official business and hurried packing was being done, a messenger arrived at the lodge. He brought with him a cable in code. The telephone service from England to Kenya at that time was intermittent and only open for a few hours a day, so a priority cable had been sent from Buckingham Palace to Government House, Nairobi. When it arrived, the official on duty could not find the code book to decipher it. (It had in fact been taken by the Governor, still on his way by train to Mombasa to farewell the Princess on her departure from Kenya.) Rather than risk any further delays, the official gave it to a messenger to take it up to Nyeri by car. By the time it finally arrived, symbolically covered in dust, all the world knew the sad message that its careful coding served to delay as well as to conceal.

Fifteen

Departure

IN THE MEANTIME Parker had been busy telephoning Mombasa and
Nairobi to try to arrange for an aircraft large enough to fly to London to be
placed at the Queen's disposal at short notice. In those days airline services
were not nearly so highly developed, and aircraft not as freely available as
they are today. Parker spoke to General Browning and the Captain of the
King's Flight, Air Commodore Feilden, both of whom were in Mombasa on
board the SS *Gothic*. Eventually arrangements were made, and approved by
Prince Philip.

By good fortune the BOAC Argonaut *Atalanta*, which had brought the
Princess out to Nairobi the previous week, was now in Mombasa. It had just
made a second trip between London and Kenya to bring out the remainder of
the Royal Household who were going on the tour and joining the SS *Gothic*.
The plane was at that moment preparing for its return flight to London.

Now they had a plane, the next thing was to get on it. The nearest airport to
the lodge was Nanyuki, about thirty-five miles to the north on the north-west
slopes of Mount Kenya. Unfortunately it was too small for use by such a large
aircraft as the four-engined propeller-driven Argonaut. For the Queen to
board the Argonaut she would have to fly either west to Mombasa or else
south to Nairobi (both farther away from England); or alternatively, they
could link up at the international airport at Entebbe in Uganda. This was five
hundred miles west of Nanyuki but over three hundred miles nearer to
London than Nairobi, so by going there they could save some precious time
on the return journey. It was decided to do this if at all possible.

East African Airways had already made all arrangements to fly the Queen
from Nanyuki to Mombasa the next day in a DC3 Dakota of their airline. The
twin-engined Dakota aircraft had won a tremendous reputation during the
war as 'maids of all work', flying anywhere and doing anything. It was an
ideal plane for East African conditions and could make the alternative
journey to Entebbe with ease. But the aircraft, named *Sagana* after the royal

lodge, was at that moment in Nairobi. The crew were located and given fifteen minutes to get the plane off the ground and on its way to Nanyuki. Meanwhile the Argonaut crew were also alerted and instructed to fly immediately to Entebbe to await the Queen's arrival by Dakota. (East African Airways were thus subsequently able to beat BOAC by a matter of hours with a claim to be the first airline ever to fly a reigning British monarch!)

Nanyuki was an army base on which last-minute preparations had been going ahead for the reception of the Princess next day. Now everything was cancelled and frantic efforts were being made instead to help the Queen's departure from the little airport. The ladies of the 4th King's African Rifles, under the supervision of the Colonel's wife, collected all the flowers that had been prepared for the Princess's retiring room. These were made into bouquets of deep-red roses and pink carnations with which they attractively decorated the cabin of the Dakota as soon as it arrived. From the food being prepared for next day, the Army also made up a cold supper which was put on the plane. It consisted of venison and ham; roast duckling with orange sauce; boiled eggs and tomato salad; and strawberries and cream.

These were not the only changes of plan to be forced on the Army. News had just come through that Ethiopian tribesmen were raiding seventy miles into Kenya, killing men, women and children. About 130 men of the King's African Rifles who were due to have been inspected by the Princess the next day were promptly sent off to the northern frontier. Meanwhile the Army also made arrangements with East African Airways to maintain signals contact with the royal plane all the way to Entebbe.

In the royal lodge it was nearly 5.30 p.m. before the travel arrangements were all finalized, the official business completed and the Queen ready to leave. There was no room for delay. It would be getting dusk by the time they reached the airport, which was not equipped with lights for use after dark. Yet despite the time pressures, the Queen insisted on saying goodbye personally to all the members of the lodge staff. They were assembled outside and the Queen presented each of them with a signed picture and thanked them for their attention. There were the chief cook, Paul Fernandes; the chief steward, Thomas Johnson; two bedroom boys, Martin and Juma; Husseim the table boy and Waithaka the deputy butler. James Cosma A. Gabatha, who had been their chauffeur in Kenya, had burst into tears when he first heard the news; now, as the Queen said goodbye to him, he knelt to kiss her shoes. Mr Richardson promised to look after the lodge until the Queen returned, when, he said, it would be 'just as lovely'. One of Prince Philip's last actions before leaving was to whistle to Turk and give him a farewell pat on the head.

Prince Philip was wearing a grey lounge suit, but he had the black tie which was part of his naval uniform. The Queen was unprepared for going into mourning, all her main luggage being aboard the SS *Gothic*, so she wore a beige dress with white hat, white gloves and white shoes. However, both wore black arm-bands produced from a little official bag that was always in the personal charge of Commander Parker. It was a bag which was never mentioned and always carefully shuffled out of sight when travelling. In view of the King's ill-health, this bag had been supplied with a few essential items for use in such an emergency, including the Royal Standard, which by now was fitted to the car.

Less than three hours elapsed between the news of the King's death reaching the lodge and the Queen's departure for Nanyuki. Despite the short space of time and the lack of communications within the rural areas of Kenya, a strange phenomenon was beginning to occur: the unexpected appearance of Africans lining the route to the airport. As the royal car drove fast towards Nanyuki, it passed many small villages of mud huts whose inhabitants frequently stood by the roadside awaiting its passage, their heads down in silent respect. How they had heard the news, and how they knew the route the car would take from Nyeri, was unknown. The former Lord Harlech, who had been at a conference up-country, was astonished at the speed with which the news travelled from village to village in his area; he suspected some form of telepathy.

The country through which the car passed was shortly to be heavily involved in the Mau Mau struggle, and even as the car reached the airport, smoke could be seen from five separate bush fires, started by arson, that marked the opening stage of the uprising. Yet these very Africans, as a personal gesture to the Queen, stood spontaneously and unasked at the roadside to express their sympathy. Repeatedly the expression was used, 'Shauri mbya kabisa' – 'The very worst has happened.'

In Nanyuki the flags flew at half-mast as the car drove through the decorated town. The sun was nearly down as the Queen reached the airport. Despite the risk of fire with the tinder-dry grass, improvised flares had been planted along the take-off path of the Dakota in case they should be needed to get the plane off the ground in the dark.

The Queen by now had a high colour, indeed was somewhat flushed. She was still elated, driven inexorably by her sense of duty. She smiled at the officials who waited gravely to receive her. They included General Cameron, GOC East Africa, who had been out shooting and was hurriedly recalled. He arrived just in time, still buttoning his uniform jacket. Meanwhile airport officials watched anxiously as the darkening of the sky was hastened by the heavy clouds of what appeared to be not one but two tropical thunderstorms, blowing up fast from different directions and converging over the airfield. Their concern was aggravated by the knowledge that the Dakota was not pressurized. But still the Queen insisted on observing all the small courtesies and formalities and had the Dakota crew presented to her. They lined up by their plane and she spoke to each one.

Finally she mounted the steps of the plane and turned at the top. General Cameron saluted; Edward Windley and Granville Roberts (present as the 'pool' reporter), standing together, bowed as she turned. It was now nearly 7 p.m. and the sun had set, but the hot air was brittle and tense with electricity. The Queen smiled and waved an acknowledgement. As she did so, her eyes swept in a half-circle, taking in the meagre party standing in the long grass, traversing way past them into the distance and settling on the mountains now almost obscured by storm-clouds. For a long moment she paused, as though in a reverie. To the watching men she seemed to be absorbing some message from this curiously beautiful and disturbing land. She stood in the gathering darkness, unmoving and totally removed. Everyone and everything was silently poised, waiting breathlessly and listening.

During this week in Africa, the Queen had consolidated and completed the process that began in Canada as she acquired a new self-assurance, a new self-confidence, which she had not hitherto possessed. It was never to leave her – and perhaps she now knew it. None of those watching could know what the Queen was thinking. But for all of them another thought began to form. Out of the depths of the past, they could hear in their minds the words of another Queen Elizabeth saying, 'I know I have the body of a weak and feeble woman, but I have the heart and stomach of a King, and of a King of England too!' To those who had been close to her, the comparison was inescapable.

But then the mood was broken by the Queen herself. She turned abruptly and, without another gesture, entered the plane. As the door closed behind her, the wheels of the aircraft started to move and then, gathering speed, the plane lifted and headed for the rapidly closing gap in the storm-clouds above.

As she entered the plane, Prince Philip had ushered her to a seat in the rear, where they could be most private. For the royal visit this particular aircraft had been refurnished and re-upholstered in East African Airways' colours of green with cream walls and ceilings, while the normal complement of twenty-four passenger seats had been reduced to ten to allow the royal party more room. The Queen had little opportunity to notice much about the interior of the plane, however, for there was still some uncertainty as to whether they would get away from Kenya. From inside the plane they watched with concern as the pilot climbed as rapidly as the aircraft allowed towards the Aberdare Mountains, already much obscured by storm-clouds. Nanyuki Airport is at an altitude of 6,140 feet, but the Aberdares rise to a peak of 13,000 feet, so there was real cause for anxiety.

With only minutes to spare, the aircraft squeezed through the gap in the clouds, cleared the mountains and set course for its two-hour flight in the dark. The Queen and Prince Philip were given strict privacy in the rear of the plane. It would hardly have been surprising if the Queen had now given way, at least partially, to her personal grief. But she did not. She was still acutely aware that in a short time she would again be exposed to formalities when they changed planes at Entebbe; they were due to arrive there at 9 p.m. and to leave in the Argonaut half an hour later.

As a consolation in her private sorrow, but as a reminder also of her new office, while the plane was *en route* to Entebbe she received a radio message from the British Prime Minister, Mr Winston Churchill, expressing his condolences and those of his Cabinet colleagues at her loss. The Queen replied to him from Entebbe, where the pause between flights was to be even more of an ordeal than expected. Bad weather *en route* somewhat delayed their arrival, but, worse still, it presaged another and much more severe storm at Entebbe than the ones they had left behind in Kenya.

The Governor of Uganda, Sir Andrew Cohen, was at Entebbe with Lady Cohen to meet the Queen. Lady Cohen was dressed in black, not for the King, as it happened, but because her own mother had just died. The Governor had been through a moment of personal uncertainty as to whether it might not be kinder to the Queen if he refrained from going to the airport but left her to herself at this time; but there was no means of communicating with the royal party, and he had no alternative officially.

As the baggage was being transferred from one plane to another, the Queen sat in the airport lounge with the Governor and Lady Cohen. Despite the sympathetic personalities of the Cohens, the atmosphere was inevitably strained and it seemed likely to be a long half-hour. Then, with abrupt suddenness, the thunderstorm which had been gathering broke with extreme severity over the airport. It had all the fearsome violence characteristic of a tropical storm, with great sheets of lightning and crackling thunder; and the rain came down in torrents.

For two hours the storm raged outside – and the airport was paralysed. In the lounge the royal party sat looking miserably out of the windows at the tumultuous darkness, at the deserted airport, at the lightning and the rain. After a night in which they had had little sleep, and a day super-charged with tension and strain, exhaustion was beginning to show in all their faces. The Cohens tactfully kept a flow of occasional conversation going, and the Queen responded. But the members of the royal party were tired and on edge and all they wanted was a chance to relax completely, even for a short time. The two hours dragged by.

All were anxiously aware of the tremendous burden of strain on the Queen; and they knew there was a further testing period ahead after she reached London. She had been so icily self-contained, so forcefully self-controlled when the original pressure was on; but now time, and the late hour, and the almost unendurably long-drawn-out period of waiting, could threaten to erode her spirit. Or so they feared.

Their fears were ungrounded. The Queen was obviously weary when, at long last, the storm was over, but she forced a wan smile of farewell for the

Cohens as she thanked them for their consideration and prepared to board the Argonaut. But even now she observed all the proprieties and insisted on meeting the crew first. Then, at thirteen minutes to midnight, the plane eventually took off for London on a flight that would last nearly twenty hours with refuelling stops. Undisturbed and in reasonable privacy, the Queen could finally relax.

Sixteen

The Long Flight Home

FOR THE FIRST LEG of the homeward flight from Entebbe to El Adem on
the North African coast, the same aircrew were in charge, under Captain
R.G. Ballantyne, as had flown the royal party in the reverse direction to
Nairobi the previous week. The flight of the Queen's plane meanwhile was
being closely followed in England by the newspapers and radio, though they
had little enough to go on. For the most part, the route lay over desert or sea
until they were practically home. But the aircrew were reporting their
position by radio every hour to the BOAC operations room at London
Airport, so it was possible to obtain some idea of the conditions. It was a long
journey, for the Argonaut *Atalanta*, though a reliable aircraft of her time, was
a four-engine propeller-driven plane with a performance that was painfully
slow and lumbering in comparison with modern jets.

Just over an hour after take-off, the plane was still at an altitude of no more
than 11,000 feet and only 214 miles from Entebbe. During the next half-hour,
it climbed to 16,500 feet and then cruised in a clear sky over the southern
Sudan at 238 m.p.h. Some five hours after leaving Entebbe, the plane was still
cruising at the same altitude and had passed Khartoum. An hour later it was
325 miles from El Adem and cruising at 265 m.p.h. in clear weather
conditions. At 0612 hours GMT *Atalanta* landed at El Adem, having flown the
2,260 miles from Entebbe in 9 hours 25 minutes.

During the long flight in the darkness, the royal party had taken the
opportunity to rest and sleep as best they could in the plane. In the refuelling
break at El Adem, they had breakfast in the airport building. A new crew now
took over, under Captain R.C. Parker. This crew also was already known to
the Queen, for they had flown *Atalanta* from London to El Adem on the
outward flight. At 7.10 a.m., the plane took off again. Within an hour it had
reached its cruising height of 16,500 feet and was past Tobruk, heading across
the North African coast and out over the Mediterranean.

The Queen was pale, tightly controlled, but rested. During the whole journey home she still showed no sign of tears, or of giving way to personal grief. She followed the route and looked with interest whenever there was anything to see. She talked normally with other members of the party, but occasionally made reference to something that had troubled her almost from the first moment when she had heard the news of her father's death at the lodge.

What she had realized immediately – as had the Duke also – was that her private life was suddenly at an end. She had been only ten years old when King Edward VIII abdicated and her father unexpectedly became King. As Duke and Duchess of York, her own parents had tried to create an informal family life and had seen much more of their children than was normal in the nanny-run nurseries of those days. The King and Queen had tried to shield their two daughters from the publicity and the interruptions of public life. The Queen succeeded in remaining both a wife and mother, but it had not been easy.

Princess Elizabeth and Prince Philip had created their own very comfortable and pleasant home at Clarence House. They were able to lead a life of comparative freedom during the early part of their marriage and the Princess had much enjoyed being a naval officer's wife in Malta. Then the King's declining health had thrown more public duties in her way. Nevertheless she looked forward to many years during which she could bring up her own children in a family atmosphere of reasonable privacy. Now all of this was finished. A glaring vista of publicity and countless public duties stretched ahead. Clarence House would clearly be impossible as a future home, and she had never liked Buckingham Palace.

Alongside the feelings of loss and grief, of sympathy for her mother and sister, preoccupation with the problems of her future home and family life were uppermost in her mind during the flight home. Fortunately she also still had some work to do on the plane. For part of the time she was busy with Charteris, studying the procedures for the Accession Privy Council which she would have to attend at St James's Palace the next day. Together they worked on her speech. The details and a draft speech had been prepared in London and were among the documents carried in the small contingency bag that was always kept carefully out of sight. Now the papers were useful to occupy her mind and also to save her time and anxiety after she arrived home.

By 9 a.m. the plane was 300 miles north-east of Malta, flying at the same speed and altitude above cloud. It continued through layers of cloud, past the toe of Italy, and hugged the Italian coastline past Naples, cruising at a speed of 219 m.p.h. During the next hour, *Atalanta* started to climb in preparation for crossing the Alps. By midday it was still flying over the sea: 115 miles north-west of Rome in a clear sky with no cloud, at 18,500 feet and cruising at 207 m.p.h.

The Mediterranean sun poured through the cabin windows as they crossed the French coast near Nice just before 1 p.m., and for the next hour the Queen watched the wonderful panorama of the Alps, including a most spectacular close view of Mont Blanc, white with winter snow gleaming in the sun. Leaving the Alps behind, the plane began to lose height again, and at 2 p.m., near Dijon, they were back to 16,500 feet, once more flying above clouds. They were still losing height at 3 p.m. as they passed seventeen miles to the east of Paris at 14,500 feet, and now flying at 173 m.p.h. At this point they were only 227 miles from London.

Half an hour later, Captain Parker reported his position again as he passed Abbeville at a height of 6,500 feet and prepared to cross the English Channel. The next report came at 3.56 p.m. from over Ashford, Kent, at 6,000 feet, dropping to 4,000 feet over Sevenoaks and 3,000 feet at Epsom – and heading straight for London Airport on Amber Airway No. 2. All other air traffic had been temporarily diverted away from the airport to allow a clear run-in for the royal plane.

Waiting on the tarmac at the airport on a grey afternoon was a group of about fifty VIPs, muffled up against the bitterly cold wind, in formal dark overcoats and uniforms, with black arm-bands. Among them were the Duke of Gloucester, the senior male member of the family, with the Earl and Countess Mountbatten, Mr Churchill, the Prime Minister, Mr Attlee, the Leader of the Opposition, other political leaders and members of the Diplomatic Corps.

The aircraft landed at 4.19 p.m. Quite unknowingly the Queen had been causing some anxiety aboard the plane, for she still wore the beige dress she had on when she left Kenya. She showed no sign of going to change into the black coat, hat and gloves and dark-green dress that had been hurriedly extracted from her luggage aboard SS *Gothic* before leaving Mombasa, and put on to *Atalanta* for her to wear for her formal arrival in London.

In fact the Queen seemed to be deferring as long as possible the moment when formality took over and she was obliged to put off her old life and assume her new role. It was only as the plane was taxiing across the airport with a police motor-cycle escort that she finally appeared in the dark mourning clothes. She sat solemnly looking out of the window at the group of VIPs as the plane drew steadily closer to them.

One of the more austere trappings of royalty which she and Prince Philip had tried to get away from was the tradition of the big black saloon car. Instead of a formal black Daimler or Rolls-Royce of the rather large and old-fashioned upright build with which royal vehicles had come to be identified ever since the notorious Queen Mary 'barouches', they normally used an Austin Princess with sharp modern lines, which had been their wedding present from the RAF. It was not, however, a black car.

As the plane taxied towards its stop, the Queen suddenly saw the line of waiting royal vehicles. Large black limousines had been sent from Buckingham Palace. Her heart sank. 'Oh Lord,' she said, 'they've sent "The Hearses".'

Seventeen

A Nation in Mourning

ON THE WEDNESDAY the whole British nation had been deeply shocked by the announcement of the King's death. At first it seemed difficult to accept, but as the news got round, so the country reacted. There was confusion over the first official news release. The two domestic news agencies, the Press Association and the Exchange Telegraph, both had their Court reporter, 'The Penguins'. These were given the announcement of the King's death with an embargo time for its release, which they duly passed on to their offices. By some misunderstanding, Exchange Telegraph sent out the message ahead of time. Reuters, alone of the international agencies, subscribed to both the Exchange Telegraph and the Press Association services.

Ranald Maclurkin, then Chief Reporter (UK) and responsible for Reuters' United Kingdom coverage, was on duty that morning. As soon as the Reuters staff saw the announcement 'KING DEAD' on the Extel machine, they prepared their own 'flash' at the Central Desk. Extel realized their mistake and within two minutes sent a rush cancellation. By that time the Reuters flash was on its way. It stated briefly: 'KING GEORGE SIXTH DIED EARLY THIS MORNING.' This was timed at 10.43 a.m., and the Africa regional desk 'flash' followed within a minute.

Maclurkin said that the sight of the Extel cancellation message promptly took several years off his life, but fortunately the Press Association report of the announcement came through just as Reuters were preparing their own 'HOLD' message. Reuters were thus able to claim a world scoop 'by luck and alertness'.

Because of the intermittent cable and telephone circuits to Kenya, Reuters had their own news radio link to Johannesburg, which took in Nairobi on the way. It was by modern standards a hazardous and primitive system, and the news messages thus relayed were printed out on a narrow band of paper with each letter being repeated three times. It served its purpose even so, and it was the Reuters message that was relayed to the royal lodge from the *East African Standard* and that was used by Kenya Radio.

The first public announcement in Britain came over the radio from the BBC, which delayed only long enough to make all its alternative programme arrangements. Using a procedure followed only for the most momentous statements, the BBC's Chief Announcer, John Snagge, came on the air at 11.15 a.m. to say, 'This is London.' He continued, 'It is with the greatest sorrow that we make the following announcement.' He then read the statement from Buckingham Palace, that the King had passed peacefully away in his sleep in the early hours of the morning, which was to be broadcast at intervals by the BBC on their home and overseas services and would be heard in Kenya by Commander Parker and used as the authority, jointly with the Reuters report, upon which the Queen was told of her Accession.

(The bringing of such important news to the Queen through the media of radio and the press – the first time that such a thing could have happened – was perhaps a presage of the communications explosion that has subsequently developed during her reign.)

After the reading of the official announcement, the BBC cancelled all normal programmes and relayed only solemn music and the tolling of bells. As the evening papers came on the streets, and as more and more people became aware of the news, conferences were interrupted. The Lutine Bell was rung at Lloyd's; and the Law Courts and the Stock Exchange both closed at noon. Flags were lowered to half-mast, sports meetings abandoned, theatre programmes cancelled. A crowd gathered outside Buckingham Palace, where the white blinds had been drawn, to watch the procession of diplomats leaving their official condolences.

At Sandringham there had been little activity to indicate to the local villagers that anything was amiss. Extra police were moved into the grounds of the park before the announcement was made, but when one of the villagers asked if the King was all right, they received the reply, 'Don't go spreading silly rumours.' Then the children came home from school saying they had all been sent home early because the King had died. The chapel to Sandringham House used by the royal family was in the church of St Mary Magdalene, on the estate and only three hundred yards from Sandringham House. The Rector, who lived in the house adjoining the chapel, knew nothing of the news until he received a telephone call from London at about 1 p.m. Only then did the verger walk over to the church and lower the flag to half-mast.

As soon as the Reuters announcement was away, Maclurkin had promptly gone as fast as he could to Sandringham to cover the story. By the afternoon he found the village besieged by newspaper and radio reporters, but very little information was available from within Sandringham House as the rest of the day went by. It was not until after the staff came off duty and had either called in at the local pub or gone home that details began to circulate. Even then it was not easy. Discretion was one of the characteristics of the staffs of the royal houses. But, on an occasion such as this, they spoke to their relatives, or discreetly to the reporters.

In conjunction with a BBC reporter, Maclurkin spoke to one member of the Sandringham staff. No financial incentive was offered or suggested. Maclurkin recalled that he was confident that his informant believed his information to be accurate. At 9 p.m. Reuters put out on their world service a story from Maclurkin with 'new matter', which was to be the 'new lead' to their running report.

BY RONALD MACLURKIN [spelling his first name incorrectly]

SANDRINGHAM NORFOLK FEB 6 REUTER – THE DEATH OF KING GEORGE SIXTH WAS DISCOVERED BY A MAN SERVANT WHO HAD BEEN GIVEN ORDERS TO WAKE HIM EARLY THIS MORNING, ACCORDING TO REPORTS FROM SANDRINGHAM ESTATE EMPLOYEES HERE TONIGHT. THE SERVANT AT ONCE CALLED COURT OFFICIALS AND THE NEWS WAS THEN BROKEN TO QUEEN ELIZABETH.

THE QUEEN WENT IMMEDIATELY TO HER HUSBAND'S BED CHAMBER.

GATHERING HER SELF CONTROL AS SHE LOOKED DOWN AT HIM SHE DID NOT WEEP, ACCORDING TO LOCAL REPORTS.

SHE KISSED THE FOREHEAD OF THE DEAD KING THEN, STRAIGHTENING UP, IS REPORTED TO HAVE SAID 'WE MUST TELL ELIZABETH. WE MUST TELL' – SHE HESITATED THEN ADDED 'THE QUEEN.'

WATCHERS KEEPING VIGIL . . .

The affairs of State had started to move more quickly. Mr J. R. Colville (later Sir John Colville, author of the distinguished Downing Street diaries, *The Fringes of Power*) was then Joint Principal Private Secretary to Mr Winston Churchill. He recalled that general arrangements for the demise of the Sovereign had been made at the time of the King's operation to restore the circulation of the blood in his legs in 1948. These had been revised and updated again only a few months earlier when he had the operation for the removal of his lung. The machinery of State therefore acted automatically and without delay. For the individuals involved it was different.

Mr Churchill had not made any preparations himself. Like everyone else at the time, the Prime Minister thought the King had made a remarkable recovery, though he expected his health to remain frail. The King's death came during an important parliamentary debate on foreign affairs. Mr Colville had sat up with Mr Churchill until 2 a.m. on the night the King died, as the Prime Minister was preparing a speech for the following day. When Colville returned to No. 10 Downing Street the next morning at about 9.30 a.m., he arrived just as Sir Edward Ford, the King's Assistant Private Secretary, was leaving. Sir Edward had gone round to No. 10, following a telephone call from Sandringham, to tell the Prime Minister that the King was dead. Colville went straight upstairs to see Mr Churchill. He found Churchill sitting up in bed surrounded by papers in a state of total misery. Tears were running down his cheeks and Churchill said as Colville entered, 'This is terrible.' He had been devoted to the King, whom he admired greatly; and equally devoted to the Queen, for whom he now felt intense sympathy and sorrow.

The last time that Churchill had met the King had been at London Airport the previous week to see Princess Elizabeth leave for Kenya. He had subsequently been rather shocked by the published photographs. It had crossed his mind then that perhaps the King was seeing his daughter for the last time; but he did not think the King thought so. Despite this, the news of the King's sudden death caught Churchill completely by surprise and came as a bombshell. He mourned the passing of the King from a personal point of view, as well as officially. 'We were very close,' he commented to Colville as the latter attempted to console him.

Over the war years and afterwards, the King and Churchill had established an intimate relationship, much on the initiative of the King himself. Churchill visited the King every Tuesday. But instead of the traditional formal early-evening audience, the King had established a special lunch-time routine which went on for some years. Luncheon would be prepared at Buckingham Palace for the two of them, and laid out in readiness. The servants would then retire, leaving the King and Churchill entirely alone, and they would help themselves, or wait upon each other. Churchill was always moved and honoured that the King should insist upon waiting upon him at luncheon as the occasion offered. During this private period, the two men would exchange thoughts and ideas on affairs of State and many other matters in a very full and frank manner. The King was a remarkably shrewd judge of popular opinion and had an unusually sure touch when it came to assessing what the people thought.

Churchill's deep respect for the King and his relationship with the Monarch were important to him personally, as well as from the viewpoint of his office of Prime Minister. Now he was much concerned about his future relationship with the Monarchy. In a dejected way, he discussed this with

Colville, who tried to reassure him by saying, 'I am sure you will establish a good relationship with the new Queen.' But Churchill replied, 'I hardly know her. She is very young. She is hardly more than a child.'

Colville for his part had been Private Secretary to Princess Elizabeth for two years, from 1947–9. He had been appointed as the first male member of her staff when she became twenty-one and the King decided that she should as Heiress to the Throne have her own Private Secretary. Previously, from 1939, he had been Assistant Private Secretary successively to Neville Chamberlain, Winston Churchill and Clement Attlee, besides serving as an RAF pilot. He was moreover the son of Lady Cynthia Colville, Queen Mary's Lady-in-Waiting, and husband to one of Princess Elizabeth's own Ladies-in-Waiting, Lady Margaret Egerton. After serving the Princess for two years, he was in a position to know – and assess – something of the new Queen's mind. He now replied to Churchill, 'But she has particularly good judgement.' He repeated, 'Her judgement is very sound.' Then he added, less formally, 'I am sure that after you have met a few times you will become devoted to her.'

Colville was right in his prediction, and he recalled later that after two or three audiences with the new Sovereign, 'any doubts that Sir Winston might have had on that score were very rapidly dissipated and he became her devoted slave in a remarkably short time'. Later the Queen offered Mr Churchill the Garter – the highest Order of Chivalry, an honour in her exclusive right to bestow. The King had offered Churchill the Garter in 1946 and he had declined it. Now, when it was offered again, Churchill accepted, partially out of gratitude to the Queen, but partially also out of his recollection of the disappointment he felt he had unwittingly occasioned the King by his previous rejection.

A Cabinet meeting was held later that morning to discuss what arrangements should be made. Both Houses of Parliament met at 2.30 p.m. and suspended all public business until after the funeral; and then adjourned until 7 p.m. that evening, when all members individually took an oath of loyalty to the new Queen. Meanwhile a meeting of the Grand Accession Council was called for 5 p.m. to be informed officially of the Accession of the Queen and to prepare for the oath-taking after her return to London. A proclamation recognizing her as Queen Elizabeth the Second was signed by all the Privy Councillors attending, by various Commonwealth High Commissioners, by the Lord Mayor and Aldermen of the City of London, and by 'other principal gentlemen of quality'.

Throughout the next day, Thursday, messages of sympathy flowed in from all over the world to the new Queen, who had not yet arrived back in England to receive them. Only once before in British history had a monarch succeeded to the Throne while out of the country, and this was two hundred years earlier in the case of George I, Elector of Hanover. All attention was now fixed on the time of the Queen's arrival back at London Airport.

At 4.30 p.m. precisely, the plane stopped fifty yards from the reception area and the Duke of Gloucester went aboard to greet the Queen. When the door reopened, the Queen was the first to emerge from the aircraft. She had been a little uncertain as to the order in which they should leave the plane, but she had been assured that on this occasion – as on all others thenceforward – she must go first. Prince Philip followed her, wearing a black coat but hatless. The Queen was greeted at the foot of the steps by Mr Churchill and the leaders of the other political parties; the Earl and Countess Mountbatten; the Lord President of the Council, Lord Woolton, and the Lord Privy Seal, Lord Salisbury. The ceremony was brief, but before she left, the Queen insisted on thanking the BOAC crew, who were lined up beside their aircraft and for whom she managed a brief smile. Then she got into the big black car to drive to London. Prince Philip tucked a rug round the Queen's feet, and they drove out of the airport past a silent crowd who waved and received a grateful acknowledgement from a black-gloved hand.

They went straight to their home at Clarence House, where the Royal Standard was broken at the mast as the Queen arrived. Waiting for them there was Queen Mary accompanied by her Lady-in-Waiting, Lady Cynthia Colville. They had driven over from Marlborough House near by. At eighty-four years of age, Queen Mary had already seen five reigns. Now she was there to pay her formal respects to a new Queen. She also came to commiserate with a granddaughter whom she loved deeply; and to receive in return some consolation at the loss of another of her sons. The last of the great traditionalists, she had a dedicated adherence to the etiquette and protocol of royalty, and so she stood, erect and dignified in the hall of Clarence House, waiting.

As the Queen entered, Queen Mary gave a deep curtsey and kissed the young Queen's hand. She, who had been Queen herself for so many years, had similarly demonstrated her loyalty to two of her sons. Thus she now also acknowledged her granddaughter. It was a moment so charged with family drama that Lady Cynthia, despite her familiarity with royal procedure, was momentarily hard pressed to keep her emotion in check.

That night at 9 p.m. the Prime Minister made his broadcast to the nation and the whole Commonwealth. Churchill, who had written the moving abdication broadcast speech for King Edward VIII, now had to speak the epitaph for the younger brother who had succeeded to the Throne. At the same time, he had to greet the new Monarch, a new Queen Elizabeth. It was an opportunity suitable to his oratory and he spent considerable time and care that day preparing his broadcast. He showed yet again how his own emotions could combine grandiloquently with his sense of a great and historic occasion. After sympathizing with the members of the Royal Family at their personal loss and paying full tribute to the late King, he said, 'Now I must leave the treasures of the past and turn to the future.' He ended his broadcast with these words:

'Famous have been the reigns of our Queens. Some of the greatest periods in our history have unfolded under their sceptre. Now that we have the second Queen Elizabeth, also ascending the Throne in her twenty-sixth year, our thoughts are carried back nearly four hundred years to the magnificent figure who presided over, and in many ways embodied and inspired, the grandeur and genius of the Elizabethan Age. Queen Elizabeth the Second, like her predecessor, did not pass her childhood in any certain expectation of the Crown. But already we know her well, and we understand why her gifts, and those of her husband, the Duke of Edinburgh, have stirred the only part of our Commonwealth she has yet been able to visit. She has already been acclaimed as Queen of Canada: we make our claim too, and others will come forward also; and tomorrow the proclamation of her Sovereignty will command the loyalty of her native land and of all other parts of the British Commonwealth and Empire.

'I, whose youth was passed in the august, unchallenged and tranquil glories of the Victorian Era, may well feel a thrill in invoking, once more, the prayer and the anthem: GOD SAVE THE QUEEN.'

During the course of that same evening, it was announced from Clarence House that the Queen had approved certain arrangements for the funeral of the late King. The royal coffin was to be brought back to London on Monday and the King would lie in state in Westminster Hall from Tuesday until Thursday. The catafalque would stand in the centre of this ancient hall, where William Rufus held his first court in AD 1099. The late King had himself stood vigil here with his brothers, one at each corner of the flag-draped coffin, when his father George V died. Upon the coffin were then – and would be again – the Imperial State Crown, the Orb, and the Sceptre. At the head would be a great cross from Westminster Abbey, and at the foot a big brass candlestick. At each corner would be four more candles in large oak candlesticks, and when the Household Cavalry stood vigil, the flickering flames of the candles would glint from the armour of their breastplates and their plumed helmets.

The way the hall breathed history was especially noticeable during the quiet hours of the night as the long queues of people shuffled through, beneath the lofty arch of the magnificent timbered roof – a miracle of Gothic carpentry built by Richard II nearly six centuries earlier. All the glories and tragedies of the past seemed to drape the walls and lurk in the upper darkness of the hall, shadowy as the mists of time.

After those three days and nights, the coffin would be taken in ceremonial procession a mile long to Windsor for the State Funeral on the following

Friday. At Windsor Castle, a royal home since the twelfth century, the King would be laid to rest in the beautiful St George's Chapel, which ranks second only to Westminster Abbey as a royal mausoleum. The King's father and grandfather have their tombs there, as have other kings and queens, including Henry VIII, who decreed that he should be placed in the vaults by the side of his beloved Jane Seymour. The State Funeral was to be the climax to a panoply of ritual ceremony going back to the Middle Ages and overwhelming in its solemnity and splendour.

For more than a week the nation was to be concerned with paying tribute to the late King. Previously unfamiliar figures were to move into temporary prominence, such as the Duke of Norfolk, Hereditary Earl Marshal of England, responsible for much of the ceremony and arrangements; a steady flow of foreign royalty; presidents and other heads of state; leading politicians and diplomatic representatives from all over the world. For a short time only during those days would public attention be concentrated principally upon the Queen, and that would be while the taking of the Accession Oath and the Proclamation of Sovereignty were carried out with traditional pageantry on the day after her return.

The Queen arose early on that first Friday morning and dealt with a number of affairs of State and certain domestic matters before driving to St James's Palace for her meeting with the Privy Council, held in the anteroom to the White and Gold Throne Room. As is the custom for Privy Council meetings, all business was conducted standing up. Some doubts existed as to the procedural status of the Duke of Edinburgh. Should he be accorded a special place as the husband of the Queen, or ought he to attend in his capacity as a Privy Councillor? He elected to go in the latter role and stood close by but apart from the Queen.

The Queen broke with tradition as she sat for the signing of her Oath of Accession. She stated in her oath that, by the sudden death of her dear father, she was called upon to assume the duties and responsibilities of sovereignty. Her heart, she continued, was too full for her to say more that day than that she would work, as her father did throughout his reign, to uphold Constitutional Government and to advance the happiness and prosperity of her people, spread as they were the world over. She concluded, 'I pray that God will help me to discharge worthily this heavy task that has been laid upon me so early in my life.'

After the meeting of the Privy Council, the Queen was proclaimed with solemn pageantry from St James's Palace where the Royal Heralds, led by the Duke of Norfolk dressed in his medieval uniform of silver and gold, with a black hat trimmed with ermine, lined up on the balcony overlooking Friary Court. State Trumpeters sounded a fanfare and the Garter King of Arms, Sir George Bellew, Herald of the Principal Order of Chivalry, wearing a crimson cloak over a velvet tabard, rich with the Royal Arms embroidered on it in gold thread, read the formal Proclamation whereby 'the High and Mighty Princess Elizabeth Alexandra Mary is now by the death of our late Sovereign of happy memory, become Queen of this Realm . . .'

The proclamation was repeated all over the country and in other parts of London as a long series of royal salutes thudded out from guns at the Tower of London and in Hyde Park; and the great bell of St Paul's began to toll. The ceremony at St James's Palace was watched by Queen Mary from a window in Marlborough House opposite; while Mr Winston Churchill craned his neck to watch it from a window of St James's Palace.

The Queen was not a spectator. She was preparing to return to Clarence House and then to drive to Sandringham, where her presence and the strength she was to bring were badly needed. For here was a small family group, bereft and lonely. The King, though quiet and unassuming, had been the male figure around whom the family revolved. His elder brother, the Duke of Windsor, was living overseas half-forgotten. In his abdication speech, Edward VIII had paid a tribute, with a note of longing in his voice, to 'the matchless blessing' that his brother had, which was not bestowed upon him – 'a happy home with his wife and children'. Now that the King was gone, three lonely queens mourned in grief.

At the big house at Sandringham on the day of the King's death, the Queen Mother and Princess Margaret had consoled each other in private while the two little children in their care were looked after by the nursery staff. Prince Charles, who was three, was bewildered by what was going on. He was puzzled that he had not seen his Grandpa and kept asking for him. He was told that the King had 'gone to sleep', but this did not satisfy him. He wandered about the disturbed house and was sitting on the stairs, sliding a toy crocodile down the polished banister rail, when he was whisked away to the nursery by Nurse Lightbody. Later he and Princess Anne were taken out into the misty grounds of the park to look for red squirrels.

That Thursday the day was very cold and cloudy. The Queen Mother and Princess Margaret, heavily veiled, went in the morning to Holy Communion at the church of St Mary Magdalene. It was characteristic of the Queen Mother that later on, despite the doubts of her staff, she insisted on playing with her grandchildren as though life were perfectly normal.

The Queen was due to arrive from London in the late afternoon of Friday, and though the weather cleared before she arrived, the country roads leading to Sandringham House and the drive itself were wet and muddy. Just before the dusk the royal car pulled in through a side-gate to avoid the crowd of photographers who waited at the main gate. At last, nearly three days after the death of her father, the Queen was able to meet her mother and sister to console them; and to be reunited with her children. Prince Charles was still asking what had happened to his Grandfather, so the Queen took him on her knee and gently told him, 'Grandpa has gone to God, and he is very happy.'

Then she went to her father's ground-floor bedroom. The room was dimly lit and the King's body lay in a simple carved oak coffin hurriedly made by the village carpenters of Sandringham from a giant oak felled on the estate some months before. The Queen entered alone, and for some time knelt by the coffin. Then she was joined by the Duke of Edinburgh.

That same evening the King's body was moved to St Mary Magdalene church, where it was to remain over the weekend with gamekeepers from the estate keeping constant vigil. It was conveyed there in the simplest possible manner. Pipe Major MacDonald, the King's piper, led the procession, playing one of the saddest of all Scottish laments, 'The Flowers o' the Forest'. The coffin, on a simple bier, was drawn by six village carpenters and behind it the Queen walked with the Queen Mother, both heavily veiled. Then came Princess Margaret with the Duke of Edinburgh; and members of the Royal Household followed, including James MacDonald, the valet who first found the King dead.

It was very cold and light snow had been falling intermittently during the past three days, though the ground was clear. Bright moonlight illumined the park, silvering the pine trees and casting long deep eerie shadows, accentuating the loneliness and poignancy of the sorrowful notes of the pipes in the bitterly cold night air. The path of the procession was lit by flickering torches carried by estate workers as they slowly wended their way through the iron gateway into the outer park and thence to the sixteenth-century church.

The coffin was laid on trestles before the silver altar profusely decorated with flowers from the estate, and a short service was held before the long night through which the gamekeepers would maintain their silent vigil. A wreath from the Queen Mother was on the coffin; one from Princess Margaret was at the foot.

At the head of the coffin of the late King, who had been, 'by the Grace of God of Great Britain, Ireland and the British Dominions beyond the Seas, King, Defender of the Faith and Sovereign of the Most Noble Order of the Garter', was a wreath of white flowers from his daughter, the new Queen, who had succeeded to all his power and titles, to the allegiance of nearly a quarter of the world's population, and who was herself now 'the Most High, the Most Mighty and Most Excellent Monarch'.

It was inscribed, simply, intimately and lovingly, 'To Papa, from Lillibet.'

Part Four

Eighteen

The Elusive Quality

MORE THAN TWENTY YEARS LATER I went back to the Sagana Lodge on a beautiful warm sunny day just after Easter, and walked down the hillside path into the river valley beside the cool stream. The gardens were still beautifully kept and even more shaded than before. In the middle of the lawn were two tall heavily branched trees soaring into the blue sky. Each had at its base a wooden plaque: one denoting that it had been planted by Princess Elizabeth, the other by Prince Philip. Their growth to great height and strength represented more than the passage of time.

During the years after they were planted as small saplings, Kenya was torn apart by a long period of bitter fighting. The Mau Mau uprising was eventually put down, but the struggle for *Uhuru* – or 'Liberty' – had been won. Amid much celebration, in which Britain took part, the country became an independent republic and a member of the British Commonwealth.

As an Independence gift, the Queen had presented to the new Kenya this historic lodge. The President, Jomo Kenyatta, thereafter used it occasionally and had the little sun pavilion on the front lawn moved down beside the creek where he could sit quietly in the dappled shade and listen to the water tumbling over the stones – like time running away. The old man, once described as 'the leader into darkness and death', had used his energies to build a new nation upon a foundation of tolerance and understanding, and he wrote a book that he called *Suffering Without Bitterness*.

President Kenyatta held the Queen and her family in especial regard and welcomed them when they again visited Kenya twenty years later. The twin bunk beds in the lodge, intended originally for the Princess's two small children should they ever visit this place, were still there. They had been kept on the President's direct instruction as a special and sentimental gesture in the hope that the children – now grown up – might use them one day. Jomo Kenyatta has gone and the lodge is now the Sagana State House for use by guests of the government.

In 1983 the Queen returned to Kenya at the invitation of President Moi and visited both the Sagana State House and the new Treetops. 'Freedom fighters' had burned down the giant fig tree and the tree house in which the Queen saw the beginning of her reign. She appeared to be very interested, but kept her memories to herself.

There was an extraordinary coincidence when the Queen revisited Treetops. On her first visit in 1952, she had had to approach close to a guardian elephant that stood watchfully at the pool. In 1983, another guardian again stood its ground near the pool: this time a Cape Buffalo, one of the most unpredictable and dangerous animals in Africa. The buffalo refused to be moved as the Queen, escorted by armed hunters, approached to inspect the site of the former Treetops. The Queen observed the buffalo, and then ignored it as she walked up to the old charred tree-stump. The buffalo stood watching, but remained stock still, and everyone breathed again. A short time later, the same buffalo had to be shot when it charged a party of other visitors.

The new Treetops, built on the other side of the waterhole, has room for over seventy guests and features flush lavatories and candlelit suppers with *pêche flambé*. It is still a wonderful vantage point from which to watch the animals coming to the waterhole at night; and, facing eastwards, it provides a splendid view of the sun rising behind Mount Kenya. But the intimacy of the old Treetops has long gone. What is there now is a reflection of modern change during the time that has elapsed.

Many of the world leaders who were in power when the Queen ascended the ladder into the tree fifty years ago are now dead. In some cases even the memory of them has faded. Prime Ministers Winston Churchill, Clement Attlee and Harold Macmillan have all gone. So have the US Presidents Truman, Eisenhower, Kennedy and Johnson. Stalin controlled the USSR, but he has departed, and so have his successors, Malenkov, Krushchev, Brezhnev, Andropov and Chernenko. Yet the Queen, now only in her mid-sixties, appearing matronly but by no means elderly, is already the longest-serving of the present world leaders and looks set fair to go on steadily towards her Golden Jubilee at the beginning of the twenty-first century, if she decides to continue until then.

Her private life from all accounts is straightforward and uncomplicated. She is reserved and unsentimental, but strongly emotional. She can be vivacious and display animation, but she is also very determined. She has been criticized for being too devoted to horses and dogs and for having rather too narrow a range of cultural interests. But these traits in a nation that likes horses and dogs, and has almost as many pets as population, remove her from the artificial worlds of sycophantic adulation and media hype and establish her as an individual with whom ordinary people can identify. She has had the usual problems that arise with children growing up, except that inevitably the activities of her family have sometimes attracted more attention than, no doubt, she would have wished.

Periodically there has been speculation about the Queen's possible 'retirement' – which would mean her abdicating in favour of Prince Charles. In the past this conjecture was premature and not to be taken seriously, but, after forty years, some consideration of it may arise again. No British Monarch ever yet 'retired' or abdicated voluntarily in this way, and there is no reason why the likelihood should be raised now, except out of consideration for the Queen and her own personal wishes. It is entirely a matter for her own decision. No one wishes to see her retire, but times have changed and it might be selfish and self-indulgent to expect her to stay on for ever. Nor should she have to feel that it is her duty to remain because it is expected of her, or because tradition decrees. She has the right to make her own choice, and her decision would be accepted, whatever it might be.

In addition to her own feelings, however, there could be other factors to be taken into consideration. The Queen Mother is still alive and well and is an extraordinarily popular personality. She has established an exceptional relationship with the public. She is everybody's favourite grandmother; the friendly smiling matriarch. It might be embarrassing to have, in effect, two Queen Mothers, although it did happen when Queen Mary was alive. But then, Queen Mary was so different in character, and so identified with a bygone period and age, that it did not seem to matter. The present Queen and the Queen Mother are much closer to each other as mother and daughter. The Queen is not sufficiently outgoing to duplicate her mother, but she is held in an affection and public respect that is unrivalled, and in their separate ways they both have a special accord with the public.

Apart from any possible desire to take things more easily – though she is still remarkably active – the Queen can have few ambitions for herself beyond continuing to do what she is doing so successfully at present. Her main remaining concern, no doubt, is that when Prince Charles does succeed her in due course, it will be under favourable circumstances.

Prince Charles has been Heir to the Throne since he was three years old. He is destined by the law of primogeniture succession inevitably to succeed to the Throne unless some major crisis or upheaval prevents it. He has never indicated any impatient desire to succeed. Nevertheless he is in an unenviable situation. Like his great-great-grandfather Edward VII, the son of Queen Victoria, who did not become King until he was fifty-nine, Prince Charles is having to spend a long time waiting. But Prince Charles has shown that he is not happy just to sit patiently or passively in the pavilion with his pads on waiting to go in to bat while the opening pair make a record stand.

As a younger man, Prince Charles was very active. He is a trained pilot and parachutist; a swimmer and scuba diver; a keen polo player and now, at his wife's insistence, an *ex*-steeplechase jockey. He is still physically fit, but upon entering middle age he has adopted more mature outlets for his interests and talents, with a philosophical approach to life more akin to that of a thinker or poet than an athlete. To develop his aptitudes and get personal creative satisfaction, he had to reconcile his feelings as a compassionate idealist with a certain desire for action that impelled him to do something to support his beliefs. He had to work this out for himself so that he did not usurp the functions of the Crown or become involved in the direct responsibilities of the government.

He must have drawn a very deep breath, for his initial forays have driven a wedge of controversy into matters that involve nothing less than the quality of life of the nation. In recent years he has been outspoken on a variety of topics which at first seemed to have little in common; and he appeared to some to be a Quixote looking for windmills. The individual trees tended to obscure the wood, and it was not immediately apparent that he was following a consistent theme reflecting some basic truths. He:

§   Is opposed to that which is ugly.
§   Encourages the creation of that which is beautiful.
§   Aims towards the highest standards of quality.
§   Urges the preservation of the best features from the past.

Prince Charles spelt out his attitude to tradition and heritage when he said, 'The fear of being considered old-fashioned seems to be so powerful that the more eternal values and principles which run like a thread through the whole tapestry of human existence are abandoned under the false assumption that they restrict progress.' Heritage, he said, assured the achievement of standards of quality that would serve our children well in the future. 'The standards are important because they help us to enlarge our awareness, to heighten and deepen our experience of life like nothing else can.'

The declaration of such high-minded principles expressed in soothing terms might well have attracted approving approbation. 'Such a nice young man!' – and then have been forgotten. But Prince Charles felt more deeply than that. He did not advocate his ideas and ideals in obscure or ambiguous terms. He suddenly came out with attacks on a series of specific examples, illustrating what he saw as fallings from grace, that rocked the recipients and made everyone sit up and take notice. The first surprise was that the Heir to the Throne should be aggressively criticizing established organizations and practitioners. An even greater shock was the blunt language and picturesque terminology he used.

In attacking the architectural profession for the ugliness of some modern buildings, he likened a proposed extension of the National Gallery in Trafalgar Square to 'a kind of vast municipal fire station . . . a carbuncle on the face of a much-loved friend'. (The design was changed and Prince Charles opened the new building.) Of the planned developments around St Paul's Cathedral, he said that when the Luftwaffe knocked down the surrounding buildings, 'It didn't replace them with anything more offensive than rubble. We did that.' He later described the new National Theatre on the South Bank of the River Thames as 'a clever way of building a nuclear power station in the middle of London without anyone objecting'.

His trenchant comments were not intended to be merely derogatory or negative. In his book, *Vision of Britain*, Prince Charles called attention to a series of positive principles, stressing that architecture should have a spiritual dimension beyond aesthetic ingenuity, structural expression or technological innovation. It should be humane and supportive of community needs, giving visual delight and creating environments that enriched and uplifted those who used them; it should respect tradition as the only true continuum upon which change could occur; and it should learn from the riches of history as a resource of limitless insight.

Prince Charles complained also about the decline in the use of the English language. 'We have rejected quality in expression, just as we have rejected quality in the buildings in which we work and educate,' he said. He deplored the popular use of English in the media, in the theatre and even in schools, which had become so impoverished, sloppy and limited that our language was reduced to 'a dismal wasteland of banality, cliché and casual obscenity'. As with architecture, he next had a specific target to illustrate his objections, a target moreover that was so sensitive that it almost bordered on a 'no-go' area: the new translations of the Bible and the Prayer Book.

Speaking in January 1990 at the Thomas Cranmer Schools prize-giving sponsored by the *Spectator* and the Prayer Book Society, he condemned the use of the English language adopted in the New English Bible and the Church of England's Alternative Service. He asked, 'Is it entirely an accident that the defacing of Cranmer's Prayer Book has coincided with a calamitous decline in literacy and the quality of English?' It saddened him that Cranmer's great work had been 'battered and deformed' in the unlikely cause of making it easier to understand. He asked: 'Whoever decided that for people who aren't very good at reading the best things to read are those written by people who aren't very good at writing?' Banality, he said, was for nobody. It might be accessible for all, but so was a desert. He added: 'We commend the "beauty of holiness", yet we forget the holiness of beauty.' If English was spoken in Heaven, he continued, the angels of the lesser ministries probably used the language of the New English Bible and the Alternative Service for internal memos.

This was strong stuff and, by comparison, those teachers whom he also criticized in deploring some aspects of the educational system came off comparatively lightly. Teachers needed to give pupils 'a vision of greatness', he said. 'If we encourage the use of mean, trite, ordinary language we encourage a mean, trite, ordinary world.'

There has been the inevitable backlash of surprise and outrage from those attacked, but also a good deal of support from others who have appreciated the more serious and fundamental undertones of what he has been saying. Prince Charles's continuing concern about the barren conditions of inner-city living and his charitable work and efforts for the disadvantaged or distressed young people have also attracted much admiration. (He is reported to have raised something in the order of £124 million for charities, making him the largest individual raiser of such funds in the world.)

The rest of the world has watched with intrigued interest as Prince Charles has used his position of great privilege to champion the under-privileged; and as certain entrenched British institutions, not held in quite the same hallowed regard overseas as they are at home, have taken a beating from a totally unexpected quarter. In his campaigns, Prince Charles has expressed himself with sufficient fluency to demonstrate that he is a forceful advocate. By his choice of causes he has shown that he is thoughtful, sensitive and idealistic. By his choice of words, he has shown great moral courage, for he must have expected the controversy he would unleash and known the risks he would run to his personal reputation.

All these qualities are admirable – but dangerous. Nevertheless it has become clear that, for someone as creative in his thinking as Prince Charles, the role he is developing for himself must be positive. He could not be satisfied with anything less. Although his roles now, and especially in the future, are not and will not be executive, they carry great influence. Moral leadership from a secular authority is a commodity that is greatly needed and not in over-supply in the world today; nor, unfortunately, does Prince Charles have much competition in providing such leadership. He may, however, run up against opposition, and this is his opportunity to test his muscles, for the time will come when he may not have the same freedom to air his personal opinions as he has now.

One day, also, he will inherit, along with his other titles, that of 'Fidei Defensor' – Defender of the Faith. Ironically this was the title originally bestowed upon Henry VIII by the same Pope who later excommunicated the King following their dispute over Henry's divorce from Catherine of Aragon. But Henry VIII retained the title as Head of the Protestant Church during the Reformation, and it was hereditary by Act of Parliament in 1544. There is no doubt that in both secular and religious affairs the Queen is inspired by deep spiritual beliefs. She does not parade her personal feelings, which remain part of that private inner-self which provides the driving force for all her actions.

Prince Charles, on the other hand, wears his heart upon his sleeve. This makes him vulnerable to those stung by his comments; or worse, to those who for various reasons do not understand him. But it is also very valuable in exposing his own inner feelings and confirming that, when he speaks, it comes from the heart as well as a flexible mind, and springs from deep personal conviction.

It is unusual (if not unique) for royalty to be so personally and forcefully controversial as Prince Charles has been. Inevitably there are those who believe he is abusing his position. On the other hand, there are those who support him for the way he is using his influence; and others still who, while wishing him success, wonder whether he can gain enough support to have any useful effect.

It is significant that in a *Daily Telegraph* poll of July 1991, an overwhelmingly majority – and especially in the under-25 age group – welcomed Prince Charles speaking his personal views in public as he has done. But the under-25 age group, while supportive of Monarchy as such, was somewhat less so than the older age groups. It is the present younger age group, however, that will be maturing into the middle-aged citizens of the future when Prince Charles has succeeded to the Throne, and the now older (and presently more supportive) groups will be disappearing.

Prince Charles has the difficult task of defining, refining and consolidating his sincerely held personal views within his public personality, and then of communicating these to the present younger generation who should provide his support base of the future. By so doing he will be moulding a changed pattern for Monarchy adapted – or adaptable – to the years of his own succession (however unpredictable in time or mode this may be at present), so that it can be received with confidence and support when that moment comes.

At the same time he must not be seen to be diminishing or contravening the present pattern and flow of the mood established and maintained by the Queen which is more acceptable to the older generation now. Rather, he should be seen as broadening the range and perceptions of Monarchy, especially in their appeal to younger people.

In due course, Prince Charles will inherit the Crown in a world which will be as different for him as it was for the Queen in the early 1950s. He will have to adjust to this, as she did. He has been feeling his way, developing his strengths and aptitudes, and honing his performance. He has taken risks, but as Milton said in his *Areopagitica*: 'I cannot praise a fugitive and cloistered virtue, unexercised and unbreathed, that never sallies out and sees her adversary, but slinks out of the race, where that immortal garland is to be run for, not without dust and heat.'

No one can foresee the future and what demands will be made upon Prince Charles. He has inherited not only his grandfather George VI's love of the countryside, but also his conscientiousness, and in the sure knowledge that one day he also will become King, he has been extending the range of his capabilities and his strengths – but not without generating some dust and heat.

The Monarchy and the Commonwealth and the whole world are presently in a state of momentous change. Power-politics of a military nature have become obsolescent. The world has frightened itself nearly to death on and off for forty years, but the horrifying costs, as much as the terrifying threat of nuclear armoury, have made it clear that negative expenditure of such magnitude is more than the whole world can bear.

A totally new factor with all-embracing power and influence has taken over and is reshaping the world: it is economic power. In the modern world, it has undermined what seemed to be the almost impregnable Communist empire of the Soviet Union and is creating new 'blocs' that are being formed and driven by economic self-interest. Eastern Europe is being transformed economically and politically. Western Europe started with the pressure of trade interests, developed into economic allegiances and is moving towards a form of political alliance. Truly, money is making the world go round.

A secondary issue, but one which could well become the major factor, is the future of the environment. At first this was considered somewhat esoteric and a matter for long hair and sandals. The realization is now being brought home most forcefully that pollution, chemicals in the atmosphere, the potential for nuclear accidents, and the spoiling and wastage of natural resources, if not all properly controlled contain the seeds for impairment of the standard of living of everyone and even possibly the ultimate destruction of large areas of the world. There is, of course, a money tag attached to this, either through the cost of protection or the loss of potential revenue. These have important implications for national economies, not to say private pockets. As Prince Charles has said, 'clarity in expression and precision in meaning' will be required 'if we are to survive competitively'. Even the intangible issues will need to be defined perhaps repeatedly, and Prince Charles has shown himself to be adept at putting his finger on sensitive pressure-points.

These new developing situations require subtle and delicate handling. The old-style concept of Monarchy is now obsolete. Just as a new form of Commonwealth has been evolving, so has a new style of Monarchy. The British Monarchy is a legacy of the past with continuing historical and emotional attachments in Britain. The British by inheritance have a possessive attitude towards the Monarchy. It is part of a thousand-year-old tradition and they can cling to it with narcissistic pride.

In the remainder of the British Commonwealth the same is not true. The former colonies are no longer British possessions. They have grown up and many have become independent. They may still hold strong feelings of loyalty to the Crown – but their motives are different. The ties of family may still exist – but they resist direction and strongly resent patronage. On the other hand, they give and expect reciprocal friendship and support. The efforts of the Commonwealth countries in two world wars to support Britain, even though they themselves were not immediately threatened, cannot be emphasized too strongly. For anyone born and brought up in Britain to go and live later in a Commonwealth country, this sense of selfless friendship and loyalty comes as a total revelation and cannot be praised or prized too highly.

During the Queen's reign, the Commonwealth has changed markedly and the role of the Monarchy has been moulded and shaped around the Queen's personality, and her behaviour and reactions have been tailored to the pattern of the new Commonwealth. This has been a success story, but it is a very difficult act to follow.

The economic forces which are driving the world today are creating new formations by *force majeure*. The convulsions in Eastern Europe and the Soviet Union; the growth of Japanese economic strength; developments in Asia and Western Europe; the question mark hanging over the potential might of China; are all redressing in their way the overall dominance of American economic power. The whole world is being given a shake-up and will take many years to resolve itself into stable new patterns.

It is now, once again, a critical period of change for the British Commonwealth. Its role is being questioned and its form and function will come up for review. During the next decade, the Commonwealth countries will come under new pressures in which they will have to make decisions about their own future self-interests.

As we enter the 1990s, the emotive date for change of all kinds is the year AD 2000. At present, self-identification and independence is an aspiration sweeping the world. This extends from adopted children seeking the identity of their natural parents so that they can more clearly know and understand themselves, and especially interpret the genes and traits of their own children, to the break-up of empires. Beyond AD 2000 is the Unknown: unknown in that it is felt it is going to be different and the start of a new era. Inevitably there will be conflict. But we are getting used to dealing with bush-fires. Hopefully the new century will bring greater stability and a constructive approach to the future.

The Commonwealth enters this uncertain future with its own groupings representing in total a substantial portion of the world's population. It has a competent Secretariat, meets regularly through the Heads of Government, has numerous inter-ministry contacts and other exchanges, and acknowledges the Queen as the titular head, even though many of the member-countries are already independent republics. Canada, which remains a Monarchy, has undergone evolutionary change involving the English-speaking and French-speaking populations. It has achieved a transformation with the establishment of a dual relationship of membership of both the British Commonwealth and the French equivalent, the Agence de Coopération, and draws strength from both.

Australia has no problems with Commonwealth membership, but it has recently been stirred into a conflict that illustrates – in peaceful form – the personal struggles that arise between the prevailing urgings for national independence and the ties of traditional loyalties. For years Australians had been relatively passive over these questions. When will Australia cut the last ties between Britain and the Crown? When will it achieve complete independence to manage its own affairs by becoming an independent republic?

The Centenary of Australian Federation will fall in January 2001. Ever since the granting of the Australian Constitution in 1901, there have been predictions that ultimately Australia would become a republic. It was felt that something would evolve eventually – rather like the famous prayer of St Augustine: 'Da mihi castitatem et contentiam, sed noli modo' ('Give me chastity and continency, but do not give it yet'). Australians have been in no hurry to face, or force, the issue.

Prior to 1975, there had never been an individual issue to raise much heat, or even much interest in a republic. The legal ties with Britain, and the powers exerted by the United Kingdom over Australia, had been gradually whittled away by mutual consent until virtually nothing was left save that Australia remained a Monarchy with allegiance to the Crown. There had been no animosity against the Queen herself, who had been, and still is, held in very high regard.

Very little thought has yet been given to the implications of change, for better or for worse; to what form a republic might take; how it should be achieved; or how it might work in practice. Some proponents of a republic say that Australia is already virtually a *de facto* republic and the centenary of Federation would be the appropriate time to recognize this formally. There has never been any enthusiasm for an American-style presidency.

In 1975, however, the then Governor-General, Sir John Kerr, acting on his own initiative and without involving the person of the Queen, used his reserve powers under the Constitution to dismiss the Labor Government under the Prime Ministership of Mr Gough Whitlam and to call a General Election. Not surprisingly, this was deeply resented by Labor supporters, some of whom 'maintained the rage' against Sir John Kerr right up to the time of his death in 1991. Kerr's action had tended to focus political attention, among Labor supporters and others, upon the Constitution and what were felt to be anachronistic ties with a Monarchy based some 20,000 kilometres away, which had the power to appoint Governors-General upon the country, and Vice-Regal Governors in each of the States, all representing the Crown.

The Constitution itself has started to come under some scrutiny. With the centenary of Federation (due in AD 2001)beginning to loom near, the

Universities of Melbourne and Sydney initiated a review early in 1991, at a Constitutional Centenary Conference. The conference did not refer directly either to the Monarch or a President, but it called for a definition of the powers of Australia's Head of State and how such a figure should be selected. Up to this point the issue had been reasonably non-political, but the whole atmosphere changed dramatically and suddenly became political in June 1991 when the Labor Party's annual conference passed a resolution that urged the party 'to begin community debate on the need to have Australia declared a republic on 1 January 2001, the centenary of the Federation'. Nevertheless, when the resolution was put to the vote, by voices at the Labor Conference, the Chairman (the retiring President of the Party) announced that it had been passed 'not very vigorously'. The mover of the resolution said afterwards that previous polls had shown no better than 40 per cent of the population in favour of a republic.

The leaders of the main Opposition Parties (the conservative Liberal and National Parties) dubbed the resolution a smoke-screen designed to cover up internal differences within the Labor Party, and said they would oppose any change from the present. The following day a new organization called the Australian Republican Movement (ARM) was formed at a meeting in Sydney. Its first President, the author Mr Thomas Keneally, expressed disappointment that the issue had become 'narrowly political' and felt that the Labor Party had done the republican movement a disservice by introducing it into the political arena. He said Australia had a special connection with, and affection for, the Monarch, but the nation's harmonious development demanded that the allegiance of Australians be fixed within, and upon Australia and its institutions. It was time to forsake the Crown. Australian politicians should swear an oath of duty to the nation; military forces should swear an oath of duty to the nation; new immigrants should swear an oath of loyalty to other Australians; and the nation should find a Head of State whose identity and function were entirely Australian.

If party-politics were to be set aside, the issue to be decided at a Referendum might well resolve itself into an emotional (or sentimental) choice between retaining links with the Monarchy or deciding to be independent as a nation. 'Monarchy', however, immediately becomes identified with the person of the Queen. The association is inescapable, and the advocates of a republic have repeatedly stressed their respect and admiration for the Queen. This is not merely political lip-service. It reflects public feeling and highlights the significance and importance of the Queen's personality. It may well be the Achilles' heel in the present republican movement.

Government House in Canberra is not a place where one would expect to find advocates of a republic. On the other hand, under present conditions of multi-cultural change in Australia, it is also not the place to look for a conventional (or platitudinous) defence of the Monarchy. The present Governor-General, Mr Bill Hayden, and the former long-time Official Secretary, Sir David Smith, are neither of them stereotypes of popular imagination. But support for the present system came in an unexpected form in January 1991, when Sir David proposed the toast 'Australia' at the Australia Day luncheon of the Australia Day Council of Victoria. He had recently retired after thirty-seven years in the Commonwealth Public Service, nine years of which had been spent in the Prime Minister's department and the last seventeen as Official Secretary to five successive Governors-General.

In his speech Sir David described the present system of government in Australia as being 'the best in the world'. It was the personal reasons he gave for supporting it without major change that came as a surprise. Even those Australians who might not agree with his conclusions would support the characteristic 'Australianism' of his approach. He explained that he is a first-generation Australian whose mother and father migrated (at different times) to Australia from Poland and arrived speaking no more English than they picked up on the boat. Their respective relations who stayed behind in Poland almost all perished in the Nazi Holocaust.

Sir David said he had been born and brought up in Melbourne and he regarded himself as *an Australian*. He refuted the argument that the Monarchy was a British one. He said it was *Australian*, and no case could be made for its abolition on the ground that Australians shared the same Sovereign with Britain or with a number of other equally sovereign and independent nations. He said: 'Australia has long since severed all legal and constitutional ties with Britain and its Government. We are an independent nation and our formal links with Britain are today no different from our formal links with any other country with whom we maintain friendly relations.' The Monarchy, he added, was an Australian one by virtue of legislation passed by the Australian Parliament in 1953 when a Liberal Government was in power. (This Act was amended significantly in 1973 when a Labor Government held office. The status of the Queen was not only confirmed, but Mr Whitlam specifically referred to her as 'Queen of Australia'.)

Sir David continued to say that the Queen had a distinct and separate role in Australia from those which she had as Queen of the United Kingdom, or Canada, or any other of the monarchical countries of the Commonwealth. He said he would 'never see the sense' in the argument that the presence of non-British migrants in Australia should be used as an excuse to do away with anything and everything that was of British origin. Virtually all the immigrants of necessity, as distinct from the immigrants of choice, had fled from countries governed by one or another of the republican forms of government. 'Is it really seriously suggested that we should therefore become another version of what they have just left behind? Maybe, just maybe, the reason they chose to come here is because of what we are, and not because of what we might become.'

The present Governor-General, Mr Bill Hayden, has surprised his critics and supporters alike in his rare public comments on the Queen and a possible republic. Mr Hayden's appointment as Governor-General in 1989 was strongly criticized on the grounds that he was a known republican – a charge he has since refuted. He said he had only once spoken in favour of a republic and that was tongue-in-cheek in Parliament in order to goad a member of the Opposition.

Bill Hayden was a Queensland policeman until he entered politics, eventually becoming Leader of the Federal Labor Party. A shrewd but self-effacing politician and a meticulous organizer, he is remembered as the architect of the Labor Party's landslide victory in the 1983 General Election. He was suddenly replaced as Leader on the eve of the campaign by the more outgoing Bob Hawke, the present Prime Minister. It was an election which, Mr Hayden said later, 'could have been won by a drover's dog'.

Until his appointment to Vice-Regal office, Bill Hayden served as a senior Cabinet Minister, as Treasurer and then as Minister for Foreign Affairs. His long-term views on his present office and on republicanism were a matter for some speculation. In 1990, well before the matter was raised as a political issue, he made two pertinent statements in interviews. In the first, after stating emphatically that he did not now hold, and never had held, republican views, he said, 'Australia as a republic is an irrelevant issue because it is not practical.' Changing the constitution, he believed, would be such an extraordinarily difficult task that he could not see the electorate supporting it. What was more, 'If you got up tomorrow morning, Australia having been declared a republic tonight, there would not be one difference to the way this country runs its affairs, or in which decisions are taken, or the independence it has. It has all these things now.'

Later, in a television interview, he said that he had encountered virtually no feelings from non-English speaking groups to the effect that an England-based Queen of Australia was divisive. 'My hunch is the Monarch, the Queen, at the moment and in the foreseeable future, could be seen as a uniting influence in this country, and, I suspect, by some of these groups,' he said.

After the republican proposals were raised as a political issue, Mr Hayden agreed to discuss with me his further reactions. He was more forthright than before, and by now seemingly somewhat impatient at what was going on. He repeated what he had said previously, but added, 'I do not think it is an issue worth expending any energy on. The Queen's standing is such that nothing is likely to happen during her lifetime on the Throne. A lot of us grew up with her image from childhood. We are unlikely to see a republic in the foreseeable future.' He then went on to back this up with one of those acerbic flashes of observation for which he is well-known. He said the republican group was just about exclusively Sydney-based. 'I talked in Melbourne with some people who I know are republicans. They expressed irritation about what seemed to them to be a little clique from Sydney "trying to take things over".'

When I said the Queen's personality seemed to be crucial to the issue and asked him for his own first-hand impressions of it, he made it clear that he had had only two longish meetings with the Queen: the first in October 1988 as Governor-General designate prior to taking up his appointment, and the second in May 1991.

It should be understood that Mr Hayden has been a very careful, thoughtful and no-nonsense politician of considerable calibre. He is a fifth-generation Australian on his mother's side. His father was an illegal immigrant seaman from America who had an Irish background. Bill Hayden would not want a title, refuses to wear a top hat, and is happy to be addressed as 'Bill'. He is proud of the fact that, from a young age and from very humble beginnings, he has made his way successfully in the world. Naturally, he was interested to have more than hand-shake discussions with the Queen and to see what she was like. 'When I first met her,' he said, 'I found her phenomenally well-briefed on the South Pacific region and the disturbances. I was enormously impressed with her grasp of detail. She was able to recall names and key figures in Fiji, who were obviously well-known to her. But it was not just a question of briefing – she *knew* – and I must confess I was a bit flummoxed in some cases – not that I am trying to put myself down. But she had done a lot of work.'

He said it was obvious that the Commonwealth was of great importance to the Queen. She watched closely what was happening, 'and she has an extraordinarily good memory'. He also talked with the Queen more widely about global matters, especially *glasnost* and *perestroika*, which were then in their early stages. 'She struck me as a very open-minded person. Very open-minded.' He said that the Queen did not allow herself to be carried away by fixed ideologies of either the left or the right and she did not start from a predetermined position. 'She looked at the issues and principles involved, and the practicalities. She looked for the best result that could be worked for, or hoped for.' He thought for a moment and then added firmly, 'She has the hallmarks, to me, of a true leader. She is very well-informed on what is taking place.'

I commented that this was the official side of the Queen. What was she like personally? There was no stiffness about her, he said. She encouraged him to express his views on a number of things. She was quite relaxed and quite prepared to talk about issues, and to share points of view, without rancour. 'She is very easy company to be with. I came away enormously impressed by her.'

The second time when Mr Hayden met the Queen was before her visit to America in 1991. She had influenza and was leaving the next day. She was preoccupied with her forthcoming visit, but, in spite of feeling unwell, she received Mr Hayden for a full discussion. After forty-five minutes, he suggested they break the discussion, as he could see the flu had a grip on her. She herself had not suggested any break. Mr Hayden said he heard later that, as soon as he left, she retired to bed.

What is there about the Queen's personality, I wondered, that produces this warm respect from men of power and high office, from Churchill to Jomo Kenyatta, from President Truman to Sir Robert Menzies? 'It is difficult to say,' said Mr Hayden. 'There is an elusive quality in her make-up. You cannot call it charm – that is a schmaltzy expression. It is something intangible.' He said he had been attracted to her from their first meeting and his own respect and admiration for her was now considerable.

I suggested to the Governor-General that from my own observations I had felt that the Queen was being objective about her own role; that she felt herself to be responsible not only *for* the Crown, but also *to* the Crown. She, too, was serving the Monarchy as equally as anyone else. He said he had never thought of it in that way before, but now it was mentioned, he agreed. He said, 'There is a sense of responsibility, that she is the latest link in the chain of monarchical succession, for Britain and for the realm. Now that you mention it I think I have unconsciously developed the impression that what she is doing is designed to maintain the role in good standing by making it acceptable.'

One builds a mental picture of the Queen as having a strong, serious mind with an excellent memory, nurtured for forty years on a diet of domestic and foreign politics through red dispatch boxes and regular briefing meetings with Prime Ministers and Ambassadors (with an expert study of bloodstock as a relaxation). As Bill Hayden said, she did not need to be told, she *knew*. The wonder is that a mind so fed on facts can retain a caring personality.

Assuming that the Queen does not abdicate and continues to enjoy good health, she will celebrate her seventieth birthday on 26 April 1996. Two months later, on 14 June 1996 – and coinciding almost to the day with her 'Official' birthday – she will have reigned longer than her namesake Queen Elizabeth I, who reigned for forty-four years, four months and seven days. On 20 November 1997, the Queen and Prince Philip will celebrate their Golden Wedding. On 6 February 2002, the Queen will celebrate the Golden Jubilee of her Accession to the throne. She will then be only seventy-five years old.

It would indeed be surprising if these anniversaries coming in succession did not increase her personal popularity. Any Australian referendum that sought a substantial majority approval from the whole population to cut the ties with Monarchy would have to be fitted in somewhere between these events. In those circumstances, Mr Keneally's comment that the AD 2001 timetable 'could be screamingly optimistic' as a date to introduce a republic might well be an accurate forecast, however appropriately convenient it might be in relation to the centenary of Federation.

If one were to assume further, that the Queen were to continue as Monarch after her Golden Jubilee, she would celebrate her Diamond Jubilee in AD 2012 at the age of eighty-five. Were she to live as long as her mother, the Queen Mother, she would have outlived and outreigned every other British Monarch by the time she was ninety. Her great-great-grandmother, Queen Victoria, died aged eighty-one, having reigned for 63 years and 216 days. The present Queen would eclipse this record by the end of the year AD 2015, when she would be only eighty-nine.

The European record for length of reign is held by Alfonso I Henriques of Portugal, who reigned for seventy-three years from AD 1112–85. The world record of length of reign as listed by the *Guinness Book of Records* was held for over 3,600 years by Phiops II, a Sixth Dynasty Pharaoh who is believed to have reigned for ninety-four years from 2281 BC. This record stood until the fourteenth century AD, when Minhti, King of Arakan (now Myanmar, and formerly Burma) reigned for ninety-five years from AD 1279–1374. His record was broken quite recently by Musoma Kanijo, chief of the Nzega of Western Tanganyika (now Tanzania), who died in 1963 having been chief for ninety-eight years.

But it will be seen that to think in terms of records of time can become somewhat frivolous if carried to extremes. Far more important is the quality of the reign and its impact upon both national and world history. As Mr Duplessis said in Canada, 'It is of great comfort to have persons in high places capable of preserving the traditions we cherish.'

The 'elusive and intangible qualities' in the Queen's character, of which Mr Hayden spoke, have their special significance. During the course of her reign, the Queen has been developing, almost involuntarily, a new concept of the role of Monarchy based upon her own deep spiritual conviction. Within an objective and disciplined approach, she has injected understanding and a sense of fairness and compassion into a complex formal position. She has created for herself and for the Crown an image and a public authority that for real worth are bound not so much by Statutes and Oaths of Loyalty as by simple trust.

This has been the outstanding achievement of her reign and, in a turbulent and restless world where too often power has tended to corrupt, it may well prove to be the rock upon which effective Monarchy will endure, especially in the Commonwealth.

In the earliest moments of her Accession in 1952, the Queen sat up in a tree in the African jungle and saw the sun rise on the first morning of her reign. A new era was born then that had no predictable sunset. Dusk settles quickly over many of the sunlit countries of the Commonwealth. But, as there was at Treetops, there has been an alternative moon over the whole Commonwealth that has imperceptibly perpetuated the light.

The source of this light has been a self-generating inspiration that the

Queen inherited from her own parents: of believing in a caring Monarchy. It has helped her to appreciate the value and importance of absolute integrity in accepting and carrying out her responsibilities.

Today, this is perhaps the most important feature of a Monarchy that does not have executive powers, or indulge in political manoeuvrings, but does possess great influence. So long as this inspirational power-source remains, the sometimes ruffled waters of the Commonwealth pool can be approached and shared by all – albeit with some patience and also with a sense of responsibility, for the latter is one of the basic ingredients of the Queen's personality. The signs of it were already clearly there on the first day when she acceded to the Throne.

Bibliography

Blixen, Karen, *Out of Africa*, Putnam, London, 1937.

Booth, Martin, *Carpet Sahib – A Life of Jim Corbett*, Constable, London 1986.

Cannadine, David, 'The Context, Performance and Meaning of Ritual: The British Monarchy and the Invention of Tradition, *c.* 1820–1977', in Eric Hobsbawm and Terence Ranger (eds.), *The Invention of Tradition*, Cambridge University Press, 1983.

Charles, Prince of Wales, *A Vision of Britain: A Personal View*, Doubleday, 1989.

Corbett, Jim, *Man-Eaters of Kumaon*, Indian Branch, Humphrey Milford, publishers to the University, Oxford University Press, 1944.

Corbett, Jim, *Tree Tops*, Oxford University Press, 1955.

Cowie, Mervyn, *Fly, Vulture*, with a Foreword by Peter Scott, Harrap, London, 1961.

Creighton, Donald, *The Story of Canada*, Faber & Faber, London, 1959; revised edition, 1971.

Delderfield, Eric R., *Kings and Queens of England and Great Britain*, David & Charles, Newton Abbot, 1966.

Fraser, Antonia (ed.), *The Lives of the Kings and Queens of England*, Weidenfeld & Nicolson, London, 1975.

Hemsing, Jan, *Treetops, Outspan, Paxtu*, Sealpoint Publicity and Public Relations, Nairobi, 1974.

Huxley, Elspeth, *Out in the Midday Sun: My Kenya*, Chatto & Windus, London, 1985.

Leacock, Stephen, *Canada: The Foundations of Its Future*, privately printed, House of Seagram, Montreal, 1941.

Portable Medieval Reader, The, assembled and illuminated by James Bruce Ross and Mary Martin McLaughlin, Penguin Books, Harmondsworth, and Viking Press, New York, 1949.

Walker, Eric Sherbrooke, *Treetops Hotel*, Robert Hale, London, 1962.

Index